# THEY CALLED US "LUCKY"

# THEY CALLED US

# "LUCKY"

## THE LIFE AND AFTERLIFE OF
## THE IRAQ WAR'S HARDEST HIT UNIT

# RUBEN GALLEGO

## WITH JIM DeFELICE

MARINER BOOKS

*New York   Boston*

HarperCollins books may be purchased for educational, business, or sales promotional use. For information, please email the Special Markets Department at SPsales@harpercollins.com.

A hardcover edition of this book was published in 2021 by Custom House, an imprint of William Morrow.

FIRST MARINER BOOKS PAPERBACK EDITION PUBLISHED 2022.

*Designed by Paula Russell Szafranski*

The Library of Congress has cataloged a previous edition of this book as follows:

Names: Gallego, Ruben, 1979- author. | DeFelice, Jim, 1956- author.
Title: They called us "lucky" : the life and afterlife of the Iraq War's hardest hit unit / Ruben Gallego and Jim DeFelice.
Other titles: Life and afterlife of the Iraq War's hardest hit unit
Description: First edition. | New York : Custom House, [2021] | Includes bibliographical references.
Identifiers: LCCN 2021038045 (print) | LCCN 2021038046 (ebook) | ISBN 9780063045811 (hardcover) | ISBN 9780063045804 (trade paperback) | ISBN 9780063045828 (ebook)
Subjects: LCSH: Gallego, Ruben, 1979- | Iraq War, 2003-2011—Personal narratives, American | United States. Marine Corps. Marine Regiment, 25th. Battalion, 3rd. Lima Company—Biography. | Iraq War, 2003-2011—Campaigns—Iraq—Hadīthah. | Marines—United States—Biography. | Legislators—United States—Biography. | United States. Congress. House—Biography.
Classification: LCC DS79.76 .G354 2021  (print) | LCC DS79.76  (ebook) | DDC 956.7044/345—dc23
LC record available at https://lccn.loc.gov/2021038045
LC ebook record available at https://lccn.loc.gov/2021038046

ISBN 978-0-06-304580-4 (pbk.)

22 23 24 25 26  LSC  10 9 8 7 6 5 4 3 2 1

# CONTENTS

DEDICATED TO

MICHAEL GRANT AND SYDNEY GALLEGO,

MY FAMILY,

JONATHAN GRANT,

AND

THE MEN OF LIMA 3/25

# THEY CALLED US "LUCKY"

# PROLOGUE

## WERE WE IN COMBAT?

**W**e measure everything in war. The distance to the enemy. The distance to home.

Our clothes are measured. Our boots. We measure the time before we leave, the time of patrols, the time until we return.

We measure ourselves.

The one thing that we cannot measure is luck. But luck is the most important factor in war. All the other measurements can line up perfectly, and yet not guarantee success, or even survival.

Without luck in war, we're all dead.

That I know in every inch of my body, in every moment's pulse. I lived it as a Marine in Iraq, enduring some of the bloodiest fighting of the occupation. I escaped death eleven times by my count, all because of luck.

I wasn't the only one who was lucky. My whole unit—Lima Company—3rd Battalion, 25th Marine Regiment, 4th Marine Division—was lucky. I was in 1st Platoon during spring 2005, high tide of the war against America in Iraq. Any conceivable thing had been made into a weapon, and the vast stretches of western Iraq transformed into a triangle of death.

"Lucky Lima" the media called us. Weeks of combat and not one casualty. Leadership considered us the golden boys, up for anything.

Remarkable, considering we were civilian Marines—members of a Reserve unit who, after our early training, met for only a weekend a month and a few weeks a year. We were Marines, but we worked civilian jobs and had "regular" lives, unlike our brothers and sisters in the active-duty components of the Corps.

We were damn lucky. Good, yes, but also lucky.

That was before the measure of our luck ran out. Before my best friend, Jonathan Grant, was killed. Before Staff Sergeant Goodwin was killed in Hell House. Before the tortured snipers. Before the amphibious vehicle I was supposed to be sitting in was destroyed and its occupants burned alive. Before we knew that Luck ran inversely against Time—the longer you stayed in a place, the less luck you had.

Time, too, is a measure in war. Its passage teases and seduces, slowing for long stretches then roaring away when you need it most.

Time heals by making you forget, but war is impossible to forget. You wouldn't want it any other way—if you forgot war, you'd forget the brothers who had your back when the bullets flew. You would forget the Bailons, or Taylor, or McKenzie. The living, as well as the dead.

You'd forget Grant, his encouragement, his easy laugh, his ability to see you through the precarious promise of luck.

You'd forget the candy and beef jerky he carried on patrol. You'd forget how he stole your music. How he helped make you the best Marine you could be.

You'd forget Goodwin's American flag bandanna. You'd forget Andre Williams's easy smile.

So you don't forget.

You walk the distance from the U.S. Capitol in Washington to Arlington National Cemetery to remember what the war revealed about yourself. You spend every Memorial Day at church, the one day of the year when you can hear God's voice, and He returns the favor. You help friends and strangers with PTSD, only to realize it took hold of you long ago.

I say "you." I mean "me." Your measure of luck may be entirely different from mine.

# McKENZIE
## SPRING 2007
### PHOENIX, ARIZONA

I'm working in a PR firm. Toward the end of the day, I get a call from my friend Jonithan McKenzie. I can tell right off from the tone in his voice that he's in trouble.

Life and death trouble.

"Ruben," he asks, "were we in combat?"

*Were we in combat?!*

God, were we in combat. Barely two years before, McKenzie and I were Marine grunts in Lima Company, 3/25—members of the 3rd Battalion of the 25th Regiment, a Reserve unit that was part of the 4th Marine Division, assigned to patrol northwestern Iraq. We were Lucky Lima, the unluckiest lucky company in the U.S. Marine Corps. In just under six months, we lost twenty-two Marines and one Navy corpsman killed in action. All told, our battalion lost forty-eight men, the most casualties of any Marine unit since the Beirut bombing in 1983, when two hundred twenty Marines died in their barracks.

That was a hell of a record for any unit in combat, let alone a Reserve unit.

Images flew into my head unbidden as McKenzie waited for an answer. Sniper bullets whipping by me in an open field. One of our amtrac vehicles overturned from a massive IED.

I saw my best friend, smiling because he was alive. The image morphed into a stuffed seabag sitting on an empty bunk—he wasn't so lucky two days later.

"McKenzie, what's wrong?" I asked, though I dreaded the answer.

In a shaky voice, he told me he was trying to get into a hospital for mental care. He was at the edge—he was sure he was going to kill himself, because he couldn't take Iraq anymore. He'd come home with me two years before, but in many ways he was still back in Mesopotamia with our dead brothers.

He knew he needed help. But the VA wasn't going to clear him, because his records said he'd never been in combat. And if you weren't in combat, you couldn't have PTSD. And if you didn't have PTSD, they couldn't help, even if the alternative was suicide.

"Of course you were in combat," I told him. "We were all in combat."

"I thought so," he said.

He said a few other things that I don't remember. Whatever they were, they were more than enough to convince me he was in very deep trouble, very much in need of professional help.

"Where are you?" I asked.

"At the VA. Are you sure we were in combat?"

"We were in fuckloads of combat. Where exactly are you?"

Albuquerque.

The more we talked, the more desperate he seemed. He wasn't just close to the edge. He was dangling from it, suspended over the endless abyss by a fingertip.

"Go home," I told him finally. "Be there as soon as I can."

I left the office, got in my car, and started driving. He was four hundred miles away across the desert. He could have been on the moon, and I still would have gone.

PEOPLE HAVE THIS IMAGE OF MARINES AS ALMOST SUPERHUMAN. WE ARE A LOT of things—well trained, highly disciplined, loyal to our country and fellow Marines. We have a proud history of courage and achievement. We value integrity, service, and sacrifice.

But we're not superhumans, not close. Metal rips through our flesh as readily as through anyone else's. We may be a bit better at handling stress and trauma than the average non-Marine, but human biology has its limits, and not even the most rigorous training can get you beyond those.

We fight. We kill. We do what we have to do. Sometimes we cry when we're done.

McKenzie—Sergeant Jonithan McKenzie—was a lot closer to the ideal version of a Marine than I was. A Navajo, he'd been in Recon, the Corps' version of the Navy SEALs and Army Special Forces. Inserted into Lima Company with a bunch of us from New Mexico to fill out the roster, he was our platoon's "Guide," essentially the executive officer to the platoon sergeant. As the second-ranking NCO (noncommissioned officer) in the unit, McKenzie worked as a floating advisor on missions. Rather than directly leading the platoon or one of its squads, he'd generally pop up where the action was, a source of experience and another set of eyes where needed.

McKenzie was the guy who had your back when you were in a bad place, and knew where you should plan on taking a left when everyone else thought you should go right or straight ahead. He'd get to you without a lot of talk, let alone hesitation.

Him calling now, and sounding the way he sounded—beyond desperate—touched off something in me. Part of it was instinct, I guess—a natural reaction as a human being to help someone in trouble. And another part had been learned and earned in the Corps: you don't leave your combat buddy on the battlefield; and on the battlefield, every Marine is your combat buddy.

Iraq had been years and thousands of miles away, but as my impulse to help showed, we were still fighting that war.

# I.

# HARVARD MARINE

Impulsive, emotional decisions are out of character for me. I'm the guy who had a four-year plan to get into Harvard even though my family was dirt poor. I don't make a dinner reservation without carefully scoping the restaurant's menu.

But ironically, my decision to become a Marine, one of the most important and consequential choices of my life, was largely spur of the moment, certainly as much an impulse as anything else I've done in life.

It was the fall of 2000. I'd flamed out at Harvard, on an enforced "pause." Though unenrolled, I was still living nearby. The administration had promised me I could reenroll, and I had every intention of doing so, proving that I was now on the straight and narrow. I wanted to resume my studies, and after graduation get a job in the State Department or the field of international relations. I had good reason to believe I'd convince Harvard to reaccept me, but for the time being those ambitions were on hold.

I was walking through Boston Common when I saw a Marine Corps recruiting office across the street.

I headed that way. Curiosity, fate, maybe boredom, took me through the door.

A Marine recruiter asked me what I wanted.

"I've always thought about joining up," I told him, not mentioning that those thoughts were vague at best. "I have some time now, between semesters. I wonder if I could?"

"You mean join the Reserves?"

I had no, exactly zero, idea what the Reserves meant, or what the difference between it and "regular" service arms were. I explained my situation and told the recruiter that I planned on going back to school in a few months. He explained how the Reserves worked.

If you've ever gone to a recruiting station, you probably realize that was a bit unusual. Many recruiters aren't all that interested in getting you to sign up for the Reserves. They have quotas to meet, and most if not all of those involve the regular service branches. But this Marine suggested I come back the next day and take an ASVAB test.

"OK."

ASVAB stands for Armed Services Vocational Aptitude Battery. It's essentially an aptitude test that identifies your basic intelligence level and what particular skills you may have.

I must have done well because his eyes were saucers as he looked things over. "Look at all these great jobs we have for you," he told me, offering everything from law clerk to something in computers. It was all nerdy stuff.

"But this is the Marine Corps," I told him. "If I wanted to be a law clerk, I could just go to the Air Force. At least there I'd get to hang around women."

Not a politically correct answer, especially since the Corps does have female members. But he took it in stride.

Then I told him I wanted to be in the infantry.

"It's hard to be in infantry," he answered.

"If I'm going to be a Marine, I want to be a *Marine*."

He claimed there were no infantry spots open.

I know now that was BS. There are *always* infantry slots open. I suspect the problem was that he needed to fill some of those other spots he was pushing, and here was the perfect candidate to help him get his attaboy.

So I left.

Then one day he called me up. "You want to be a mortarman?" he asked.

"What's a mortarman?"

"You're in the infantry. You have a mortar."

Sure, I told him. Sounds good.

He was pleased. The only catch was, I had to sign and leave in five days.

"If you help me move out of my apartment," I told him, "I'll take it."

A day or two later, he showed up with a few recruits and helped me get my stuff over to my fraternity, Sigma Chi, where I could store it. Less than a week later, I reported to Parris Island for boot camp.


THE WORDS "HARVARD" AND "MARINE" SEEM ALMOST CONTRADICTORY THESE days. Colleges in general are assumed to be liberal, and members of the military—Marines especially—are presumed to be conservative. Those assumptions are clichés—Harvard has a number of veterans who are undergrads, and I know Marines who are even more liberal than me—but there is truth in them. The idea of a young adult going to college as an enlisted man rather than an officer seems like even more of an oxymoron, especially if that college is an elite Ivy League institution. Like many schools, Harvard has an ROTC program, but the aim for a Reserve Officer Training Corps candidate is to become an officer. After all, in most people's minds, being an officer is better than being enlisted, and if you're good enough to get into Harvard, then surely you're good enough to be an officer instead of a grunt.

It's not my purpose here to disabuse people of their erroneous assumptions, or even point out that seven percent of our enlisted personnel these days have college degrees and a significant number of other men and women are working toward them. Speaking strictly for myself, I chose to become an enlisted man because of the commitment I was willing to make. I wished to serve my country, but I didn't want the military to be a career, or even a very long-term commitment. As a Reserve Marine, I could expect to spend less time over the course of my service deployed. I would have flexibility to pursue my education and my actual career. I had no interest in becoming a career military officer—though I could opt for that down the line if I changed my mind.

Two things were important:

One, I wanted to be a Marine. No slight to the other services, but the Corps is the best. Period.

The Marines had always held a special place in my mind. Among Latinos and Hispanics there is a strong tradition of joining the Corps, and undoubtedly I absorbed that growing up. It's almost like, if you are going to go into the military, then being a Marine is or should be the default choice. The Corps has generally reciprocated, and its ranks historically have included more Hispanics and Latinos percentagewise than are in the general population.

Two, I wanted to be a fighting Marine. All Marines are riflemen, true. But if I was going to be a Marine, I wanted to be on the front line, seeing action.

Even though I was signing up for the Reserves, I knew that it was very likely I would be deployed. This was before 9/11 and the invasion of Iraq. I don't claim any sort of clairvoyance, but the Marines traditionally have been called to the front lines of any conflict, big or small. Being a relatively small branch it was highly likely that the Reserves would be activated and rotated to the front. I had no problem with that; on the contrary, I was excited by the prospect.

Did I want to kill people?

No. I wasn't a sociopath; I didn't want to kill people. Frankly, the Corps wouldn't have taken me if I were.

But were I to be in combat and the situation called for it, I would absolutely do my duty. That's what war is about.

## BOOT CAMP

Like any smart recruit, I kept my head down as much as possible in boot camp. I've never been very athletic, so the physical training was difficult for me. But the aim of that portion of basic training is to get a recruit in decent condition, not make the Olympics. Do what you're told, and you'll become physically fit. I ended up in the best shape of my life.

It's possible that some recruits succeed on innate ability, and others do well because of experiences they've already had in civilian life. I succeeded because I was not going to fail, and if that meant extra work to master a task, I went at it. One of the cardinal lessons you're taught in boot camp is how to handle and take care of your rifle. I'd never fired one before, let alone cleaned or assembled one. I practiced those skills in the dark until I could identify each part by touch, and put them together blindfolded.

It took time, but I wasn't going to fail.

One thing I didn't do: mention Harvard. I knew that I would invite a lot of ribbing and worse, so I kept it to myself. It wasn't until the third or maybe fourth phase of our training that my cover was blown.

One day at mail call, a package arrived for me. If you had a package, one of the drill instructors would be present when it was opened. Recruits are only allowed to have certain items while training, and the drill is going to make sure no contraband sneaks in through the mail.

Fair enough.

This happens in the squad bay with the rest of the unit there, and even the most innocuous items can generate a great deal of humor.

I hadn't gotten much mail while I was there, so I was surprised when the drill instructor called my name. He had a box in front of him. He opened it and looked inside.

"Recruit, do you go to Harvard?"

"This recruit does not go to Harvard," I answered truthfully. Because technically I wasn't enrolled.

You can't get around a smart drill instructor.

"Did you go to Harvard at some point?"

"This recruit attended Harvard for a year and a half," I said, hoping to limit the damage.

"Do you intend on going back to Harvard at some point?" he asked, pointing to a course catalog my friends had included in the box.

I had to say that, yes, I was aiming to finish my degree there when I was through with boot camp and the training that followed.

"Why the hell aren't you an officer?" he demanded. "Are you stupid?"

I forget exactly what I answered. I'm sure it didn't really matter; I was already marked.

We weren't done. Besides the course catalog that had given me away, the box contained a variety of contraband, apparently sent in innocence by my friend, Shay Sahay. There was a bottle of Jack Daniel's, a flask, a carton of Marlboro Lights, a *Playboy* magazine, a *Maxim* magazine, three small Godiva chocolate mice, and a can of red-hot peanuts. All were confiscated.

Later that evening, I was called into the drill instructor's hooch, where I saw my three chocolate mice lined up at the top of his computer screen. Two of our other instructors were there, trying to hide their smirks.

Top Hat asked if I wanted the candy.

"No, sir," I answered quickly.

He wasn't taking no for an answer. He told me to go get two of my best friends and return to the office so each one of us could have a candy.

Knowing this wasn't going to end well, I went out and came back with two recruits I didn't particularly like—sorry guys. My feeling was that it would be better to have them mad at me than to lose a friend.

The drill instructor produced the red-hot peanuts. The DI then instructed us to take a handful, put them in our mouths, and then sing "Three Blind Mice." If we didn't lose our shit, we could have the chocolate.

It wasn't a request.

Those peanuts were hot. Tears were streaming down our cheeks before the end of the first verse. I guess it was a pretty funny sight, because one of the instructors had to duck outside so we wouldn't see him laughing.

To this day, I can't hear the song "Three Blind Mice" without tearing up a little. And not in a good way.

## POOR TRASH

Needless to say, Harvard became something of a theme over the next few days. But I wasn't razzed any more than most of the other recruits, and fortunately the end of boot camp was in sight.

In a lot of ways, I was more of a typical Marine than a typical Harvard student. My background was "disadvantaged"—a nice way of saying poor—and I genuinely was looking to both serve my country and make something of myself, both in the service and later as a civilian.

I was born in Chicago in 1979. My mom's family had come to America from Bogotá, Colombia, when she was a teenager. Her father had lost his small shoe factory after some financial reverses and came to the U.S. to work. He eventually brought the rest of the family to Chicago to settle. You can see the difference good nutrition and health care make by looking at my aunts—none of the four born in Colombia stand over five feet tall; my other four aunts, born in the United States, are considerably taller.

My dad also emigrated to America during his very early teens. His family had a farm in Mexico, but he was a bit of a black sheep, the youngest of a large family, and largely on his own. He got a job working construction in the Chicago area.

My parents met at a local dance when Mom was eighteen and Dad was a little older. It wasn't love at first sight—he was more interested in her sister. But within a few months they were dating seriously and soon married. I was the second of four children, the only boy in the marriage. When I was two, we went to Mexico to help my ailing grandmother, who was living on a small farm in the mountains of Chihuahua; we stayed until I was in second grade. At that point, my father brought us back to Chicago and opened a small construction business. When the school year was over, I'd generally go back to Mexico to help on the farm, cultivating beans, watermelon, and corn. It was literally in the middle of nowhere, and I could spend hours wandering, either on foot or horseback. I captured a baby coyote once and turned it into a pet—as much as you can make a pet out of a coyote.

It's funny. In Mexico, I was taunted by the kids for being American. In the U.S., I was taunted for being Mexican. As a little kid, I remember a lot of fights. I've always been on the small side, especially as a kid, but I won more than my share—I fought dirty. That's fair, in my book, when you're outnumbered or your opponent is bigger than you.

Around junior high, my mom and dad divorced. My mom, myself, and my three sisters moved to an area just south of Chicago, an apartment so tiny that I slept on the floor of the living room rather than a bed. We wouldn't have had money for a bed even if there was space.

My father's construction business had gone bust. I found out later that he and one of his cousins had begun dabbling in the drug trade. If my father was making any money from his involvement, we never saw it. Eventually, my father was busted and found guilty of felony possession with intent to sell cocaine and marijuana. My uncle made out worse—he was shot and killed in Mexico. I never found out the details, and don't care to.

Being poor is one thing. Having a dealer for a dad—that's a different level. I always knew we were poor. There was no shame in that. You worked hard and things got better. But now as a young teenager, I felt we were trash.

Lying on the floor of our apartment one night, hungry and tired because I worked after school earning money to help my mother pay for things, I told myself this was not who I was. I was not going to be poor trash the rest of my life. I was going to college, no matter what it took.

What college?

The best: Harvard.

## HARVARD

I had some excellent teachers in high school, a fine principal, and good friends who let me use their computers to complete assignments. I supplied the hard work and, most of all, the motivation.

I knew that if I could get into Harvard, they'd give me a scholarship that would probably pay my way. So I got really nerdy. I called up Harvard students and asked what they did to get in. I put together a four-year plan and showed it to my guidance counselor.

"You know, kids from here don't usually go to Harvard," he told me.

"I understand it's hard," I said, "but I am the kid who can."

He may have been doubtful, but he didn't discourage me. I was elected class president. I took every AP class available. I made the high school baseball team, though I mostly rode the bench. I found a scholarship that sent me to Greece for several weeks—in theory studying, though a good amount of time was spent with a girl I met there. My real standout activity was the school quiz team, where my command of trivia—fueled by reading free editions of an encyclopedia from cover to cover—helped immensely. We'd only gotten editions up to the *N*'s, but I killed on any answer that started with the first half of the alphabet.

I had a variety of outside jobs to earn money—cashier at a pizza place, janitor, low man on a construction crew, line cook at a small grill. I can still whip up a pretty good Chicago hot dog.

And if you have to ask what a Chicago-style hot dog is, you've obviously never had one. Here's a hint, though—they're beef, neither grilled nor boiled, and the lettuce is generally considered optional.

A lot of the kids in my school were from working-class, Irish-American families, and more than a few brought their parents' racist attitudes to class. It was a time when Rush Limbaugh was just getting started as a national broadcaster, and his rants were gaining popularity. A smart Latino kid who was not afraid to voice his opinion rubbed a lot of my classmates the wrong way.

Most of the time I ignored them, but there were a few fights. I remember one where I showed up at the alley after school and to my surprise discovered a packed house waiting to watch me get beat up.

There was even a guy playing a guitar on the neighbor's rooftop. My pummeling was going to be the week's entertainment.

I glanced over at the bully, a good head taller than me. He had broad shoulders, hams for fists, and a confident smirk. I figured my goal was to get a punch in and then pray I wouldn't be too shattered before someone rushed in to break it up.

Things didn't go exactly that way.

"I don't really want to fight," I told him.

He answered with a hard right to my face, and another to my body. Then he kneed me in my stomach.

Rage spun up inside me. I jumped up from the ground, grabbed the bully's hair, and threw him to the ground. I jumped on top of him and started swinging.

His body went lax.

Fight over. I let him up.

"We're done," I said.

"No, we're not," he insisted.

He punched me again. I ducked his next swing, but not quite all the way—his fist caught the back of my skull.

Being hardheaded has its advantages. My head broke his hand.

The bully staggered back, pulling his arm up to hold his hand. I jumped on him, grabbed his neck, and now there was no mercy. When I finally let him go, he had no more fight left in him.

He showed up the next day in a cast. I can't remember being challenged to a fight after that.

HARVARD WASN'T THE ONLY COLLEGE I APPLIED TO, BUT IT WAS ALWAYS MY FIRST choice. I did well on the college exams and was offered interviews with local alumni. I remember taking two different trains and a bus to get up and over to northwest Chicago for my first one. The woman was very nice. When we were done, she asked when my mom was picking me up.

"She's not," I told her. "She's working. I'm catching the bus to the train. It's six blocks away."

That apparently shocked her. She studied me a moment, then offered to give me a ride to the Metro.

A few months afterward, Harvard offered a scholarship covering all but about $4,000 of my housing and tuition. I spent the summer working at a meat-packing plant to cover most of those and other expenses.

My ambition at that time was to either go to work at the CIA or join the State Department.

Yeah, I wanted to be a spy, even though I had no concrete idea what working at the Central Intelligence Agency was really like. I'd at least met a diplomat when I traveled to Greece, which made the State Department a more realistic career goal. I liked traveling, and getting someone else to pay for it isn't a bad way to go.

That did eventually happen, though not quite in the way I'd imagined.

MY DORM SUITE AT HARVARD HAD TWO BEDROOMS, A BATH, AND A LIVING ROOM shared among four guys. That's standard at American colleges these days, but it was exciting to me—it was the most space I'd ever lived in and the first bed I'd had in six years. I made my way past the Mercedes and the moving vans, dropped my single bag of clothing, and became a Harvard undergrad.

The whole thing was culture shock, but mostly good. I was one of the few working-class kids, and certainly a minority as a Latino. While most of my classmates were out partying the first week, I was looking for work-study slots and an outside job. I ended up as a custodian in the dorms and picked up needed cash and the occasional cookie doing odd jobs and shoveling snow in the local neighborhood. I probably was the only person in Massachusetts praying for heavy snow every winter night.

My classes were the normal survey courses you take as a freshman, except for a class that focused on the Maya and other precolonial South American history. I'd never known much about my ancestry—I'm about twenty-five percent indigenous Mexican, according to a family DNA test—so every lecture was a revelation about my past.

I studied hard enough to pull Bs and B-pluses—quite a difference from the As I got in high school, but the expectations were higher here. Occasionally there were classes where my background hurt a little—try writing a composition about golf without knowing the most basic facts of the game—but the social aspects of school were far more difficult to master. I'd take a girl out, have a great time, then say I'd see her the following week.

"Why wait a week?" she'd ask.

I'd answer truthfully: *I have to work a week to get the money to take you out and get paid again.*

The inevitable answer to that:

*Why not just put it on your parents' credit card?*

I was probably as much of a culture shock to them as they were to me.

The class differences were more important when it came to things like internships, which were strongly encouraged even for freshmen. I remember a classmate casually mentioning that he was going to intern that summer at the UN, thanks to an arrangement his dad had made. There was no way to even apply for that internship as a freshman. I had to spend the summer working for school, though I did manage to land an internship at a local law firm back home with the help of my old junior high school principal. In sophomore year I moved in with some friends, and to be honest, spent probably too much time partying. My grades slipped a bit, then a bit more. There were broken rules and extenuating circumstances, but the bottom line was I was "asked" to leave school, though they said I could reapply in a year.

It was devastating. I thought about tucking my tail between my legs and going home. I talked to my mom, and while she was very comforting, I realized that going home meant giving up. I decided to stay and try to turn it around.

I couch-surfed for a while, found a stable if not well-paying job, and got an apartment.

A few months later, I walked down through Boston Common and saw the Marine recruiting station.

## FATHER

I should mention one fact about my enlistment—I had to lie to get in.

Not about drugs or anything criminal. About my leg.

I'd been in a car accident when I was very young. It messed up my left leg bad. To fix it, the doctors broke my femur in half. The result was that my knee was not terribly stable. In fact, it looked a little funny to the doctor who examined me when I joined.

I told him I'd been born that way.

Whether he believed me or not, he could see that I could walk, and cleared me for training.

The National Anthem sounded a little different the day I graduated boot camp. I felt proud, ready to serve my country in an organization that has a long history of courage and sacrifice. It wasn't a macho thing. It was more belonging, and patriotic. I've always believed in the idea of a great America, where people can come and achieve more than they might have elsewhere. I was proof of it. Now I was in a position to pay the country back.

At some point during the graduation ceremony, I looked out into the audience and saw my mom and one of my sisters. Still scanning around, I happened to catch a glimpse of my father in another section.

I couldn't have been more shocked. I hadn't seen him in years.

Even before the divorce, my father and I had a strained relationship. One of my strongest childhood memories was going with him to McDonald's, where he criticized me for eating my French fries one at a time. More than criticized—he reached across the table and slapped them out of my mouth, then told me I was gay for eating them like that.

Obviously, issues.

Seeing him at the graduation enraged me, and still does. I felt as if he'd come to steal some portion of my achievement, as if he was responsible for all the work I'd done to get this far. He hadn't supported me or encouraged me in anything to that point—not high school, not Harvard. And now he somehow wanted a piece of this.

Fair or not, that's how I felt. I avoided him, staying close to my mom and sisters, avoiding any possibility of contact. I've barely heard from him since.

GRADUATING BOOT CAMP IS JUST THE FIRST PHASE OF YOUR MILITARY CAREER. MY next stop was the School of Infantry, where I learned the basic tactics and procedures all infantrymen follow. I also learned the basics of my specialty as a mortarman.

I loved it. As a mortarman, you're part of the infantry, right in the middle of the action. At the same time, there's a lot of math and quick decisions involved—perfect for a thinking fighting man. Brains as well as brawn.

You do have to hump with more gear—mortarmen have a regular infantry load, plus their mortar. A 60 mm mortar has a tube that's a good fifteen pounds before you add in the tripod. You're always under pressure to get the mortar up and ready to shoot—within forty seconds. It's impossible when you start; child's play by the end of training.

Another of those "in the moment" things. There's no time to be distracted by other thoughts. Especially when you realize everything in the military is made by the lowest bidder, and all that is between you and disaster is a very thin metal tube.

I had one month of training. I had to pass everything on time before returning to Harvard, which had re-accepted me for the winter semester. If there was any conflict between the Marines and Harvard—if I got rolled back or failed training—the Marines would win. Fortunately, I flew through the course and reported to Harvard with a few hours to spare, thanks to the Greyhound Bus Company.

I think a lot of my friends at Harvard thought I'd wash out of the service, or maybe not come back to school. It was just unusual—Harvard's such a strange place that we didn't think twice about going to school with movie stars (Natalie Portman was a student while I was there), but no one knew anyone at college who was *enlisted* (as opposed to being in ROTC or an officer) in the Marine Corps. I was also more liberal than the average Marine, so nothing seemed to add up. But probably the biggest confusion for my friends was this: they knew I don't like being told what to do. And that, almost by definition, is what being in the service means.

In truth it wasn't a problem. I understood the purpose of the orders I was given as a Marine. *Liking* an order wasn't part of the requirement.

The truth is, I felt free in the Marines. I had taken ownership of my life. It may seem contradictory, but joining the Corps was something I had done on my own, with no expectation or pressure to conform with what society expected from me as someone who got into Harvard.

The achievement came with commitments. I had a six-year contract. I knew I'd be activated at some point; it only made sense. I've never understood the people who sign up for the Reserves but believe, sincerely, that their unit will never be called to active duty, and that they themselves will never have to fight.

Don't join the military if you're not prepared to fight.


HARVARD WAS EASIER THE SECOND TIME AROUND. MORE GROUNDED AND LESS awed by my surroundings, I focused on getting through school and moving to the next step of my life.

The Corps and Harvard coexisted peacefully for the most part.

There were times when they clashed, though. Like in the basic introduction to Greek civilization class.

Talking about Greek heroes during one lecture, the professor made the point that these men were willing to die for a greater cause. To me, though, they were willing to die together because that's what they were trained to do, just like a Marine. They were fighting for each other at least as much as they were fighting for ideals.

I mentioned that in class. He told me I was wrong.

Obviously, he'd never served in the military. I'm sure he knew a lot about Greek literature and culture, just not so much about warriors.

But those moments were more the exception than the rule. I settled into my new routine—classes, work, drills once a month or so with my unit in New Hampshire.

Then one morning, the future changed.

## WAR

"I think you're going to war."

I opened my eyes. It was September, one of the first days of class in the fall 2001 semester. My girlfriend was hovering over me.

"What are you talking about?" I asked.

She pushed the laptop toward me. I watched a video on CNN .com showing an airliner hitting one of the World Trade Center towers. Moments later, a live feed showed the second plane striking the other building.

"Oh shit," I said, "this is an attack."

I called my drill center, asking what I should do. They told me they weren't sure, but for the moment I was not to report.

I spent most of the day with a friend who was Indian, but who thought he would be mistaken for a Muslim and targeted. We eventually went to a bar for drinks, spent much of the day talking about what might happen. No one mistook him for anything but a tipsy Harvard student, and the day passed without confrontation.

A week or so later, having lunch in the luxuriously decked-out Harvard dining hall, a friend sat down across from me and asked if I wanted to report for duty if called.

"Yes, of course I'll go."

He scowled. "I didn't ask if you would go. I asked if you *wanted* to go."

"Of course I do," I told him.

Obviously not the answer he wanted. He lectured me on how America was really responsible for the terrorist atrocity.

I got a little heated answering. He kept going, even telling me that the capitalist system was responsible for the outrage.

His argument lost a bit of luster against the backdrop of the well-polished wood panels and elaborate stained-glass windows. Irony was obviously not his strong point.

"Just remember," I told him finally, "for every capitalist who was in that building, there was a janitor, there was a firefighter, there was a police officer. You get to enjoy the next couple of years because other people are going to go to war for you, and yet you'll look down on them. It's very nice. Very nice."

It wasn't just talk. I was ready to go. My seabag was already packed. I wanted to fight. I wanted revenge. The fact that al Qaeda had killed innocent Americans on our home soil was a shock to my psyche.

Most everyone on campus was just as shaken. Everyone thinks Harvard is a pacifist, antiwar place, but really it's not. Later on there would be some very small antiwar groups—the idiot who confronted me in the dining hall was a member, I'm sure—but for the most part people were either apprehensive that there might be another attack, this one on the school, or wanted revenge as I did. Or both.

I HAD A RESERVE TRAINING SESSION NOT LONG AFTER THE ATTACKS. I'D BEEN AS-signed to Bravo Company, 1st Battalion, 25th Marines. The unit specialized in mountain fighting and operating in cold weather—qualities we all knew would come in handy in Afghanistan, al Qaeda's training ground. That first weekend, there was a lot of cigarette smoking and officers coming by to see if we were ready to fight.

We wanted to be part of whatever was going to happen, but no one would tell us anything. It was frustrating—and even more so when we went home without call-up orders.

When I got back to campus, I walked by Memorial Hall, which has a list of Harvard students and graduates who died in war.

The list stopped at Vietnam. That may be largely due to the fact that America has fortunately lost fewer men and women in combat since the twentieth-century wars, but to me it was a re-minder of how much had changed in our society. It emphasized how alone and different I was, an enlisted Marine at Harvard.

The disconnect between enlisted grunt and Harvard under-grad wasn't conservative versus liberal, as most people probably believe. It was more subtle, more class and expectation based.

Students in my foreign policy seminar—most of whom un-doubtedly hoped to join the National Security apparatus someday—would talk for hours about moving assets and using strategic forces when what they really meant was making war. Killing people. Hav-ing your countrymen die. The discussion didn't get to the ground level—at best, casualties were a necessary price of police.

During one session, we gamed out the Afghan war. My fellow students talked about accepting X number of casualties as an ac-ceptable exchange.

The Marine grunt in me rebelled.

"Those are real people," I said. "We have to understand that when we're saying this, we're talking about real people."

The class got quiet after that. But I doubt there was much lasting effect.

THAT SUMMER, I GOT AN INTERNSHIP WITH THE STATE DEPARTMENT IN WASHINGton, D.C. My section dealt with South and Central America; I answered phones during a two-day mini-crisis over the value of the Uruguayan peso, which had plummeted due to errant remarks by one of our under-secretaries. The controversy wasn't a résumé builder, but it was exciting to play even a tiny role in handling a real crisis.

Everything about that internship was exciting. Career diplomats freely shared advice and stories in the cafeteria. At any point you could pass Secretary of State Colin Powell in the hallway. More importantly, there was an air of optimism among the young people I worked with. The terror attacks had galvanized world opinion. Not only were countries condemning terrorism, but they were willing to take steps to correct the conditions that encouraged it, like poverty. My peers and I believed that, in the wake of 9/11, America had a chance to forge lasting peace and stronger alliances around the world.

That would soon change.

## BOUGHT AT AUCTION

The fall of my junior year, Harvard's fraternities decided to raise money for the Red Cross by selling dates. If you're going to be both politically incorrect and somewhat self-serving, then your only saving grace is to do it for charity.

I was enlisted for the auction block at the last minute, not because of my sleek Marine physique, superior intellect, or ruggedly good looks. No, I happened to live right next to the bar where the event was being held, and when one of the assigned dates didn't show up, my fraternity mates rushed me into service.

The bidding was torrid. It rose to the grand sum of $43. When it looked like a woman I'd already dated was about to win, I decided to spice things up by offering to pay half if there was a higher bid.

Kate Widland took the bait. She got me for $44, half of which I paid. With inflation, I'm sure I'm worth $25 now at least.

Kate grew up in Albuquerque, New Mexico, where her parents had moved after living in Chicago. She was an environmental studies major, at least partly because she suffered from asthma as a child. Harvard helped her complement that interest with an understanding of how public policy can shape solutions; ultimately, she would combine science with politics.

We hit it off on our first date and things blossomed from there. She was pretty, smart, far deeper and more well-rounded than many of the girls I'd met at school. We both loved *Casablanca*. I was on a very limited budget, but she loved my creative date ideas. Within a month we were an item.

IT FEELS ODD TO TALK ABOUT KATE IN THIS WAY NOW, TO TALK ABOUT ROMANCE and young love. Not to give the entire plot away, but we get married and inevitably drift apart and finally divorce at what outsiders might think is the worst possible time. Yet we remain friends, share in each other's lives, and we certainly support each other's careers. But the terms of our relationship now are utterly different. Our romance was pre-Iraq; our marriage came in the crucible of my floundering attempts to come to terms with Iraq.

I don't dare say I'm beyond dealing with Iraq and the war. It's not superstition. It's an acknowledgment that intense experiences shape you intensely, and are never really done with you, even though you wish to be done with them.

THE AFGHANISTAN PHASE OF WHAT WAS NOW CALLED THE WAR ON TERROR RATCH-eted up quickly. In the space of a few months, U.S. bombers and a handful of American Special Forces men on the ground helped what had been a ragtag resistance movement overthrow the Taliban, sending al Qaeda leader Osama bin Laden into hiding and eventual exile in Pakistan. Meanwhile my unit still wasn't activated for deployment.

Then we started hearing about Iraq. The Bush administration claimed that Iraq's leader, Saddam Hussein, was working with terrorists and actively developing weapons of mass destruction—nuclear bombs—that could be used against the West.

I thought it was bullshit, to be honest. Why would Osama bin Laden be working with Iraq? The evidence was not convincing at best and manufactured at worst. Iraq is largely a secular Arab nation; Muslim extremists, and bin Laden especially, certainly did not align themselves with Hussein.

It didn't add up. And yet there was a rush to war. The arguments became more and more ridiculous.

By now I was a senior, months away from graduating. Unlike before Afghanistan, there were big protests on campus. I had mixed feelings. I was against the war, but I didn't feel I should protest. It would be too weird—if my unit was activated and I had to go, of course I would, so why would I protest beforehand?

I understand I had a right to; every American has that right. But it just would have felt incongruent. Or weird, take your pick.

A lot of people knew I was the only Marine reservist on campus—in fact, our campus newspaper interviewed me for a story. Classmates would come up to me and say, "Hey, if you get activated, take care of yourself." A few would try to talk me out of reporting if I got activated. I didn't get into any arguments; there was no sense.

Toward the end of 2002, I got the word: my unit would be activated the first week of January. I was to report for active duty and join the unit for our "workup"—the specific training and preparation for a mission—prior to being sent overseas. I would miss my final semester.

My activation was coming during the Christmas holiday but before final exams. One of the advantages of being a very old institution is that Harvard has dealt with a wide variety of situations, including something like this. I met with my professors and was offered the choice of either taking the grade I had to that point in the semester, or taking a proctored exam, which according to Harvard rules meant I would be supervised by a chaplain while taking the test.

There was one class where taking the exam might make a positive difference—Intro to Shakespeare. So I carried around my huge Shakespeare anthology during the workup for our deployment.

I humped all thirty-seven plays and one hundred fifty-four sonnets with me to the field. I didn't recite iambic pentameter between mortar rounds, but I did contemplate the fact that the book was thick enough to stop a bullet. Maybe even a mortar shell.

I got a B+. It made up for all the crap I took from the guys around me.

Lugging around Shakespeare was arguably the most difficult thing I did on that deployment. After about six months of training in the Carolinas, they called a company formation and informed us that we were going to Okinawa, Japan. We were to sit there and be ready in case North Korea went off the rails.

In retrospect, I guess it was better than heading to Afghanistan or Iraq, which was where we all thought we were going at the time. But I resented it. I was one semester away from graduating. If I had to miss school and put my civilian life on hold for a year or so,

I wanted it to mean something. I didn't want to be a dogcatcher waiting for the Eternal General Secretary—aka Kim Jong-il—to do something stupid.

It was a low-priority job, to be honest. Safe, maybe—but you don't join the Marines to get safe or low-priority jobs. I had trained for war, expected and wanted to go. I was disturbed by the bogus reasons the Bush administration gave for going to war, but I wanted to fight. Sitting around in Japan felt like mostly a waste of time.

Upper command seemed to agree—they sent all the ROTC kids home in time for their next semester.

Me, because I was not going to be a fancy officer, had to put off graduating another year.

We spent the time training and trying not to be bored. Jungle warfare training was the best. Zip lines were fun. Bug eating was . . . different.

The ants were the best. Mealworms in a pinch. Here's a hint: use a straw if you can. It goes down quicker, and you think about it less.

Okinawa itself was a fascinating place. I mostly stayed on the base, but every so often I'd head into town and check out the food or the night scene. We found a club that featured a contest to the death between a tarantula and scorpion. (The scorpions generally won.)

Kate took some time off and flew out for about a week, arriving in Tokyo in the middle of a typhoon. She managed to get to Okinawa after spending the night on the terminal floor, and we had a fun time, driving around the island, snorkeling, visiting tourist sites. My being deployed overseas was a new experience for her as well as me. Her family did not have a deep military tradition, and as far as we knew, I was the only deployed enlisted Marine at Harvard.

She could be very understanding. Like the time I lost track of what time she was arriving for a visit, and she walked into the middle of a rumble in the squad bay. There was a military reason: one of our fellow Marines had missed a crowd control exercise, and so we brought him up to speed with the help of pepper spray and impromptu wrestling and boxing techniques. Just like they trained us.

A Valentine's Day to remember, I'm sure.

I made lance corporal that year.

There's a belief that sergeants in the military run everything, but in my experience, it's really the lance corporals who make the show. They're the ones who do all the hard work. So, making lance corporal was a milestone. Authority-wise, it let me take charge of work parties—not exactly a glamor position. But it also made me a member of the so-called Lance Corporal Underground, the Corps' informal information network, a place where advice and intelligence flow freely.

If you want to know what's going on, see a lance corporal.

When you make E-3, you get half a blood stripe—an homage, in a way, to the "full" blood stripe worn by E-4s and above on their uniforms. The exact nature of the E-3 ceremony can only be divulged to actual lance corporals, but suffice to say that the congratulatory pounding of my new chevrons produced an ample flow of red.

Incidentally, the official blood stripe for NCOs and officers commemorates Marine Corps heroism at the Battle of Chapultepec, where the Marines led an uphill assault on a heavily fortified position in Mexico City, ultimately taking the hill despite tremendous losses. The battle helped secure America's victory in the Mexican-American War.

Having spent a lot of time in Mexico as a child, I also know the other side of the story: a heroic stand by a vastly outnumbered force consisting primarily of teenage military cadets. When the cadets ran out of bullets, rather than surrendering, they wrapped themselves in flags and threw themselves off the cliff. They are honored in Mexico as the Niños Héroes.

Which version of the story you prefer depends on your perspective.

Attitudes toward gender and sexuality have been controversial in the U.S. military for quite some time; maybe forever. I served during the "Don't ask, don't tell" period, which was supposed to be a compromise from previous explicitly antigay policies. If you didn't say you were gay, you wouldn't be bothered—or kicked out of the service.

In practice, things were a lot more complicated. This isn't a book on policy, and the issues of gender and sexuality extend far beyond the Marine Corps. Being an organization of mostly young men—women were not admitted to combat arms until 2016—there was quite a bit of unspoken anxiety over gayness and gender identity. While we were in Tokyo, I went out to a bar with some fellow Marines. One of our number—and ironically probably the most homophobic—fell under the sway of a lithe young creature with a fairly prominent Adam's apple—apparently invisible to him in the dark. When he finally understood the nature of things, he went outside and threw up.

Later, he spent quite a lot of time asking if I thought the attraction made him gay.

Drunk, yes. Gay, probably not. Though to mess with him I had to say "yes."

Doubts about sexuality, attraction, identity—they're never going to be eliminated in a culture where those things are controversial or even under question. The Corps reflected that.

The only combat we saw that activation was in an Air Force enlisted men's club, where Air Force servicepeople decided to test Marine Corps mettle. Legend has it that three Marines took on one hundred fifty Air Force—there may be some exaggeration on both sides. I got out as soon as the MPs showed up—I don't mind fighting, but the paperwork involved when you've been caught is a bitch.

There were a few times on that deployment when I was stuck with the modern-day version of Shore Patrol—the unhappy saps who have to respond to a situation before the actual MPs get called. You basically have all the authority of a crossing guard. You can't make an arrest, and the likely reaction of any Marine when called out is a pair of fists in your face.

Which of course must be answered, which leads to the MPs or police being called. And a lot of paperwork.

I took an entrepreneurial approach: I'd give a guy ten bucks to spend at a bar down the street. Problem solved, and no blood or paperwork besides.

3/25

Our Japan deployment meant that the unit would not be reactivated for at least another year. That was the good news. The bad news was that I still had a semester to go at Harvard and had missed the early round of job interviews customarily granted to seniors. Here I was twenty-four, not yet a graduate, not yet in the permanent workforce. I did work my last semester as a bouncer at a bar in town, often hauling out classmates who couldn't hold their liquor or their tongues. But I felt a little stuck, behind where I should be.

Looking back, I don't mean to downplay what I'd achieved with the help of my family. Statistically, you won't find many young Latino males raised by single women in households with sketchy backgrounds getting college degrees, let alone from Harvard. The odds were far better that I'd be in prison, or even dead. I'd worked hard to get where I was. But that hard work had gifted me a quandary—what exactly was the next step?

Due to my activations, Kate was now graduating with me, and we decided we would go back to her home state, New Mexico, and try to find jobs there. We'd work on some campaigns—it was 2004, a presidential year with a lot of elections in need of young workers—and then put together a long-range plan. Maybe I'd take the Foreign Service exam; maybe she would go to law school. Working for a few months outside of the college bubble would help us decide.

I should mention that I'm a Democrat and was looking to work on a Democrat's campaign. I grew up poor, took advantage of things the Democrats championed like Pell Grants and school lunch programs, and in general found myself in line with the party's aims. Critics call those programs handouts. They're more like helping hands, giving people an opportunity to reach more of their potential. When you succeed, you feel a debt of gratitude to the country, and you want to pay back in any way you can. Even though I was already a serviceman, I still felt I needed to contribute more to my country.

I found a job working in Santa Fe for an independent, union-sponsored organization called America Coming Together that was aiming to help John Kerry's campaign. I was a field organizer, going house to house getting people registered to vote.

Kate's hunt not only took much longer; it took her to Arizona, where she was hired by the Democratic Party to work on campaigns.

We now had a long-distance relationship. Just as importantly, the move affected my Reserve status. Because I could no longer attend training in New Hampshire, I needed to join a unit closer to home. That brought me to Company D of the 4th Reconnaissance Battalion of the U.S. Marine Corps, a headquarters and service company that supported a Marine Recon unit.

Known as "Marine Raiders," the Recon forces are roughly the equivalent of Navy SEALs and Army Special Forces soldiers, though generally tasked with specific Marine Corp missions. Things have changed a bit since I served, but Recon then and now consists of highly trained Marines who can operate behind enemy lines, perform special missions, prepare assaults, and do a lot of what SEALs and Green Berets do, just not with the same PR blast.

Even these guys need units supporting them, and that was the job of the company I reported to, Company D, or Delta Company as we would refer to it in the military. The unit included Marines who were in the Recon pipeline or training program but had not finished. There were also men who had been candidates for Marine Recon but ended up dropping out and being reassigned to Delta for one reason or the other.

Let me make this clear: the admission standards for Recon are every bit as hard as those for other special operations units. The guys who dropped out of the program were still pretty awesome Marines, self-selected to be the cream of the cream. I was not one of them. I was just a regular infantryman.

Shortly after we moved, I went out to see the first sergeant to introduce myself and get a feel for the unit. He gestured to a chair.

"We're going," he told me. He was calm and matter-of-fact, but also very direct. "This is your chance. If you don't want to go to Iraq. Don't join this unit."

Delta had been tasked to augment, or "fill in," another unit in the 4th Division that was short of manpower, 3/25.

Civilians tend to focus on divisions as the major units of the military. If you're in the service, though, your identity generally comes from the smaller units that make up the division.

Units and men can be moved around depending on need and mission, but the general organization of infantry units in the Marines starts with a four-man fireteam. Three of them make a squad; three squads make a platoon. Three platoons make a company, along with a weapons platoon and a headquarters section. Three companies make a battalion; three battalions make a regiment. There's a weapons company, headquarters, attachments—Marines with special missions like engineers, for example—as well.

As an infantryman, the highest level of organization you're ever involved with is the battalion; you might once in a blue moon wave at someone from regimental and dread an inspection from the division general. Three-Deuce-Five, as it was often called, was the 3rd Battalion of the 25th Regiment, part of the 4th Division.

Both Recon and 3/25 trace their roots to World War II. The Scouts fought in several Pacific battles, perhaps most famously at Iwo Jima. Three-25 saw action in the Pacific as well, fighting at Saipan and Iwo Jima. There were no easy battles in that war, but the fight on Iwo was ferocious enough to have burned itself into not only Marine memory, but our nation's as well. The victory there is commemorated in the famous photograph of Marines hoisting a flag during a lull in the battle. (Full disclosure: the Marines in the photo were from 2/28, not 3/25.)

While Delta and 3/25 were members of the same division, they had not trained together as far as I know. The battalion's men mostly lived in the area around central Ohio—think Columbus, though there were subunits in Pennsylvania and Tennessee. While some thought had been given to using Delta as an integral unit, by the time I got there plans were already underway to spread the members of the company out among 3/25's own companies and build a stronger cohesion among the overall unit.

If I'm remembering correctly, the sergeant told me I had an option because my orders had not yet come through. I could have easily stayed with my New Hampshire unit for a few more months, or even found another unit that wasn't set to deploy.

But that isn't the Marine way. It wasn't mine either.

I took a deep breath. It's not like I was a gung ho guy. I didn't want to kill anyone. But if I didn't go, then someone else would go in my place, and that was unfair.

And it wouldn't have felt right at all.

"It'd be wrong not to go," I told the first sergeant. "I'm in."

# II.

# FLYING IN

## McKENZIE

Racing to McKenzie felt like plunging from my present to my past.

I had left New Mexico permanently after the Iraq war, largely because the place was too filled with the memories of my friends who had died. Going back now, I thought more of who McKenzie had been—an experienced Marine who was something of a mentor—rather than who he was now, a civilian down on his luck and in turmoil.

I thought of who I'd been as well: a young man, coming of age, proving myself as a Marine, and as a human being.

McKenzie was Diné (pronounced "din-eh"), or Navajo, and had been living on the Rez—the Navajo Nation Reservation—before we were activated. There was a small but significant core group of Native Americans in the New Mexico unit. Beyond the fact that many Navajo live in New Mexico, there is a strong tradition of service with the Corps in their community. Illustrious examples, such as the Code Talkers of World War II, are not only respected, but at the time of our activation were well-known neighbors of some of the men.

While stories of war exploits were plentiful, McKenzie had joined looking for career opportunities rather than medals. The Marines offered a way out of poverty for him, his wife, and two daughters. Initially discouraged from becoming a Recon Marine because he didn't meet the physical requirements, he'd worked out ferociously until he could qualify. Before our deployment, he had attended the schools in the long-term training program and was helping a handful of other men in the Recon pipeline.

The path through Recon was arduous; sticking to it showed stubbornness as much as skill and ambition. None of those things were evident in his voice now.

I kept him on the phone as I drove, believing that as long as I had him talking to me, he wouldn't do anything stupid. He'd be alive when I got there, and together we could get him some help.

The irony was, there had been plenty of opportunity for him to die in Iraq. The same for me. Anyone with a death wish could easily have had it fulfilled.

But back then we all were desperate to stay alive. We wanted to do our duty and be good Marines. Most of all, we didn't want to let the guys next to us down.

As darkness fell on the highway, I thought the members of Lima 3/25 had achieved those things. With one exception: we hadn't all stayed alive.

## THE RIVER AND THE DAM

We flew into Haditha Dam the third week of March 2005, having spent several weeks training in the States for our mission. Iraq was still hypothetical to us at that point, a place we'd seen on TV and in videos, but not experienced.

I couldn't see much from where I was sitting in the helicopter, and it was already getting dark anyway. The noise in the helo was so loud talking was difficult, so mostly I imagined all the possible ways we could crash and burn before we got to our destination.

Mechanical failure. RPGs—rocket-propelled grenades. Anti-air missile. Stray bullet shots. Run out of fuel. . . . The possibilities seemed endless.

Even if it had been daytime, the terrain below wouldn't have offered much of a diversion. Light tan desert punctuated by a meandering river—the Euphrates. Buildings collected around the river's banks, mostly in small clusters, though occasionally in sprawls large enough to suggest a city. Every so often a small grid city built by Saddam for industrial workers.

Greenery at the desert's edges, where the watershed could support farming. Barely.

This was the Iraq we were coming to stabilize. Hundreds of miles of it, mostly empty.

I'd told Kate I'd probably have to deploy the same night I found out. It happened to be the day of a presidential debate in Arizona; she was there on another campaign, and was backstage when I called her.

On my end, it sounded like she took it well. I found out later that she started crying the moment she hung up. Supposedly that got the Secret Service agents there pretty nervous—why was this woman, to this point calm and highly organized, now suddenly falling apart?

That passed. I can't say her fears for me did. It had been difficult knowing I could be deployed immediately after 9/11, but this was far worse.

My knee throbbed as the helicopter banked to follow the path to the dam. I'd spent several weeks trying to build up the muscles around the joints in hopes that would relieve some of the pain, but all the exercise did was make it hurt even more.

But in a way, my messed-up knee was a good thing. It's how I got to know Grant.

## GRANT—FRIEND, MARINE, CANDY STORE

I can't pinpoint the first time I met Jonathan Grant, but it would have been soon after I reported to Delta. Most likely I had some food in my hand. It was rare for Grant to pass up a snack, and he wasn't shy about asking others to share.

It may also have gone the other way. Grant—how I knew him, how I knew most Marines, by their last name—was a constant supply of candy and assorted junk food, a big guy with seemingly endless pockets. Everybody liked him. He was affable, easy to talk to, a genuinely nice man.

Soon after I'd arrived at the Reserve unit in New Mexico, I took a physical fitness test and ended up not being able to complete the run portion in the allotted time—I did the three miles in something like thirty-five minutes. The minimum standard for my age group would have been under twenty-eight. I began working out to strengthen my leg and endurance, and Grant volunteered to help. He lived near me in Santa Fe, and he became my unofficial trainer.

We would do weight work, and hike in the mountains near Santa Fe to strengthen my knee. We'd hump thirty or forty pounds—far less than a full combat pack, but a weight you felt nonetheless, especially after the first mile. Grant could be a hard-ass trainer: at lunch, he'd sometimes arrive with a full bucket of chicken, which he'd eat while I exercised. No food for me on his watch since I had to lose weight.

He lightened up after workouts—when all the chicken was gone. He loved to listen to my music, borrowing my headphones to groove on whatever playlist I had going. So there were benefits back and forth.

He had a toddler and an infant at home. When we gathered to leave New Mexico, I held his baby while he and his wife hugged to say good-bye.

"Take care of him," Grant's wife told me as I handed the little one back.

"Of course I will," I told her, knowing it was far more likely that he would be watching out for me.

## HADITHA DAM

The dam we were approaching was huge—not Hoover Dam huge, but massive just the same. It held back what was now a large lake at the northern stretch of the Euphrates, and contained sizable turbines and a sizable number of offices. Approaching from the riverside, it looked like a wedge of concrete squares and rectangles shoved into a sandy hill.

The towering cement and earthen structure supplied hydroelectricity to much of the northern portion of Iraq. Constructed in the late 1970s and 1980s, the dam flooded a pair of significant archaeological sites. Ceramics extracted from one before the flooding were dated to 1800–1700 BC; people have been living and farming in the area a very long time.

Because its destruction could have caused catastrophic flooding, the dam had been seized by U.S. forces at the outset of the war. In 2004, the turbines that generated electricity were put back online, and by the time we arrived, the facility could generate 650 mV (millivolt) of power. That's enough electricity to power a good-sized city in the States, and then some.

Troops from Azerbaijan provided security at the dam, part of an attempt by the Bush administration to make the occupation seem like an international effort. The Azerbaijani troops were notorious for being trigger happy; we quickly learned to make sure they knew when we were coming and going, and to carefully identify ourselves at their checkpoints. The 4th Assault Amphibian Battalion—Trackers, we called them, since they would drive the amtrac vehicles we got around in (I'll explain in a bit)—had arrived ahead of us to set up our transportation. It was also an occasional home to special operations guys who kept completely to themselves. Iraq workers came in to work and went home at the end of their shifts.

The area below the dam and to the west was al Anbar Province, our patrol area. In the immediate aftermath of the 2003 invasion, the province had been relatively quiet. Most of it lay far from Baghdad and, except for the banks of the Euphrates, was mostly desert.

But the recent calm was deceiving. Saddam had strong family and tribal ties here, and many supporters among the Sunni population. The southern part of the province around Fallujah and Ramadi had always been a rebel stronghold. Four U.S. contractors were killed and their bodies desecrated in April 2004, setting off not one but two major battles there. In a fierce campaign that November and December, Marines pushed most of the insurgents out.

Much of Fallujah was destroyed during the siege, which presented the fledgling Iraqi government and the U.S. with the additional problem of rebuilding the city. Warned of the impending attack, many of the civilians had left to avoid being swept up in the battle. It would take years for the city to be rebuilt and for its population to grow close to its prewar size. Nor did insurgent activity completely end in the city, though it had been severely curtailed.

The U.S. used different tactics in Ramadi, another insurgent stronghold and the capital of the province. The overall tactics in Fallujah had been relatively conventional for urban warfare, with quick strikes at strongholds and a progressive sweep from one side of the town to the other, pushing out insurgents as they were forced against units preventing their escape—hammer and anvil tactics, to use the phrase historians often adopt. Though greatly augmented by advances in technology, the general approach would have been familiar to a military man a hundred years earlier.

These tactics, however, caused a great deal of destruction. Official U.S. estimates report that about fifteen percent of the city's buildings were completely destroyed, and judging from photos taken of the city after the battle, it's easy to conclude that's an underestimate. Few corners of the city remained unscathed. Civilian casualties were nearly impossible to estimate, but the number had to be significant.

In Ramadi, the idea was to keep the local population and government in place to whatever extent possible. Coalition troops would target known insurgents, sweep areas where they were believed to be hiding, and patrol the city. It took far longer and success was difficult to measure by traditional means—body counts and territory gained were meaningless. There was a string of key battles, with each being relatively small or isolated when viewed against the entire backdrop of the war. Ultimately, though, the campaign helped establish the setting for the Sahwa al Anbar, or Great Awakening, of the Sunni tribal leaders in the region. Their alliance against the insurgents was critical to the uneasy peace that eventually settled over the Sunni Triangle.

But that lay in the future. Ramadi was calmer than it had been when we arrived that March, but hardly subdued.

Most, though not all, American military leaders and the Bush administration concluded that the victory in Fallujah had decimated the insurgents, and that insurgent activity throughout the province would be light for the foreseeable future. This would turn out to be a critical mistake. While many insurgents had died, enough escaped the city or managed to lay low long enough to survive. Many of the survivors were able to join or start cells in other parts of the province. They trained new recruits and learned from earlier mistakes. Others arrived at a steady pace, generally sneaking in from Syria, which bordered the province.

THE INSURGENTS WE WOULD FACE WERE A MIX OF DIFFERENT GROUPS. SOME were ex-soldiers once loyal to Saddam Hussein who still opposed us. Other locals were motivated by religion or tribal loyalties, and attacked us because they thought we supported their rivals. The area was majority Sunni, though some cities had large populations of Shia Muslims. As a rule, the Sunni and Shiite factions did not get along and usually would not ally on an operation; occasionally they fought each other.

By far the most formidable enemies were foreign fighters who had been recruited to fight "infidels"—Americans. Most operated under the banner of Tanzim Qaida al-Jihad fi Bilad al-Rafidayn—known to us as al Qaeda in Iraq or al Qaeda in Mesopotamia. These fanatics were usually adherents of extremist Sunni teachers and leaders, most especially Osama bin Laden. As far as they were concerned, they were fighting a holy war to eliminate us; dying on the battlefield led directly to Paradise.

Most of the province outside of Fallujah and Ramadi had been quiet in the days after the initial invasion in 2003. A lot of Iraqis had welcomed U.S. forces openly.

They did that rarely now. The slow evolution of violence would spike exponentially in the coming months.

## THE FEELING OF WAR AND MAGIC SAND

Nobody says "Good luck" when you tell them you're being activated and headed toward a war zone, or least no one did to me.

They do, however, ask how you feel.

*Fine.*

*No, how do you fee-eel . . . ?*

It was a weird question. How was I supposed to feel? Like I was going to do my job, I guess.

Like I was going to war.

Part of me thought we'd end up guarding a chow hall or something, staying mostly way behind the lines, second stringers. And that part of me was fine with that; I'd do my time, then come home and get back on my career track, such as it was.

Another part of me wanted to do what I'd been trained to

do—be a Marine. Fight. My mother knew my knee was still messed up, and she encouraged me to see a doctor with the hopes that I would get released from the deployment. I told her I couldn't do that. My father even called from Mexico to urge me to cross the border and go AWOL. I doubt either of them thought I would take their advice; it was more a way of expressing concern for my well-being.

A few nights before the deployment, I went out to a local bar and started talking to some older veterans who happened to hang out there. A handful of Navajos who had served during Vietnam and afterward got really deep and philosophical with me. They explained some of their traditions and customs dealing with warfare and especially the dead. They gave me advice, then took me to one of their homes for a spiritual cleansing ceremony, so I could be properly prepared for battle.

One of the men built a small fire in the backyard. I watched quietly as he added large amounts of what I believe was sage to the flames, singing the green leaves. Surrounded by thick smoke, I stood motionless as he prayed for my safety. Whether the simple ceremony was ancient or ad hoc, it was extremely emotional, and I left feeling as if I had been gifted a powerful protection by generous elders.

Not long afterward, I made a pilgrimage with my mother and a sister to Chimayo, a sanctuary sacred to Catholics as well as Native Peoples in New Mexico.

Chimayo is a small Catholic church that dates from 1816. The adobe chapel at the center of the churchyard is very small— fourteen hundred square feet, less than many tract homes. Though filled with lush trees and a carefully tended garden, the grounds are on the same scale. Yet you feel an overwhelming spiritual presence as soon as you pass beneath the adobe archway to the property and enter the church. A row of crutches line the nave's wall, left by people who have been cured miraculously following a visit.

I walked to a small room off the side and bent down to *el pocito,* an ancient well now filled with sand. Anyone taking a fistful is said to be protected from evil. Either by miracle or with the aid of dutiful priests, the hole refills itself each night, making the sand always available for those who believe.

I'm not sure exactly what I believed at that moment, but I knelt nonetheless and grabbed some sand, pouring it into a baggie I would carry through the war.

## 185 MARINES

Three-Deuce-Five had three infantry companies. Two were designated to largely pull security at fixed bases in the province; the third, Lima, was assigned to do sweeps and go on various operations.

I was in Lima, with one hundred eighty-four other Marines. The bulk of the guys had been in the Ohio unit, but there was a good mix from New Mexico. For all intents and purposes, Delta Company no longer existed; we were all Lima now. Generally, we fit in.

I was in 1st Platoon, where Grant and some of my other friends were. For unexplained reasons, myself and another Marine had been inadvertently left off the rosters when the unit was adding the New Mexico guys, and so were given a choice: join Infantry as a rifleman or join Headquarters.

I took Infantry, which was the only job I knew besides being a mortarman, and it would guarantee that I would be close to Grant.

The other Marine, Sergeant Michael Marzano, went to Headquarters, slotted to a mobile platoon. Sergeant Marzano was killed in May by an improvised explosive device, or IED, in Haditha.

It could have been me. Would have been me.

My choice of unit was the first of several lucky breaks that kept me alive. I'd count eleven of them when I got home.

They sent me to Lima Company's 1st Platoon, 3rd Squad. Grant was the platoon's communications guy, handling the radio for the platoon commander. That meant he was rarely with me on patrols, but most of the time when we were transporting to or from an op, he'd be sitting next to me, handing out candy and stealing my earbuds. He was nearby in the helo the day we flew to the dam.

As the last to join, I was low man on the fireteam—the machine gunner's assistant. That's the worst job on the team, since you have to carry the gunner's extra ammo—you're basically the gunner's bitch. Most times, that's a job for a private without much experience, but I couldn't be choosey. The extra weight I had to carry didn't bother me, really.

Our fireteam leader was Andy Britten. Very down-to-earth kind of guy. He could be pretty sarcastic, though not toward his guys. He had one standout quality in a firefight: he was extremely calm. When everything is going to shit, a steady voice and a matter-of-fact gaze mean everything.

The assistant team leader was Trevor Smith. He was always joking around. We bonded out in the field in Iraq when nature called to him and he couldn't remove his body armor—I helped hold him up as he squatted to answer the call.

Fun times.

Even the most life-and-death maneuvers could be a game with him. He called his legs Thunder and Lightning. We'd stack up near a door, ready to enter a building suspected of holding a weapons cache, and he'd yell, "Which is it going to be? Thunder, Lightning? Thunder, Lightning? Thunder . . ."

You had to guess which leg. He was an equal opportunity kicker; I can't say he played favorites.

For the record, I kicked in doors as a lefty. I write lefty, though I do shoot right-handed.

Smith was a great impressionist, known for his completely inappropriate routines spoofing everything from ethnicity to mental health. Probably not funny out of context, but when your context is live rounds and IEDs, inappropriate humor becomes an acceptable form of entertainment.

Our machine gunner was Peter Batchelder. He was a quiet Christian boy—often read the Bible, rarely swore, and probably didn't even drink. Atypical for a Marine, but a good guy.

Gerald "Gary" Norris led the second fireteam from my squad. He was a bit of an Eminem character, a white guy with a dew rag who laid down a rap once or twice while we were on patrol. Their machine gunner was Hawkey—imagine a pothead in the Marine Corps. He didn't actually smoke pot, but he had the aura of someone who had.

Corporal Brent McKitrick led the third fireteam. An old, crotchety man with crotchety sayings—that's how he came off, though I doubt he was too far past twenty years old. In civilian life he worked as a corrections officer back in Ohio.

My other friends included Cheston Bailon—a quiet, smart-as-shit Navajo kid. I'd met him and his brother John, also in the company but not in our platoon, back in New Mexico; they'd started talking to me one weekend during maneuvers because they were Democrats and heard I was working on the election.

The Bailons are Navajos, who sometimes described themselves as "Irish twins"—close in age, and close in life. John was a little more than a year older, but Cheston was built a little smaller. You find a high percentage of Native Americans in the service, especially in the Marines. In the Bailons' case, enlisting had felt like "the right thing to do," at least partly because of their heritage and the warrior culture they'd grown up with.

Both men had a strong ethos; you could count on them in a fight. Both had been in the Recon pipeline but had dropped back to infantry for different reasons. Though as a general rule the

Marines would not let brothers serve in the same unit, somehow their relationship had been overlooked until just before we shipped out; Command had put them into different platoons as a way of lessening the chance that both would be injured or worse during the same operation.

"You're an intellectual with a Marine Corps wrapper," John liked to tell me. I took it as a compliment.

Our squad leader was David Jolly from Montana. Jolly was his name, not his disposition. You could joke around with him for hours and not get a laugh. Not a bad guy, just not given to humor.

Andy Taylor led 2nd Squad. He was an irreverent jokester from the Cincinnati area. We called him T Rex because he had this habit of keeping his arms close to his body when he was in full combat rattle; with the vest and all, he looked like the killer dinosaur.

Before I got to Lima, Taylor had been the platoon sergeant, the highest-ranking NCO in the platoon, and the squad leaders' boss. Thanks to some college classes, Taylor had a smattering of Arabic, which was more than anyone else in the platoon had.

A member of Taylor's squad, Lance Corporal Sajjad Rizvi, spoke Urdu, thanks to his family's Pakistani background. Urdu and Arabic are not related at all—they aren't even distant cousins—but his background helped him puzzle out what was being said.

Sometimes.

For the most part, we ended up relying on hand gestures and very simple words, unless we had interpreters or Iraqi National troops with us.

More friends:

Scott Bunker—great Marine, now a firefighter/EMT. Originally planning to become an officer and a Marine pilot, Scott joined as an enlisted man after 9/11. He intended to finish his education after the deployment, graduate, and then enter an officer training program. While we were in Iraq, he did a stint with a Marine sniper team and was invited to join the sniper unit when he could get clearance from Command; those plans would never be fulfilled.

Hillbilly—Andrew Hildebrand—a really good-natured guy from Ohio.

Gilbert Miera. Also from New Mexico, Miera was a lance corporal when we deployed. He was quiet, stoic, a good friend of Grant's. He was an avid hunter in civilian life and would occasionally open up and tell us about some of his trophy kills.

And of course McKenzie. He was only a few years older than I was, but in terms of life experience, he was far older. He was the son of a Christian missionary, though he wasn't a Bible thumper by any means. He'd trained for artillery before trying out for Recon and was a big guy—six-one. Like the rest of us, he was gung ho about our assignment, excited to be finally getting a chance to put everything he'd learned into practice. It would take a while, but eventually that enthusiasm was tempered.

ABOUT A MONTH AFTER WE ARRIVED, STAFF SERGEANT ANTHONY GOODWIN JOINED us as platoon sergeant, bumping Charles Hurley up to platoon commander. If you had to design the archetype bigger-than-life Marine, it was Goodwin. I can close my eyes and see him on the top of an amtrac amphibious vehicle wearing an American flag bandanna around his face to fight off the swirling sand and dust.

You could tell he was grinning, though.

He was made for combat. You'd be running for your life and he'd be up on an amtrac, smiling at the machine-gun fire. His bandanna would slip and he'd poke a Marlboro into the side of his mouth.

I never had trouble with him, but Goodwin rubbed a lot of the guys the wrong way. He could be way too gung ho and, frankly, a bit of a prick. Some of that was needed at times—the company tended to be too easygoing when we first deployed—and at times it was a bit of an act, part of his goal of keeping us motivated. Goodwin seemed to relish the role of bad cop to others' good cop when dealing with his Marines. And as he told a fireteam leader before the war, "sometimes you have to be a dick so the Marines focus on you rather than the situation."

Our deployment would give him plenty of opportunity to put this to the test.

And then there was Charles Hurley.

Hurley was about forty years old when we deployed. He'd first joined Lima in the late 1980s or '90s—the Stone Age as far as we were concerned. While he'd never been in combat, he'd served in several different locations and circumstances. He'd left the Reserves briefly, rejoining after 9/11 because he felt it was his patriotic duty. His enlistment ran out, but when he heard the unit was going to Iraq, he reupped in time to deploy. He wasn't going to let his guys go without him.

Ordinarily Marine platoons are led by an officer, generally a lieutenant, but an exception was made in our case. Hurley certainly had a lot of experience, and in most instances the platoon sergeant informally runs things anyway. He almost always has more experience than the officer holding the title of commander. (Mustang officers—men and women who become officers after spending years in the enlisted ranks—are the exception.)

Anyway, Hurley had plenty of experience for the job and proved himself over and over again. He joined us as a staff sergeant, but was soon promoted to gunnery sergeant, aka Gunny. Later on, an officer came in as commander, with Hurley taking over as platoon sergeant—but I'm getting ahead of myself.

We called Hurley a lot of things—Old Man Hurley, Gray Hair Hurley—but he was probably best known as Gunny—the universal tag for E-7s in the Marines.

Gunnery sergeants have a special place in the Marine Corps infantry. Working as platoon sergeants, they are officially the unit's operations leader, working with the officer or officers and supervising the sergeants and other enlisted Marines under them.

But that doesn't do them real justice. For most infantrymen in combat, "Gunny"—whoever that may be—is maybe a notch below God, and in some circumstances may outrank Him. Lore holds that Marine Corps gunnery sergeants are the toughest, smartest, most bad-assed Marines on the battlefield, and generally they live up to that legend.

Hurley surpassed it.

He'd been raised in the Corps the old-school way—Marines in command were to keep aloof from the men they commanded. But Hurley had a touch for looking away at just the right moment—like when Taylor ordered pizza during a training exercise just before leaving for Iraq. More importantly, Hurley was very much a lead-from-the-front Marine. When the shit hit the fan, he was generally in the thick of it. I have a lasting memory of Hurley leaping off the top of a vehicle under fire to tell me to get my butt moving and direct other Marines to follow. Hollywood couldn't have scripted a better scene, or a better character, for that matter.

He may have rubbed some of the sergeants below him the wrong way, as he could be a hard-ass. A few thought he was a micro-manager. But he had a grandfatherly vibe going with the guys on the line. In my experience, he was pretty tolerant, and if not exactly easygoing, you could joke around with him and even occasionally prank him without his scorching your head off—something a few gunnery sergeants are known to do.

One of the squad leaders thought it was a riot one night when he had one of his Marines take the radio and call in for a routine check. The thing was, the Marine—Collen West—had a bad stutter, and talking to Hurley made it worse. That twenty-second radio call had to have taken five minutes at least, and left the guys on our end rolling in the sand. West, by the way, never ever stuttered or hesitated under combat; you could count on him in the shit.

Gray 99—another of our nicknames for him that referenced his alleged age—may have had a different opinion. Then again, getting your chops busted is just a sign your Marines love you.

Our company commander was Major Stephen Lawson. He had two strikes against him in the opinion of most of the company: One, he replaced a very popular commander who'd moved up to battalion as executive officer. Two, he came over from a Supply position rather than Infantry. A lot of times we got the feeling that he was putting us out on missions all the time to earn points with his commanders. Whether that was accurate or not, it became a popular explanation in the ranks for the high tempo we were put through. It seemed we were always going out on missions, and in fact we would rack up more than most if not all similar-sized units at that point in the war.

IN REGULAR MARINE UNITS, FIRETEAMS ARE GENERALLY LED BY CORPORALS; sergeants lead squads, lieutenants lead platoons, companies are led by captains, and lieutenant colonels head battalions. In our case, like many Reserve units, we had a strong roster of noncommissioned officers, which meant that senior sergeants held jobs that might otherwise fall to less experienced though still highly qualified NCOs. The officer ranks, however, were much thinner.

Taylor once explained to me that part of this is due to the nature of the Reserve community. Essentially, it's far more common for NCOs to join the ranks of the Reserves after coming off active duty, which he did himself. Officers, however, have different commitments to the service and generally different career paths or aspirations once they leave. Lima and 3/25 had gone through several officers in the year or so before deployment, the men coming and going for different reasons. Not everyone had the sort of experience in infantry that you would find in the regular divisions. On the other hand, that meant we had captains in some cases as platoon leaders, and sergeants at positions they were ordinarily overqualified for.

In combat, you don't check a guy's résumé. You make your judgment about his ability by what he does, not the rank on his uniform. And you always follow orders.

THE TRAINING WE HAD IN THE STATES RIGHT BEFORE DEPLOYING WAS SERIOUS, BUT it was hard to gauge how prepared we were for actual combat. A couple of weeks with actors playing the part of Iraqis—how realistic can that really be, since you know you'll live in the end?

I heard about a sergeant who'd seen combat and came back to train a fresh platoon. He busted ass hard, ran them back and forth, drilled them until they couldn't walk. He was hated by one and all.

Until they got to combat. They realized his drills were an attempt to give them every advantage he could to survive.

They loved him even more when they all came back.

There's so much truth in that story. And yet . . .

One thing I was to learn as time went on in Iraq was this: even the best get killed. Hard training and good leadership increase your odds. But we all have a finite store of luck that eventually runs out.

I had to learn that the hard way, but I should have realized how important luck is and isn't back in the States.

Just before we left for Iraq. They gave us liberty in Las Vegas. I spent hours in the gambling rooms, playing roulette.

Winning.

One of my sergeants was standing next to me as my pile of chips mounted higher and higher. I was on an enormous hot streak, a crazy run of good luck. I couldn't seem to lose.

"We gotta go," he said finally. "You gotta cash out."

I wanted to keep riding that, but an order's an order. I took the chips and left the table hot. I came away with over two thousand dollars.

Kate was waiting, wanting to make a big good-bye, kisses and hugs.

"I have to go hit the bathroom," I told her. "I'll be right back."

I went out to the lobby and kept going, love as well as luck suspended. I couldn't deal with a big good-bye scene, even if it meant making her angry and disappointed. More importantly, I didn't want to jinx myself.

It may sound silly now, but what I was thinking was: every war movie has a romantic good-bye scene, and without fail, that's always the first guy to die.

## VIRGINS

Not more than three or four guys in the entire company had been in combat when we landed in Iraq. The rest of us were popping our cherry together.

Wind whipped through the interior of the CH-46 Sea Knight helicopter as we approached the dam. The rear hatch had been open the whole way. I had so much gear between my butt and the seat that I could hardly feel my legs, but I could definitely feel the cold.

The gunner at the side tossed his last cigarette and braced himself as we landed. I felt a surge of relief as the helicopter set down. In combat, I can control many things, but once I get into a vehicle—helicopter, tank, landing craft—I'm a passenger. That's the worst place to be: out of control.

I shouldered my backpack and followed the others out of the helo, into a chaos of dust rousted by the propellers. The first thing I saw to my left was an Azerbaijani soldier, up on the dam, staring with his weapon pointed straight at me. Fortunately, we'd been briefed they were there, or I would have thought Saddam's old soldiers had taken over the base.

The helicopters lifted off, leaving us standing in the starlit night, trying not to feel too cold or too scared, unsure where we were going to go next. Finally, Gunny Hurley got orders, and we headed to a doorway in the dam complex. Through the door, we found stairs and began descending, walking down and down forever. It was like walking toward Hades: the stench of sulfur (a by-product of the hydro conversion and turbines) became stronger as we went. It was a damp hell, though, and cold. So close to the river it held back, the concrete structure couldn't help but feel sodden, its air moist.

The dam complex had a total of four entrances, one each at the base and top on either side of the river. No matter how you came in—that first day we entered from the top—you had to walk many flights up or down to get to your quarters.

We trudged on with our combat gear and full packs, all the way down to the basement area, maybe ten floors below. The hum of the turbines was a low rumble—when all were working, which turned out to be hit or miss, it was like sitting next to a line of jets waiting to take off. That night it was more numbing than ear-shattering, one more thing we weren't used to.

We started looking for places to sleep, checking with flashlights whose main effect was to (briefly) chase the rats away. We finally found an empty spot and plopped down.

A day or two later, we moved upstairs to the middle of the dam, taking over the rooms vacated by the company we were replacing. The hallways were cavernous. The rooms off them were good-sized as well; originally intended as offices, they had been repurposed with bunks and very little else. These weren't en suite—the toilets were a half-dozen porta-potties down in the basement. If you needed to take a leak in the middle of the night, you had a long hike.

Shower?

Those were in the basement as well. The drains worked with reluctance; you were usually standing in a puddle of water left from the last Marine. And of course the water was cold. I came to rely on baby wipes, cleaning up as best I could rather than dealing with the showers. Later on we'd find places to clean up on patrols, often when we went "firm"—stayed the night in a house. We'd shower with our clothes on, outside with a hose or sometimes inside in the bathroom. By then, our uniforms would be so full of salt from sweat I swear they'd stand up on their own, so we'd be washing them as well as ourselves.

The dam's chow hall was up on the seventh floor, three or four stories away. The meals were . . . tolerable, generally. Dinner wasn't bad; we'd get stir fries with rice, along with some kind of fruit. Every so often there would be steak or crab legs, five-star meals compared to what we were used to.

Breakfast, in most of the company's opinion, was inedible. Taylor compared the potatoes to warmed-over pencil erasers; he was being generous. After a while, a lot of guys wouldn't bother making the morning trek, relying on power bars and whatever they could scrounge from care packages sent from home for breakfast. Those did for lunch as well—even at the dam, the standard lunch consisted of MREs. Officially, the abbreviation stood for Meal, Ready to Eat. Unofficially, it was Meals Rejected by Everyone—and far worse pseudonyms.

Rats weren't the only animals we shared the dam with. There were camel spiders large enough to ride on; a few guys would hunt them for sport.

Not me; I try not to mess with anything that can bite back.

Bats would come out at night; I was such a city boy the first time I saw them I wondered what all those night birds were called. The bats themselves weren't that bad, assuming you overlooked their habit of dive-bombing anyone who was smoking, but their guano was everywhere.

The platoon's squads mingled together once we chose our

rooms, and Grant came in with me. When we walked in, I pointed to a pair of bunk beds.

"I'm taking the top," I told him, looking at the rickety structure. I figured if it collapsed, we'd both have a chance of surviving. No way would that happen if I was on the bottom.

Part of the reason Grant and I bunked together was our friendship. The other part was that I was the only one who could deal with his snoring. I'd wake up some nights to a low rumble that sounded halfway between an earthquake and a gangsta-rap bass line played at half speed. I'd reach down and push him a bit. He'd stop. I'd go back to sleep.

Usually. But there were times when his snores got so bad other guys would throw crap at him to get him to shut up. I eventually tied some 550 cord to him. "Five-fifty" is a versatile and strong paracord or rope, used for all sorts of things in the service, though curing a snorer may have been a first. When he'd wake me at night with his honking, I'd give him a yank.

All things considered, I slept well at the dam. I don't remember having any nightmares, not even later when people started dying. My brain saved them for when I got back.

There wasn't a lot to do at the dam. There was a TV, but it had no reception and the supply of videos was limited. A few guys had video game consoles—one of the medics had a PlayStation 2—but only two could play at a time. Things could get crowded and fairly loud when a game was going, which tended to annoy anyone in the room who wasn't interested.

There were card games, board games. I played a lot of Trivial Pursuit until I was banned for being too good.

Mostly, I'd read. If Grant was around, he'd try grabbing my music. I'd end up "splitting" it with him—I'd let him listen on one of the buds while I listened on the other. We could sit for hours talking about things back home, and future plans—what we'd do after the war. We were going to live near each other and be best friends, raising our families together. The wives would get along, and the kids.

There'd be an endless supply of snacks. The future was bright.

## AMTRACS, IEDS, AND ENEMIES

A day after we arrived, we were introduced to our vehicles: lightly armored, tracked personnel carriers officially known as AAVP-7A1s, more often called AAVs (for Assault Amphibious Vehicle) or amphibs, and known throughout the Corps as amtracs, or just tracs. They looked like the lower half of a tank with a big hatch at the back and gun turrets on top near the front. The tracs were designed to swim to shore during a landing from the sea. Once on the beach, they could disgorge up to twenty-five Marines while covering them with heavy machine guns and grenade launchers from a turret near the front.

Back during our workup, we'd practiced mock battles using vehicles available at the base—pre-up-armored Humvees. I thought at the time they were the worst possible vehicles to fight in. Their armor was about the level as what you'd find on a typical pickup truck in the States. Naturally, I assumed the actual vehicles we'd use in combat would be better—safer.

That's what I thought. I was wrong. The tracs were worse than unarmored Humvees. They were, for the chosen job, close to the worst choice you could make.

They carried more men and had a higher firing position than you'd find on a Humvee. But they were not meant to operate in a desert, let alone a hostile city filled with IEDs. Calling them obsolete death traps is kind.

The AAVP originally entered Marine Corps service in 1972 as the Landing Vehicle, Tracked, Personnel-7 (LVTP-7 AAVP-7A1).

The designation changed with an upgrade program in the early 1980s, but they were basically the same vehicle. The upgrades may have dramatically improved the engine, maneuverability, and weapons, but they were still water-going trucks designed to do a very different job than what we were using them for.

The best thing you could say about them was that this was what we had.

They could move a lot of men. The official specs say they can fit twenty-one plus a three-man crew. We generally had a squad and maybe a few attachments—fifteen guys, I'd say on average, plus the crew. We squeezed together, sitting shoulder to shoulder with barely enough room to wiggle our fingers. We sat on small metal benches against the side, sometimes for hours and hours as we drove through the desert. Gear—and drinking water—would be stuffed anywhere it would fit inside and outside, hanging off the flanks. Engine exhaust would flow in through the hatchways on the top. The noise when they moved sounded like the roar of a bus that had mated with a bulldozer and lost its muffler in the process. You shouted to be heard, even by the guy next to you.

We had a few "hacks" to make our trips slightly more bearable, like wrapping small water bottles in wet socks and sticking them on the top as we drove. Air cooling got the water to an almost acceptable temperature—which was anything below scorching. When we could find cushions or pillows in some of the towns we'd buy them and put them on the metal benches. Still, on any ride that lasted more than an hour, your body parts would go numb.

There's an old saying in the Corps that goes like this: How many Marines can you fit into a vehicle? One more.

We lived that.

The vehicle crewmen—"trackers"—were very good. They were reservists as well, based in Louisiana, with accents so thick it was sometimes easier to understand the Iraqis. They not only kept the tracs going, but were genuinely in it with us, not just taxi drivers who got rid of their riders at the first sign of trouble.

I think it was Taylor who asked about the vehicles' armor early on.

"Pretty thick, huh?" he said to one of the commanders. "RPG'd bounce off."

"Hell no," said the commander, or words to that effect. "RPG hits us, we're all fucked."

IEDs?

"That's even worse."

The tracs might have looked like tanks, but they were made out of aluminum barely thick enough to stop a bullet. And while they were amphibs, they couldn't cross water higher than a trickle. Worn out by the war, they were no longer watertight and lacked the plugs and other gear needed to swim through anything deeper than a good-sized puddle. We were riding to war in glorified beer cans.

I SHOULD EXPLAIN A LITTLE ABOUT IEDS, THE "IMPROVISED EXPLOSIVE DEVICES" that were the enemy's most effective weapon and our biggest source of grief in Iraq.

The term refers to an explosive device that is fashioned from something not originally designed to operate the way it is used. In many ways it's like a mine, the primary difference being that the mine was built to be used as a mine. An IED could have many types of triggers. It could be exploded either remotely by cell phone or a wired trigger, or by something interacting with it—say, the pressure of a vehicle riding over it.

The actual explosive could be anything that blew up—artillery and mortar shells were common in Iraq. Saddam's army had been well supplied with them before the war, and there were countless left in the country after he was defeated.

Many of the IEDs U.S. troops faced in Iraq were buried by the side of roads. They were harder to spot in the dirt, and could be planted relatively easily. An insurgent could hide a decent distance away, watching for the opportune time to hit the trigger.

Building IEDs was a skill that could be taught and perfected, and as the war of occupation went on, insurgents got better at making them. They got larger, more deadly, and sometimes harder to find.

Insurgents also learned to use them as part of an attack or ambush. An initial explosion might do minimal damage but still cause a force to stop, leaving it vulnerable to attack. Because they came in different varieties and could be planted in a number of locations, you could never be sure that the explosion that just missed you meant you were safe; there was always the possibility that a ground attack would follow, or that more IEDs were planted around you.

U.S. forces and our allies were not the only ones injured by IEDs. Any explosion in a crowded city area would naturally harm anyone nearby. Those that self-triggered didn't discriminate between soldiers and civilians.

IEDs were everywhere. They weren't always fatal. Some number of them were duds, and many others were so small that they couldn't do a lot of damage even to an unarmored vehicle.

And then there was luck. Later, during one sweep, Scott Bunker, a fireteam leader in Taylor's squad, was assigned to pull security with his men for a pair of Abrams tanks operating with the platoon. Bunker took a position in the shade near the crossroad where the tanks had set up a position. After sitting on a pile of rocks for two hours, he got up and started across the road to swap with another member of the team—they would share time in the direct sun and shade. As he crossed, he noticed a wire in one of the dirt tracks left by the tank treads when it turned.

Bunker picked up the end of the loose wire and followed it back to the side of the road. It led to the rocks where he'd been sitting.

An IED sat there in the rocks; the only thing that saved Bunker was the broken wire—apparently the tank had inadvertently cut it when it turned in the dirt.

Luck. Or fate. Whichever.

The bomb controller was probably sitting nearby somewhere, punching the kill button repeatedly, wondering why it never went off.

Speaking of the enemy: we faced a wide range of them in Iraq, of varying abilities and loyalties. In general, I'm going to call them insurgents or mujahedeen—or the far more common slang, muj (pronounced *mooge*), unless being specific makes a meaningful difference. Technically mujahedeen refers to a warrior engaged in jihad. The Iraqis loyal to the government and opposed to the insurgency would cringe when they heard the term, since in their minds it legitimized the people trying to kill them. But pretty much that was the term we used, at least among ourselves.

What did the Iraqis call the insurgents?

Ali Baba. Usually as part of the phrase "No Ali Baba here."

How exactly terrorists got to be named after the folk hero of "Forty Thieves" fame seems to be a mystery. But it was universal in the areas we would patrol.

## GOING TO WORK

Our first "mission" was a two-hour orientation ride at night. We drove through the desert and came back without incident—and without getting out of our vehicles.

Easy.

All I saw from the back of the AAV were large walls and sand dunes. We had a guy with us from the unit we were replacing who was tremendously relaxed. "This whole area is really safe," he told us. "Don't worry about it."

Then he popped his head out the top hatch to have a cigarette.

That was the first big clue that our training and the reality of Iraq were two different things. We'd been told throughout training not to smoke at night, since the light from the cigarette could give your position away.

That rule was quickly abandoned. Given the size and noise of the vehicles, it'd be obvious where we were. Even dismounted in a city, our presence was rarely if ever a secret. If smoking helped you handle your anxiety, there was no real reason not to.

The distance between theory and reality would continue to grow.

Throughout our deployment, patrols would range from relatively small affairs with just a squad to full-scale operations involving the entire company and beyond. Aside from major operations to take control of insurgent-held areas and clear the insurgents out, there was usually a correlation between the size of the unit making the patrol and the distance from the dam. If we were working near the base, just a squad—twelve men typically—would go, often on foot. Farther away, the entire platoon or even the whole company might be involved. Other things being equal, the size of the unit on any particular patrol or mission had to do with the ability of the unit to sustain itself before help arrived if things went bad. In that case, a unit or units on alert as a Quick Reaction Force, or QRF, would ride to the rescue. The QRF's size and location would depend on the mission.

The most common mission for all Marine infantrymen in our corner of Iraq was a "presence mission," where a unit patrolled an area, making it obvious that we were around. The theory here was that by letting ourselves be seen often in the area, insurgents would never feel comfortable about establishing a base. The unofficial name for these patrols were "F-Us"—fuck you, bad guys, we can go wherever we want and there's nothing you can do to stop us.

Almost as common were "sweeps," where we would go house to house in a city or village, searching for weapons and possible insurgents. There were a few missions where we would be given specific instructions to take an individual in for questioning. And finally there were much larger missions where we were part of complex operations to either engage the enemy or clear a specific area of insurgents.

Any mission could be dangerous, given the nature of the enemy and the war. IEDs could blow you up whether you were strolling through a supposedly quiet town or charging a well-prepared hornets' nest. Mortars could strike you whether you were going house to house or sitting back at the base. While we would learn to think of the dam as our safe haven, insurgents tried at least once to place bombs inside. And across Iraq there were plenty of instances of insurgents making direct, bold attacks on U.S. bases thought to be secure.

We tended to think of a mission as easy or difficult based as much on how long it lasted as on whether we had any contact. Taking casualties, though, always meant it was a hard one.

## BABY STEPS

The training wheels were off for our second op in Iraq. We drove out in the middle of the day to a village near the dam where government workers lived, dismounted from the tracs, and started a sweep. We knocked on doors and politely asked to enter and search. Everyone was compliant, even welcoming.

Iraqi Guardsmen accompanied us. I was with one of the Guardsmen when he started gesturing toward a store. I went in with him; he bought a chewing stick—a kind of natural toothbrush. Though it's popular in many places around the world, I'd never seen one. It was fascinating.

When we came, Jolly berated me, yelling that I could have been kidnapped and not to trust the Guardsmen.

"This guy is a Shia." I tried to explain the deep rifts between the Shiite and Sunni branches of Islam, and how that division ran through the country's politics and the terror groups. "These guys," I said, gesturing to the Guardsmen, "would never help the mujahedeen here."

Jolly wasn't having it. Maybe he was just being overly cautious. But he also didn't seem to have been briefed on one of the most basic facts of the country's politics and culture.

What else was he missing? What else were we missing?

Nearly everything, from religion to dental care. He wasn't unique. We didn't even get a good orientation about where we were in Iraq. If you were a grunt, you'd see a map or maybe a satellite image of the city you were to patrol, then you'd board the trac, ride for whatever time it took, then hop out and do the patrol. As far as you were concerned, you might be in northern Iraq or central Iraq or maybe Timbuktu. We never got a good feel for our location.

Would that have made a difference?

In the moment of battle, I suppose not. But I can't imagine the Marines at Iwo Jima not knowing where on the island they were, or crashing the Halls of Montezuma without a basic understanding of how far away the American border was. We operated in a context-less void.

A different issue: the satellite maps we used when hitting a city were out of date. You'd expect that with the war, of course, but it was a bit galling to come across an insurgent who had a Google Map that was more up to date.

DURING OUR WORKUP, WE'D HAD A CROWD CONTROL SIMULATION WHERE WE FACED a group of angry locals. Our ROEs—rules of engagement—directed that we were not to fire our weapons, not even for warning shots. Outnumbered, the inevitable happened—some of the locals grabbed one of our guys and made off with him. We stood around with our guns, not knowing what the hell to do—we weren't supposed to shoot the people. How could we stop them?

No one knew. Someone should have given us an order or at least a suggestion: *Form up a formation. Go get him.*

Instead, we just stood around.

The briefers told us later forming up and going after him was the right solution to the problem. But under the ROEs, that wouldn't really have worked—all the townspeople would have had to do to stop us was stand in the way. The real answer would have been not to let them grab him in the first place, even if that meant firing, ROEs be damned.

Warning shot first to separate the crowd, and then whatever had to be done to get our guy back.

We'd all seen the images of American contractors captured, tortured, and hung from a bridge in Fallujah the year before. My suspicion is that if anything like the simulation had happened for real in Iraq, there would have been plenty of shooting. I know I wouldn't have let one of my fellow Marines get taken to have his head chopped off and his body dragged through the town for YouTube. And I sure wouldn't have let that happen to myself without a hell of a fight.

We had plenty of conversations among ourselves on what should be done in case it happened. I won't tell what everyone else's preference was, but I made it clear to my team to not let them take me alive. I wasn't gonna put my family through that pain.

We didn't reject the ROEs completely; on the contrary, we were very careful to follow them. It was just that we knew that in the worst possible case, we weren't going to let them keep us from doing what we knew in our souls was right.

It was hard to put those images of the contractors out of my mind the first few times I patrolled. The Iraqis, though, weren't anything like the hostile crowd we'd trained against. Even as we expanded our operation and started patrolling in towns less friendly to Americans, most Iraqis were never openly hostile. They would ignore us, or at least try to. The men especially tried not to make eye contact. They were more used to us than we were to them.

Those first house searches went easy. We'd knock on the door. The man of the house would come and lead us inside. The women would go into the sitting room, covering their faces. Meanwhile, whatever kids were around would play outside. Sometimes they'd watch us like we were a TV show; sometimes they'd be looking for candy.

The houses were all the same—small, one-story, generally with only four rooms. They were easy to check, and because a lot of the people working here were working at the dam, they tended to be cooperative and even hospitable.

If there was no one home, we'd break the lock and search. We were supposed to take pictures of anything we broke; CAG—Civil Affairs Group—would then compensate the owners for the damage.

We got back to the dam without having encountered any trouble or contraband. If the rest of the deployment was half as easy, it'd be a breeze.

## GOING TO SCHOOL

A few days later we briefed a mission to sweep Haditha, south of the dam on the west side of the river. My platoon was tasked with clearing a large technical school on the outskirts of the city that would be used as the headquarters for the operation.

As soon as our squad got our orders, I began rehearsing in my mind what I would do. I saw myself going through the building, gun ready, alert, taking the corner of a hallway, hitting a door, clearing a room.

That was my general mode of operations—I'd try to envision what I might find, mentally practicing not so much to eliminate surprises, but to cut down on mistakes. I didn't want to make a mistake and let the rest of my team down.

I'd see myself dumping a mag and reloading, firing, dumping, reloading.

See it again. Rehearse it over and over.

Meanwhile, I packed my gear with ammo and as much food as I could stuff into my pack, pockets, or webbing. I'd have about eight magazines of M16A4 ammo, not counting the "oh shit mag" taped to my gunstock, for use in an extreme emergency. Besides that, I humped four hundred rounds for the squad's machine gun and its extra barrel, three fragmentation (or "frag") grenades, and two flash-bangs. I didn't want to have to rely solely on MREs, so I'd carry along canned chicken, salsa, protein bars, and whatever else came to hand.

Occasionally I carried the bazooka, depending on the mission. (It was actually an AT4, the modern bazooka. Never got to shoot it in combat but fun as hell in training.) My rifle had an optical laser sight, or ACOG. It projected a perfect red hatch on a target. I also had a laser pointer attachment to my rifle. It was infrared and you could only see it with night vision goggles (NVGs). We largely used it at night to point out objects of interest to other Marines. And maybe draw penis designs on walls.

I had my first-aid kit, some zip ties to detain prisoners, and my sunglasses—a pair of Ray Bans I guarded jealously. They were critical equipment in the desert. For the first few weeks, I wore gloves, their fingers removed so I could handle my weapon properly. Eventually the weather was warm enough and my hands would be sufficiently calloused that I tossed them aside.

As we rode in the trac to an op, I listened to my music. So many Marines and soldiers listened to heavy metal and hard rap when going out on a mission that it's a cliché. They wanted to get pumped, jacking their adrenaline. But I sought the opposite—I wanted my head clear, my body as calm as possible. So I went in the opposite direction. I'd listen to the Buena Vista Social Club, Cubano music with an easy rhythm akin to Latin big band jazz. Or even Sarah McLachlan, a bluesy alt-pop singer. I'd wager I was the only one in the platoon with that playlist.

WE WERE PUMPED THAT NIGHT AS WE WAITED. OTHER PLATOONS HAD MADE CONtact with the enemy already, and we were hoping we'd get ours, anxious but excited.

Midnight came and we loaded up. Smoking was one of the few things I could control and so I lit up a Marlboro Light.

If we'd driven directly, we'd have gotten to the city in twenty minutes. But that night it took more than an hour to get to the outskirts, with all the maneuvering around the desert and then the city to approach from the south without giving the original destination away. Bumping along on the hard metal bench, occasionally smacking my head on the trac's side, I practiced loading and reloading, my fingers dancing along the rifle.

Suddenly, the engine's pitch changed, revving high. The trac smashed through a gate and we shoved out, racing to the building.

Our fireteam had been tapped to get in first, and so we ran straight to the building, pausing at the doorway—the front door was gone.

We stacked to go in, tucking against the wall near the jamb. Smith first, then me; the others right behind me.

*Go!*

I went in behind Smith, tensely checking the first hall. It was a massive building, pitch dark and silent. We walked with arms tucked in, crouching slightly like we had drilled thousands of times, making sure to keep our steps even and light so our rifle would stay steady in front of us in case we had to fire. I regulated my breathing—can't breathe heavy or your rifle moves and you lose your aim. Stay calm, and move.

*Something?*

No.

We moved slowly, using our flashlights to peer into the first rooms, not knowing what to expect. "Slow is smooth and smooth is fast" was drilled into our heads when we were taught how to fight in urban combat.

*Empty.*

We moved on.

Move, search, move, search.

I got more confident the further we went. Still, I knew the biggest danger was to get complacent, start cutting corners or drop my focus. Our team stopped and switched off with another, took a quick break, then moved back to the front. All the time I reminded myself to go slow, to be watchful. Being nervous was better than being overconfident.

Smith and I alternated leading the way into the rooms. Part of that was to keep sharp, part of it to even the odds on who might get shot. Yet even with all that, with all the reminders and the constant checks in my brain, my mind began to wander. I remember standing in the hall, waiting to go in, and thinking about what might be going on back home.

*Focus, focus, focus!*

The M16 was too long when you were turning a corner or entering a room. The enemy could see it long before you saw them.

*Focus, focus, focus!*

It took two nerve-racking hours to clear all three stories. But the place turned out to be empty. Bright blue walls, desks, chalkboards, a few with writing on them, as if we'd interrupted lessons. There was no enemy, no cache of weapons. The big find was a stash of English-language anti-Semitic literature in one of the rooms.

## THE REAL SHIT

The shelling started the next day.

They were mortar rounds, launched from within the city. The school was directly in line with a radio tower that could be used as a marker for whoever was aiming at us.

Being a mortarman, I knew exactly how you'd do it. All it took was a little math. You know where the tower is, where we are in relation to the tower, and where you are—crunch the numbers, adjust the weapon, let fly.

And keep them coming, zeroing in as you went.

The shells got closer. I recognized their technique from my own training—fire a round to get your aim, then follow with a quick volley on target. We'd work with three tubes at a time. The lead would fire, home in, get on point, then pass the directions to the others and fire for effect. Nine rounds and that was the end of whatever you were shooting at.

These guys weren't Marines, fortunately; all their rounds missed. They were smart enough, though, to pack up quickly after firing a few salvos and take off.

We took turns standing watch on the roof. The city in front of us consisted mostly of low-rising, simple houses, with a couple of taller buildings farther off. We could see people in the streets, going to market or work, with kids running around the yards and road, playing. Meanwhile, Marines were working their way through the streets, knocking on doors and going in, making sure there were no stores of guns or explosives.

That was one of the things that always seemed weird to me, and that I never really got used to: normal life continued while we swept. The bad guys mixed with the civilians without anyone giving them away. I'd see kids playing, then a man with a gun nearby.

Third Platoon found a guy planting an IED; someone shot an RPG at Taylor's squad but missed.

I was on watch later when I saw something blow on one of the roads. It looked like a mine strike, a low explosion followed by a small plume of rising smoke. It was a mine—a vehicle carrying the headquarters platoon had hit it while driving toward us.

I tensed, ready, expecting an attack.

None came. A Black Hawk helicopter flew in and evacuated the injured. One of the men in the trac lost his leg.

Meanwhile, kids continued to play. A few gathered near the school, staring in our direction, curious like I suppose kids in the States would be. Just kids in the middle of a war.

EVENTUALLY WE WERE ROTATED OFF SECURITY TO WORK "SEARCH SWEEPS" through the city. We'd start on one end of a block and move our way down the street, knocking on every door and checking every house. The residential area we worked reminded me in many ways of the ranch area where I'd lived in Mexico and the American Southwest. Thick-walled houses, dusty roads, nothing that might be considered ostentatious in the yards or buildings. Depending on the part of the city you were in, the streets could be relatively straight, but the maze of alleyways and walls made for plenty of potential ambush spots and crooked routes in and out of the main thoroughfares. This was typical throughout al Anbar Province.

We'd block off the roads so there wouldn't be any traffic while we worked. The cars were generally what you would see in the States, albeit much older and far dirtier. Sand and dust made everything filthy. The thickness of the sand varied depending on where we were, but there was always grit to rub against your eyes and potentially clog your weapon. Near the river, there could be thick foliage; large, tropical trees—and still enough muddy grit to coat every part of you, even your tongue.

Dust was everywhere and litter usually lined the streets, but Iraqi homes were very clean inside; the women made sure of that. Cleanliness helped on a search—if you looked carefully, you might see a line of dust where a bookcase had been moved recently, indicating a panel hidden in the wall.

Dust wasn't the only thing you scanned for, of course. You also observed the people inside, looking to see if there was someone who didn't fit—a lot of men who were clearly not family members, for example. As the deployment went on, we learned to quickly spot those sorts of things.

Most people were pretty good with us. They'd answer quickly if we knocked and let us in. No answer meant we kicked in the door and went in anyway, though a lot more wary.

We always tried to deal with the oldest male of the house, and rarely with any of the women. That was a cultural thing. In a very patriarchal society with a strict pecking order, to ignore the man's authority would have been an insult. The male would accompany us as we searched, a statement of his authority in the house, and for us a practicality—he was the most likely to answer our questions, or behave in a way that made it obvious we wanted to ask more questions.

Surprisingly, I felt comfortable close up and personal with most of the Iraqis. I didn't feel as if they hated me, much less that they would try and attack me.

Somehow watching them go about their everyday lives had lessened my sense of danger. That's not to say that I thought everyone was my friend, or that I wasn't aware there were mujahedeen terrorists lurking in the city. I just got the sense that the population at large didn't hate us. I think some were genuinely glad that we had kicked out Saddam, and most of the others looked at our presence as something to be endured with as much grace and as little grief as possible.

A lot of Marines demonized the Iraqis. For them, that made it easier to be on patrol, easier to deal with the enemy. Our company seemed to be different.

I had a small Arabic dictionary with me, and for a brief time on the Haditha sweep I took on the unofficial role of translator for some of the squad—which basically meant pointing at different lines in the little book and then trying to puzzle out the answer I got. I would flip through pages desperately, trying to find something that might make sense.

I doubt I was very good at it. There's only so far a Harvard education will get you. Later on we worked with actual interpreters and the Iraqi National Guard, and were far better off for it.

Iraqi houses almost always had flat roofs. Generally, a fireteam would be posted on one to watch the area as the rest of the squad moved through from house to house. Depending on the city, the houses were sometimes close enough to go from roof to roof; occasionally we'd use a roof entrance or a back door or whatever to get into places where we expected trouble. But most often we went in through the front door. Knocking in most places, but if the circumstances called for it—say a locked storage building or a bombmaker's shack—a shotgun aimed at the lock or a trusty sledgehammer worked just about as well.

When we weren't going door to door, we patrolled the streets. Occasionally you'd come across an Iraqi offering to take you to the bad guys in exchange for cash. Maybe some of those offers were real, but they seemed more likely to be cons or even traps, so we didn't take anyone up on the offer.

Either that day or the next, we got a call over the radio that someone had spotted a man on a rooftop with a rifle.

We rushed to the house, adrenaline pumping. The house had already been searched and cleared, but that only made it more dangerous—it was in the rear, a supposedly safe place.

Smith and I rushed to the door. One of us kicked it in— probably me, as I remember charging forward.

A man stood in the room in front of me, a rifle in his hand.

I pointed my M16 at his chest, then barely kept myself from firing.

He was holding a broom, not a rifle. Had it taken me another moment to see it, he would have been dead.

We both knew it. He stepped back, pale. I tried calming the kids standing behind him as the rest of the team searched the house. There was no one on the roof; the report had been false— probably a mistake when someone saw him sweeping up there.

Later in the occupation, a drone might have been available, or the overwatch might have been bigger and more sophisticated. But the mix of fear and adrenaline would always be present. Command certainly didn't want us shooting civilians. But they were also clear that we had to take care of ourselves first. We could always defend ourselves if we felt under threat. And we had stricter rules of engagement than the average police officer.

AS THE OPERATION WENT ON, WE STARTED TAKING OVER HOUSES AT NIGHT. "GOING firm" to sleep. This became common as our deployment continued.

It was a bit scarier than being in the school, and far less safe than the dam. There were always less of us in a house—sometimes just a squad or two. The houses were vulnerable to attack by suicide vehicles or even old-fashioned ground assaults. Our nearest reinforcements were generally several blocks away—a vast difference in the middle of a firefight.

We learned to pick the houses carefully—elevation, an open area around the structure . . . and whenever possible, a satellite dish.

The satellite dish meant there was a television and potential entertainment at night.

We spent eleven days out, patrolling not only Haditha, but Haqlaniyah, Dulab, and Barwana, which was over on the east side of the river. The battalion discovered and cleared several IEDs and foiled a plot to use a car bomb as a suicide weapon—an SVBIED in military parlance.

For me, though, it was mundane, almost routine, not pulse-raising—except for the man with the broom.

Even the mortar attacks had begun to seem routine. They continued, the mortarman packing up after firing a few shots. Someone gave him a nickname—Three Fingers Ali.

Why Three Fingers? I don't know. Maybe whoever coined it thought he always missed because he'd lost those other two fingers.

Eventually, a motorized company got him. But by that time, I was on my way back to the dam.

III.

# IN THE SUCK

## McKENZIE

With darkness settling in, I struggled to see the edges of the back roads as I hurried toward McKenzie. Despite taking every short-cut I could find, I had over two hundred miles still to go. The distance seemed to grow in the darkness, multiplying my fears that I wouldn't make it in time.

I thought of all this as I drove. I had to keep him talking; I had to get there before anything rash happened. He was depending on me.

As I had depended on him.

McKenzie's question about whether we had seen combat or not was not quite as bizarre as it seemed. It was a result of a bu-reaucratic snafu that probably affects a lot of people. It hit me, too.

Without going too deeply into the different regulations and qualifiers, VA benefits are different for reservists and servicepeople who have been on active duty. Being activated and seeing combat entitles a reservist to a much wider range of benefits. Getting high-level treatment for post-traumatic stress through the VA required having seen combat.

So the reason for denying McKenzie admission to a VA hospi-tal unit for PTSD would have been along the lines of: your records don't say you were in combat, therefore you are not entitled to this benefit for an ailment you received in combat.

The problem apparently lay with our unit command, which inexplicably had not forwarded the information about our deploy-ment through the proper channels.

A year or two before, I had gone to the VA hoping for coverage of my banged-up knee. They told me I hadn't seen combat. Getting that straightened out was a nightmare.

The record has been updated—I now have my Combat Action Ribbon (CAR), issued years after the fact. But how many people in a similar situation could afford to wait or blow it off?

Not McKenzie, surely.

Talking about problems with the VA wasn't a good strategy. What else?

The war. But my memories were scattered, bits and pieces of action, jumbled together. Memory is never a straight line, and under duress it's worse.

Random images and thoughts flit into my head. In Iraq, McKenzie would say stuff from left field sometimes that made no sense. You'd be talking about something and he'd be listening intently, then all of a sudden he'd go, "That's what your mother says." I guess it was intended as a joke—a random non sequitur. But McKenzie was ordinarily so serious that these comments were more like electrical shocks. It was as if the earth had suddenly skipped a beat on its rotation. For a moment, everything seemed out of kilter.

Then you'd catch on, and laugh.

I saw him next to me, a massive man, one of the biggest Navajos I've ever met in my life. Just his presence commanded respect.

What could we talk about?

Inevitably, I came back to the war.

"Do you remember Outer Banks?" I asked. "Barwana and the rest?"

"Oh, yeah," he said. "That was a tough one."

## SEX AND THE CITY

We were feeling pretty good when we reached the dam at the end of River Bridge, the Haditha mission. Marine records give Lima credit for four insurgents killed. A large number of weapons caches had been located during our sweeps. Most importantly, our company had not suffered any casualties.

Hopefully, it was a harbinger of what was to come.

Our assignment was more serious than I thought it would be before we landed in Iraq. Gone were the illusions that we would roam some hypothetical Camp Cupcake pulling guard duty, sitting in a dusty outpost far from the real war. Still, if things continued like this, the deployment wouldn't be that bad. Nerve-racking at times, surely, but ultimately not nearly as dangerous as what had happened in the rest of the country the year before, let alone the assault on Fallujah.

We went to our hooches and kicked back.

Someone back home sent us a huge care package. Inside were a bunch of DVDs, including *Sex and the City*. Grant and I started watching it; soon the entire squad was hooked. We came to look at Carrie, her friends, and love interests almost as family.

*Sex and the City* was a late 1990s/early 2000s television show about a young woman looking for love in New York. It was squarely aimed at women, and probably among the last things you would figure Marines to latch onto. But we were hooked. Discussions about what might happen next on the series were lively, and even took place while on patrol.

*I don't think she should go out with Mr. Big. He's an asshole.*
*He'll break her heart.*
*That other guy's a real dick.*
*But he's got money. Women like that.*

I'm sure we could have scripted another ten seasons if the producers had asked.

*The O.C.* was another popular TV show we got a copy of. A kid from the wrong side of the tracks ends up living with some rich folk in Newport Beach, Orange County (O.C.), California. Not close to the typical Marine experience, but still rife with possibilities. It was ironic that we identified with shows from two areas most of us had never been to—I didn't realize till later the O.C. was a real place.

During one show, Mischa Barton's character began making out with Olivia Wilde—the hootch went insane. From that point on, watching was mandatory.

## HEARTS AND MINDS IN OUTER BANKS

Operation River Bridge ended around March 26. On April Fool's Day, we started a new operation: Outer Banks.

Outer Banks was similar in design and intent to River Bridge, but the towns were generally smaller and farther from our base. The platoon would go secure and search several places along the river: Barwana, Baghdadi, Abu-Hayat, Al Muhammadi, Kubaysah, Haditha, and Haqlaniyah. It was slated to last a little more than three weeks. Farther from our base, in an area generally less friendly to Americans, it turned out to be more involved and more deadly than our earlier ops.

Our first stop was Barwana, along the east side of the Euphrates. The town was tightly packed, very active with Iraqis. We patrolled the center area for a few hours, then headed to a two-story school building where we went firm and rested for lunch before getting other orders. All told, there were probably two platoons worth of Marines at the temporary post, a little over eighty men.

My fireteam went upstairs to a room and dropped our gear.

I'd just taken off my vest when we heard a sharp crackling noise outside.

No one knew what it was. We'd never heard real machine-gun fire aimed at us before.

The crackling continued. Finally it dawned on us: we were under attack.

It seems like it took forever to reach that realization, though most likely it was only a few seconds. We grabbed our rifles and ran to the roof.

Goodwin was already there, lining up a defense. The gunfire was coming from the south, near a bridge that crossed the river. The mujahedeen had AKs and at least one RPK, a light or squad-level machine gun that can put out a good volume of fire but is light enough to be easily mobile.

Looking north, it became clear that we didn't have the advantage of elevation—the building was situated below a hill populated with houses and small farms a short distance away. Goodwin realized that the attackers could flank around and attack us from the higher ground.

He turned to our fireteam and pointed. "Get up there!"

We took off, racing up the steep hill dividing the school from the farms. Smith and I trucked up the slope. After a few dozen yards, Smith came to a barbed-wire fence. He barreled into one of the posts, bending it and holding the strands of wire down. I stepped on his back and hurdled over.

I ran up to a building and saw a head pop out. Before I could bring my weapon to bear, I realized it belonged to a young kid, obviously curious about what the hell was going on. He jerked back and I began sighting back in the direction of the enemy, getting my bearings. The enemy was still to the south, on the other side of the building.

The rest of the squad came up; we cleared and took up firing positions, nervously waiting for the ambush to arrive.

Meanwhile, the Marine mobile weapons platoon responded from another part of the city and charged at the attackers. The volleys stopped a few minutes later; the muj had fled across the river.

The engagement felt as if it had taken hours. In actual fact, it lasted less than twenty minutes from start to finish.

I was pumped, full of adrenaline. I was also proud of myself and the rest of the team. To an outsider, the engagement would surely seem inconsequential. No one was hurt, and the threat ultimately was insignificant. But emotionally, it was huge. I had proven to myself I wasn't a coward. I could react under fire, follow orders and my training without question or hesitation.

And I hadn't shot the kid.

Every infantryman has a question about what they will do when bullets fly in their direction. Until you face combat, you just don't know. History is filled with stories of seemingly well accomplished soldiers freezing or otherwise failing the first time they face real bullets. I'm not saying I wasn't fearful; I'm saying that I performed despite whatever fear might have played in the back of my mind. I'd focused on the task, on my job, what was around me, what I had to do. It was a rite of passage that is difficult to fully explain unless you've faced it yourself.

*What's going to happen when the shit hits the fan?*

Goodwin truly impressed me. He stood calmly on the rooftop as the bullets sailed past. More importantly, he'd quickly sized up the situation and directed us into place. He'd seen a vulnerability and dealt with it swiftly and efficiently.

That's what a combat leader does. That's why you respect him and do what he says. It doesn't automatically come with the stripes or insignia. If I'd ever had any doubts about him, they vanished that day.

—

THE ATTACK WAS THE MOST EXCITING THING THAT HAPPENED TO US IN BARWANA that trip. Later, we were called out to hold a portion of the city while another element of the company tracked a group of insurgents. Somebody spotted a black-clad sniper watching us from a roof, causing all sorts of a stir—a helicopter was called out to take him down.

Which it did.

Unfortunately, the "sniper" turned out to be a black sheep kept on the roof of an Iraqi house. We paid for the animal and the damage.

IT MAY SEEM ODD TO CALL AN ENCOUNTER WHERE YOU COULD EASILY DIE "EXCIT-ing," but there's nothing like combat to pump your adrenaline. If you get through it without anything bad happening—without deaths or injuries, holding your ground, achieving whatever objective you were after—then it can feel like an incredible high.

Churchill had a saying along the lines of: *There is nothing more thrilling to getting shot at and living.* For a long while, combat was like that for Lima. Almost a video game, or even the Super Bowl—enormous fun. Knowing that it didn't have to go well added to the elation when it did.

One of our other units found a vehicle poised to be used as a suicide weapon. An even bigger find that day was a safe house used by insurgents that had a weapons cache and torture room. The house sat next to a hospital, apparently also used by the muj. Engineers blew up the house and the cache inside. (The hospital was off limits due to our ROEs. It wasn't damaged.)

According to Taylor, they left a note on what was left of the house:

*Dear Muj, we stopped by to visit and you weren't home, Sorry about the mess, USMC.*

THREE OR FOUR DAYS LATER WE FOUND OURSELVES IN BAGHDADI. WE'D HEARD about the place beforehand—not a good sign, since it meant an attack had occurred there. But the city—more like village-sized to a city boy like me—turned out to be calm. Surprisingly, it had extra wide streets, which seemed entirely out of scale not only for the town but for most of Iraq.

The highlight of our stay involved moving a half-dozen or so new Ford Explorers from one parking lot to another so we could use a building as a temporary headquarters. It was really kind of comical—Marines gunned the SUVs a few hundred yards maybe down the road, spitting dirt and smoke as if we were back home on a dirt track on a Saturday afternoon.

I found it hilarious.

You had to be there. In war, a lot of strange things strike you as out of place, and therefore funny.

And yet, that can be true of things that aren't out of place, and are deadly serious. Arriving in Abu-Hayat a few days later, our fireteam was tasked to run from our trac, cross a wide field, and secure the riverbank. I was hungry, tired, and a little on edge—we'd dodged an IED attack on the way in that had damaged one of the other vehicles.

I was about halfway through the field, out on point, when something whipped by.

And again.

*I'm under sniper fire.*

*Damn, I am not going to run. I am not going to stop. But I am not going to run.*

The shots were fired at my vicinity, but obviously from far off and not accurately. I gave the guy shooting at me the finger and kept walking. Someone closer could deal with him.

Smith was behind me. As I walked out of the palm grove, I spotted a little building ahead with elevation—a perfect spot to pick us off. Smith and I instinctively charged it, realizing we needed to take it before they opened up on us.

If there was someone inside, they snuck out the back before we got there. Which maybe was lucky for us, because the house was stocked with rifles, ammo, RPGs, and the raw material for IEDs.

There were also shackles, and dried blood—it was some sort of strong point or headquarters, as well as a place to manufacture IEDs. There was writing high up on the wall of one of the rooms. Goodwin and some of the intel guys came in, trying to figure out what the hell it meant, if anything.

It appeared to be a date: 12-10-2000.

The intel guys were baffled.

"Maybe they messed up 9/11," said one.

"No," I finally told them. "It *is* a date, but it's written in Arabic order."

I explained how to move the numbers around so they could be read properly: 10/12/2000.

"Why that date?" asked the intel guy.

"The USS *Cole*," I told them. "These guys are al Qaeda."

On October 12, 2000, seventeen U.S. Navy sailors were killed and another thirty-nine injured when a boat loaded with explosives rammed into the guided missile destroyer USS *Cole* while she was docked in Yemen. This was a landmark event for al Qaeda, their first successful attack on a U.S. military asset. My nerdy ability to remember random things finally came in handy.

The date pretty much identified these guys as al Qaeda, or at a minimum strongly influenced by them. It also suggested they were Yemeni, where the incident took place.

In any event, it was a clear sign that we were dealing with foreign fighters and al Qaeda.

"That's why I fuckin' love reservists," said Goodwin as I walked away. "They're so damn smart."

Command decided we'd blow the building, and a team of Marine engineers came in and set up charges while we were pulling security.

"Hey, you want to blow it up?" asked one of the Marines after inspecting our find.

"What?" I asked.

"Do you want to blow it up? You found it."

"Hell, yeah!"

They wrapped the place in C4 and det cord.

"We're going to be behind that berm," they told me, handing me the plunger. "We got thirty seconds on the cord. We'll be filming you."

Great, I thought, I'll have a Hollywood-style video of me walking, cool as ice cream in Alaska, while the thing blows up behind me.

I picked up the device—it was no bigger than a Pez dispenser. I pushed the plunger, stuck a cigarette in my mouth, and started walking nonchalantly toward the berm.

The techs started freaking out. "The det cord jumped! It's gonna go! Get over here! Run!"

I leapt forward, expecting to be airborne. I dove over the berm—only to discover them laughing their butts off when I opened my eyes.

The house had not exploded, by the way.

They'd pranked me, capturing true fear and great speed on video. The building blew a few moments later—it was a good blast, completely obliterating the structure as well as the ammunition.

MARKINGS INSIDE BUILDINGS WERE ONE WAY YOU COULD TELL TERRORISTS HAD used it as a post. Other giveaways would be pictures of bin Laden, propaganda leaflets, and literature. But there were plenty of signs of insurgencies outside buildings that showed they were active in the town. Anti-American graffiti would be sprayed on walls by insurgents. One of the favorites was an American flag with a boot over it—not exactly subtle.

At some point we started spray painting over them. A favorite tag: USMC.

Think of it as our gang insignia. I avoided joining gangs on the South Side of Chicago; now it looked like I was part of one.

WE STAYED IN THE CITY A FEW DAYS, AND THEN HELPED WITH SOME "HEARTS AND minds" ops—Civil Affairs got some soccer balls to pass out to the kids. We were escorting a Civil Affairs team when I started talking to a group of Iraqi men on the street. I happened to be carrying a laser pointer that I used to signal the rest of the fireteam; one of the Iraqis pointed to it and asked what it was.

As I was taking it out, Grant came up nearby and mentioned that we had a "show of force" on the way—meaning a low-level demonstration flight meant to impress both friendlies and enemies was inbound.

"Watch this," I told the Iraqis, miming the words. I pointed the laser skywards and clicked a few times.

Just then, an F/A-18 flew low on the deck, afterburners flaring, its engines shaking the ground with their roar.

The Iraqis freaked out, diving for cover while I stood nonchalantly, suppressing a laugh.

"Can I do it?" gestured one of the Iraqis. They had quite logically concluded that my pointer had made the aircraft appear.

"No," I said. "Too powerful."

I genuinely enjoyed talking to some of the Iraqis on these sorts of missions, and one of the Civil Affairs officers took notice. Ricardo Crocker was a major in the Civil Affairs unit, a reservist like myself, and a state trooper back home in California. We chatted a few times and became friendly enough that he came over one day to see if I'd be interested in coming over to his unit.

I told him thank you but no thanks.

"I can't leave my fireteam," I explained.

He understood—few Marines in combat are going to walk out on their brothers. But he was so friendly and open, I felt bad about turning him down. I told him I'd be happy to help where I could.

"I'll remember that," he promised.

A few days later Lima was tasked to patrol Kubaysah, a village about a hundred miles south of the dam and a dozen or so east of Hit. The location and nature of the operation made trucking down there by trac impractical, so Command ordered up some helos to transport our company.

Except me.

It was nothing personal. Goodwin came up to me while we were getting ready. "Listen, your fireteam was going to talk to you about this, but I'm doing it. You can't go on the mission."

"Why?"

"Weight. Space. You're the low man. It's just the way the roster works."

What he meant was, there wasn't enough room in the helicopter for the whole team. I had the lowest rank and least seniority, and therefore by Corps calculus and helicopter physics, I was staying home.

I was pissed. I was livid.

"What are you saying about me?" I demanded. "I'm a good Marine."

"No, it has nothing to do with you. It's just the way the roster worked."

"Damn. God damn. Fuck this, fuck the Corps. You have useless POGs going from HQ and I have to leave my team behind. Half those fuckers haven't even left the wire and you are putting them on a helo op? Do they even know how to clean their fucking rifles?"

"POGs" stood for "people other than grunts" and was a term we used for office Marines, rather than the even more derogatory though highly accurate "REMFs," rear echelon motherfuckers.

Besides taking up valuable space, they largely did (admittedly necessary) paperwork. Attached to Command HQ, they lived the life of Reilly. They had better food, better sleeping quarters, and generally no patrols. They also got the same pay as us.

This sums up our attitude toward REMFs: we promoted one Marine from our platoon to HQ not because he was good at paperwork but because he was a horrible infantry Marine, and inevitably would have gotten us or himself killed.

I was so pissed. My fireteam came over and couldn't console me. It wasn't meant as an insult, but I took it as one. It doubly hurt to think that my guys were going to be exposed to danger and I couldn't help. I knew nothing about Kubaysah, but I was sure it wasn't going to be a picnic.

I spent the first day they were gone sulking. Fuming and sulking.

Our motorized weapons platoon had stayed at the base as well. They were tasked to help provide security for Crocker on a CAG mission, so I volunteered to go along as a gunner.

I ended up as vehicle commander in a souped up—as in up-armored—Humvee.

Let me step back and explain the nomenclature: Humvees are HMMWVs, "High Mobility Multipurpose Wheeled Vehicles," the modern-day versions of your grandpa's Jeep. Also called Hummers, they were originally meant as very light vehicles, without meaningful armor. Experience in Iraq showed that the lack of armor increased casualties in a war where the enemy's weapon of choice was a shrapnel-producing IED. So some of the vehicles were fitted with light armor—not enough to stop a missile or tank round, but at least offering protection against a spray of metal. At the same time, a number were equipped with crew-fired weapons, such as the 40 mm grenade launcher and light machine gun ours fielded.

As for my rank as commander: It came down to where I sat in the Humvee. Literally.

Milling around the vehicle before the operation, I was probably the lowest-ranking person there, a lance corporal amid sergeants and officers. Once the mission began, however, my role took precedence over what we might call "regular" rank. For clarity and efficiency in combat, the Corps designates the Marine in the front righthand seat of a vehicle as that vehicle's commander. As commander in the vehicle, he or she outranks everyone else inside, no matter how many stripes or stars they have on their uniform. The commander tells the driver (in this case, Sergeant Dale Fox) where to go, and the others what to do.

We were leading three other vehicles, when a bitch of a sandstorm blew down through us. It was so bad, we had to stop; it was just impossible to see.

Moments later, an IED went off down the road, right where we would have been had we not stopped. Whoever was working the remote on the explosive had thought we'd kept driving ahead.

Luck.

I would have been dead had we proceeded. The explosion was massive, and it was on my side of the road.

I started shouting instructions—as the vehicle commander, I had the responsibility of getting everyone out and prepared for a follow-on attack.

There was a large dune to our right as we exited the vehicle. I grabbed another Marine and told him to run up the dune with me, taking one side while I had the other to guard our flanks.

Unfortunately, the Marine I grabbed was a captain. Even more unfortunately, the captain was a bit of a dickhead. While I was waiting for the mission commander to decide whether to continue to our objective, I glanced behind me to check how he was doing.

He was nowhere to be seen.

*WTF! Where is he! Our flank is exposed. . . .*

I rushed to where I'd set him out not a minute before. I expected to see a pack of sand ninjas scurrying off across the desert through the whipping sand. Instead I saw nothing—until I noticed a figure in the wadi below.

"Sir, get up here!" I yelled.

No response.

*"Sir!"*

Nothing.

"Hey!" I shouted. "Get the fuck up here!"

Captain Dickhead finally stomped up the hill.

"Don't give me orders," he sputtered.

"I'm vehicle commander. It's my job. You left our flank exposed."

I said some other things as well.

He told me afterward that he had gone down to check something out, which still didn't make it the right thing to do. He also complained about me to my XO, who basically told him to pound sand.

About an hour later, the mission commander put us back in motion. The bomb had been exploded in the middle of the desert, so we thought it had been detonated by someone in a vehicle or that he might have tried escaping in a car. We set up a vehicle checkpoint in hopes of catching the IED maker—a forlorn hope—and stopped a few vehicles, turning them inside out to no avail. Then we drove on into the city where we delivered food, medicine, and soccer balls to a bunch of kids.

That was a typical juxtaposition in my war—almost getting killed one minute, giving toys to the kids of maybe some of the would-be killers the next.

But if anything made me uneasy in the little town, it was the fact that I didn't really know the Marines with me and how they would react during a firefight. That's not a slam on them; I'm sure they knew their jobs very well. But we had never worked together, and more importantly, they were used to fighting and patrolling in the vehicles; they weren't ground grunts. They never stayed in one place very long. Being an Infantry Marine is a different thing.

Case in point: we stopped in the middle of town, and the guys began handing stuff out right away.

"Hold on, hold on," I told them. "If we're going to be here for a while, we have to check these buildings out. We have to make sure there's nobody inside who'll harm us, or the kids. And we need to find a safe spot in case we're attacked and have to go firm."

Completely instinctual to me—after several weeks in Iraq, that is. But foreign to them.

They saw the logic, though, and we quickly cased the area. Major Crocker came with me into two different buildings. We confiscated a few rifles, but otherwise found nothing alarming.

AFTER I LEFT THE WAR, THOSE INSTINCTS HAUNTED ME. I COULDN'T STAY IN ONE spot for too long. I'd get anxious, not knowing what danger might be in a nearby building or even room.

You can't clear everything around you, not in peacetime, not alone.

That day with the guys on the CAG mission, we'd had twenty Marines all together—we could have fended off anybody. Back home alone, God knows.

I felt that way for years. Still do at times.

REUNITED WITH LIMA A FEW DAYS AFTER THE HELO MISSION (WHICH TURNED OUT to be a nothing burger), we arrived at a small settlement around the Haditha train station, working with some engineers to search lockers on the roof of the station building. The engineers began systematically working on the lockers, using shotguns to blow off the locks. All of a sudden we heard the zip-zip of rounds flying in our direction.

It took us a moment to realize the gunfire was coming from the

American unit tasked at the settlement nearby, apparently mistaking our guys for the enemy.

We popped blue smoke—the universal sign for "hey, stop firing at us—we're on your side and you're messing us up."

The gunfire stopped and we went back to work. We found nothing—a boring day nearly perforated by blue-on-blue disaster.

## HAQLANIYAH

We inserted into Haqlaniyah in the middle of the night April 21. It was a ghost town.

We were tasked to inspect a house suspected of being a weapons cache. We were carrying a special tool we'd appropriated somewhere along the way: Thor.

Thor was a large sledgehammer. Thor liked to pound things. Locks and doors especially. Thor was carried by Miera. I am convinced Miera used it as a pillow. He loved that thing.

We got to the house quickly, left security in the middle of a nearby crossroad, and went to work.

Thor said, let me in.

The door said no.

Thor laughed.

A few seconds later, we pushed into the house. The intel had been good. While there were no insurgents inside, we discovered a radio device used to set off IEDs, weapons, and the ingredients for bombs.

And Thor found a companion—a good-sized crowbar.

Love at first sight. A perfect pair.

Thor and Crow weren't needed too often—mostly on lockers and industrial-type buildings—but they came in handy when they were. They were far heftier and more efficient than the tools Command had supplied, which looked like something a very small fire department might have at the back of the basement, gathering dust. Now that I know how defense procurement works, I'm sure millions of dollars were put into research and development of those tools, only to be supplanted by things we appropriated in the field.

TWO FEMALE MARINES, A LIEUTENANT AND A CORPORAL, JOINED US SOON AFTERward as we began patrolling the city. To that point, we hadn't been able to search women for weapons; they were with us for those searches.

Hurley and Goodwin briefed us just before they came in. It was more like a dressing down: *There's not to be any bullshit. No hankypanky. No funny stuff. No bullshit. We know you guys are animals. But you will treat them with respect and no stupid fucking comments.*

The lieutenant was a good Marine. She never flinched. She was especially good with kids, and would calm Iraqi women almost instinctually, speaking gently and patting them on their backs, as if consoling a grieving mom. It was something no one in Lima could have done.

The female corporal had never been in combat—I think her actual job was working on vehicles—and had some tough moments adjusting.

The first time an explosion went off, she lost her shit. To give her her due, it was a nearby explosion. An IED or something had been discovered and was blown by engineers. They were so close when it went up that we were rocked back and forth from the air blast and thump.

"Don't worry," we told her. "It was a planned demolition."

"Why do you think this is normal?" she asked.

"Because it *is* normal."

Thinking about it now, I realize we were the crazy ones. It wasn't normal at all—except there. But if we lost our shit every time something went boom, we'd have gone insane weeks before.

It was on that same mission that we got intel about IEDs in a nearby field. We were sent to find them. We went there, formed into a V-shaped formation, and started walking through, looking carefully at the ground.

"Hey, I think I found one," said somebody in the squad.

Then he reached down and grabbed it.

Cue the moment of heart-stopping, gut-wrenching silence. Because picking up a booby-trapped IED can lead to only one thing.

Fortunately, it turned out to be just a mortar round that had been randomly left in the field.

But the telling thing is that we just kept going after that, walking on, looking for an IED that *could* blow us up.

We were blasé, but not that blasé. It was a strange mix.

In Haditha, we went out to patrol the downtown area before the sun pushed over the horizon. On this one particular street, we climbed stairs to a small, elevated market area that extended maybe a couple hundred feet.

The markets in Anbar Province towns tended to be very small, unlike those you might find in more developed (and touristy) areas of the Middle East, and certainly unlike supermarkets or even the farmers markets you'd find in the States. In this case, they were a collection of stalls guarded by locked metal doors, little more than niches carved in brick or adobe walls. Thor would break the locks; we'd haul up the doors and inspect what was inside.

I'd just come up the stairs when I spotted a grocery bag with wires sticking out of it. Typically, there are bags all over the place when a market is open, and even closed there were usually a few scattered around. But this one drew my attention because something white was poking from the top.

*Wires?*

Definitely wires.

I peaked in and saw the outline of an explosive.

*Yes!*

Our unofficial official SOPs or standard operating procedures kicked in. We quickly cleared the market area while Gunny called in the Explosive Ordnance Disposal (EOD) technicians. We set up a cordon, waited, waited, waited—the engineers generally had a long list of assignments and it might take them hours to arrive— waited, waited, and then finally watched as the demolition guys secured the IED. As soon as they took it away, we resumed our patrol as if nothing had happened.

Why was the bomb there?

My guess is that whoever had made it was on his way to plant it somewhere, heard us coming, and decided discretion was the better part of valor—he dropped it and ran.

It's also possible, though, that the bomber hoped to catch us on patrol and hadn't realized we'd be up before he was. If we'd slept in that morning, he would have killed or maimed dozens of Iraqis as well as a few of us.

For many terrorists, any deaths to the locals would have been considered unfortunate at worst, inconsequential at best. While we were always the prime targets, the al Qaeda–trained or backed fighters who came from outside Iraq lacked family and tribal connections in Anbar. Their radical religious convictions convinced many of them that the Muslims they were living among were nearly as bad as we were. They were infidels, not following the one true way.

The local Iraqis realized that they were disposable and even targets, and did resist when they were able. Eventually, there would be a movement of the different family tribes in the area known as the Awakening, where they organized to help get rid of al Qaeda. But at this point, resistance was still uncoordinated, and perilous. Shortly before we arrived in March, the Haditha police chief had been kidnapped and beheaded after organizing raids on the al Qaeda cells. The memory of that and other attacks against prominent local Iraqis weighed heavily, and the fear that America might pull out in the near future reinforced Iraqis' reluctance to risk their lives openly opposing the terrorists.

THE GUYS PLANTING THE IEDS COULD BE DAMN CREATIVE. DEAD DOG, HOLLOWED-out curb, random bag—you never knew. At times, a detonation could be the signal for an assault, the terrorists following up with an attack to kill survivors or anyone responding. So we'd have to wait and watch, prepare for the worst while hoping the device or devices we'd found were the only ones there.

This could be for four or five hours, waiting for EOD to arrive. The sun comes up, the heat rises, you're sitting in the same place so long it's easy to be targeted by mortars . . . and all the time you're not doing the other ten or twenty things you were supposed to do that day.

After a while, we started blowing up IEDs ourselves. A grenade launcher did the trick nicely; a tank's gun was even better. Obviously, we couldn't do that where it would hurt a civilian, but otherwise it was a good alternative to screwing the timing of an entire sweep.

EOD did have some nice little robots, though. We called them Johnny Five, after the star of *Short Circuit*.

After watching them in action, I began wondering whether they couldn't be used to check houses out before we went in—stick a couple of cameras on them and send them through the door while we watched. I even suggested that to one of our commanders.

By that time, Command universally figured I was crazy and didn't pay any attention. But I want a piece of the royalties when the idea is patented.

WE'D LANDED IN THE RAINY SEASON, ENDURING A FEW DOWNFALLS DURING OUR early days. The worst thing about the rain was that it turned the fine sand covering most of the country into a pasty sludge that clung to everything, from the bottom of your boots to the inside of your nose. McKenzie called it a toxic slime.

The weather quickly improved. The rain stopped. The cold nights became far warmer.

And then everything got really dry, and really hot.

How hot did it get in Iraq as the summer came on?

Hot enough that some guys had their butane lighters explode in their pockets.

That hot.

## PIT STOP AT AL ASAD

After River Bridge wound down, we ran a brief mission much farther south, and our itinerary allowed us to rest overnight at the American base at al Asad. We came in hot and sweaty, dirty—naturally since we'd been out primed for combat for a couple of days.

Entering al Asad was like crossing into another country. This was a large base—in my mind, it's the size of Boulder, Colorado, and if that's an exaggeration, it's not much of one when you look at its amenities in the context of our war. The place had ice cream and real food. A Burger King. Computers you could sign up to use. Email. All the modern amenities.

Did I mention ice cream?

The strangest thing about the base, though, was the fact that other Marines were walking around with their M16s slung over their shoulders with no magazines. I couldn't imagine doing that now, except back at the dam. We were granted permission to keep our weapons with us and loaded—personally, I wouldn't have felt safe otherwise.

The Marines assigned to the base looked at us like poor relations who'd been wandering in the desert for weeks. Maybe that was an apt description.

I went with Britten, my fireteam leader, to see a movie—in an actual movie theater with an air conditioner! It was one of the *Transporter* series. I kept waiting for the hero to pick up a gun and end the fight.

With our brief sojourn coming to a close, we headed over to the PX to stock up on things we couldn't get back at the dam. We were standing on the checkout line when a second lieutenant came in with a team bearing shiny uniforms and even shinier M4s. They were going to go up the base towers and stand watch.

I couldn't help but be jealous about the M4s. We absolutely could have used those during house searches. Which may have added to the aggravation when the lieutenant had his men cut the line.

Apparently the base had a rule that people who had to stand watch soon could cut. I looked at my watch, fearing I was about to lose everything—cigarettes, a *Maxim* magazine, a bunch of munchies, and other goodies. I kept my emotions to myself. Then the lieutenant crossed the line.

"You guys are a disgrace," he said to one of us, or something to that effect. "Your uniforms are out of line, you need to shave . . ."

I was just about to go off when Goodwin appeared. Out of nowhere, he walked up to the lieutenant and got in his face.

"You need to shut the fuck up," said our platoon sergeant. "Do not talk to my Marines that way. While you were leading around your little poogie-baiters and fucking around in Pizza Hut, we were in the shit."

There was more. I doubt the lieutenant had ever been dressed down like that, certainly not by a staff NCO.

Goodwin directed us to cut back into place, pay up, and leave. Which we did, quickly, running to the vehicles like a bunch of pirates who'd just robbed a village.

Goodwin covered us by arguing, loudly, until the last of us was done, then executed a controlled repositioning—Marines don't retreat—to the vehicles.

If the lieutenant ever figured out who we were—or recovered from the heart attack Goodwin had surely induced with his lack of decorum and ass-kissing—we never heard.

## COMBAT VETERANS

The variety of our missions over those few weeks had given us confidence and experience. While the pace to date had been heavy, we had proven that this Reserve unit could do the job of active Marines. We had also become "tighter" as a group, developing a rhythm in the field. I think if you asked any of us what we were feeling about our deployment, the response would have been along the lines of "We got this." We weren't overconfident, but we trusted each other.

Trust comes with experience. Experience shows in many different ways, and not just in combat. Grant, for example, had upped his game on the snack front. I'm not sure how he did it, but he somehow managed to procure Slim Jims in addition to the usual candy and chips. Being his close friend paid dividends.

We'd grown a lot because we'd done a lot in a short time. But one downside of our mission pace was fatigue. There were times going through a patrol where I felt like I was walking through a thick fog or wading into an ocean, as if every part of my body had to push extra hard just to stay in motion. In the space of roughly a month and a half, we'd patrolled through roughly a dozen different places, been mortared, survived IED attacks, and engaged several muj. We'd discovered and secured what seemed like hundreds of booby traps and arms caches. Not one of those incidents would rate mention in a history of the war, but each exacted a toll in terms of stress. Simply training your attention on a dozen points of possible ambush while humping down the street of a crowded marketplace taxed your brain as well as your muscles.

Possibly the other guys were more physically adapted to it. I'm not a naturally coordinated person. I'm the kid on the Little League team who didn't get a hit his first two years. So even though I was a combat veteran now, I continued practicing as much as I could, doing things like miming how to load the mag into my rifle under fire and in the dark, over and over. Rehearsing the way to move through a field or a house, where to be if ambushed—I thought of everything that could go wrong, rehearsed solutions, went over the simplest procedures and routines again and again in my mind.

It was a way of compensating for clumsiness, but it was also kind of soothing, a routine that assured me I knew what to do and could do it under pressure.

## OPERATION TEDDY BEAR

Overall, our squad had claimed at least thirty-two insurgents killed and forty-six captured, including a general who'd served in Saddam's army during River Bridge. But some of our guys thought we were somehow getting shortchanged: *Why are other platoons racking up serious firefights and we're not?*

I thought that was crazy. We'd been in several scraps; people had tried to kill us.

If you go to a war zone and don't come back with a CAR then you're not a real Marine. I figured we'd already earned ours.

Some of this was silly. A few days later, we did another sweep through Barwana, and Goodwin honestly told us to act like Army soldiers.

Come again?

He meant, smoke cigarettes, be loud, be obvious, maybe even

a little sloppy—try and draw the enemy out by thinking we were easy targets.

While we were attracting attention, Marines on higher ground would be waiting to counterattack when the muj showed themselves.

So we followed orders at three a.m. Talking loud, sounding almost drunk, smoking—the whole time I was thinking *this is crazy*.

Sure, we'll end up beating the enemy, but who's going to get it first?

No contact.

What are you going to do?

FIREFIGHTS OR NOT, THERE WAS CERTAINLY NO SHORTAGE OF DANGER—SOME OF IT even self-induced.

Taylor and I were getting a little desperate for alcohol, as we hadn't had any since leaving the States. A copy of *Maxim* magazine was circulating within the company, and inside the issue was a recipe for prison hootch. The list of ingredients was neither extensive nor exotic—I think oranges were the most prominent.

We procured and fixed up the ingredients, put them in a bunch of white garbage bags to ferment, and left them while we were out on an operation.

Returning to the base, we cut open one of the bags.

Everyone nearby evacuated, just about puking from the scent. I think we made somebody taste the concoction, though Taylor insists now that it was too awful smelling to even do that. His memory on that is undoubtedly more reliable, given that the stuff surely would have been fatal, and company records do not list "death by hootch" among our casualties.

Most people might give up after such a disaster, but not Marines, and certainly not Lima Company. Following a thorough debrief, we launched Operation Teddy Bear—a resounding success.

The basic idea was simple. Alcohol was definitely contraband and could not be shipped to us from home.

Stuffed animals, on the other hand, were not on the forbidden list.

Kate coordinated activities back in the States with my best friend Shay. She quickly learned that size matters—you don't want to send too small a bottle, but a large teddy bear might attract too much notice. You had to match the delivery vehicle to the payload as efficiently as possible.

She got some of our friends and her coworkers to help, supplementing their regular care packages of salsa and the like with furry little critters stuffed with liquid gold.

The first teddy bear did not raise eyebrows. I took it into our squad room, did a little surgery, and extracted an airline-sized bottle of whiskey.

We went on from there. Within weeks we had an extensive network of suppliers back home, and an impressive collection of stuffed animals. People got creative. Gatorade bottles filled with alcohol. Hand sanitizer that was vodka.

Then leadership found out.

Our punishment? We had to share.

A lot of people were in on it from then on. For all I know, Defense Secretary Donald Rumsfeld was getting a cut.

Everyone was in on it *except* the people doing the mail call. They started looking at me funny around the third bear.

Everyone in the platoon would just laugh when they tried to give me shit.

*Gallego, he's just weird.*

*Can't sleep without his Teddy.*

*Loves the bear.*

In the meantime, Taylor had sent a letter to the Thompson Cigar Company, a cigar wholesaler back home, asking if there might be some free samples to support the troops; they responded with a massive case of high-end smokes.

We weren't expected to go out for a few days, so we partied hardy that night. There was even a dance-off on the top of the dam with NVGs.

## OUR FIRST FIREFIGHT

Missions followed one after another as April wore on. I'm sure they were distinct to the commanders, with their own objectives and tactics, but to me on the ground, it was one town after another, different but the same. Toward the end of April, we were tasked to do security on a CAG mission in Barwana, where the Community Affairs guys handed out soccer balls. That finished, we headed back across the river to Haqlaniyah to patrol before returning to the dam.

I hopped out of the trac, in the lead of the fireteam, starting to patrol not far from where we'd tried to draw a firefight some days before. I realized right away that something was off. Ordinarily, the place would be bustling with Iraqis going to market or doing chores, etc. But the area was almost completely empty. The lone Iraqi I saw, about a block away, locked eyes with me.

I hadn't seen that in Iraq before. I walked on warily.

There was a building between us. A few steps later, I popped back to a spot where I had a view of where he was—he was still there, and still staring at me.

*Something is weird here.*

Another man ran across the street ahead. He was dressed in black, knees and below exposed, carrying a tube on his back.

*What the . . . ? A tube?*

*RPG!*

"Gunny!" I yelled to Hurley, who was in the trac above me. "Someone just ran across the street with an RPG."

"If you think it's an RPG, get the hell out of the road!"

In the next moment, I saw this black dot hurling toward us.

I threw myself down into a ditch. The RPG round hit the ground and bounded away.

My memory is that it was a dud, or hit something before it had flown far enough to load its fuse. Hurley remembers it blowing up behind him before he had a chance to duck. One way or the other, I escaped unscathed, when very likely I should have died.

Neither one of us had much time to fix the memory in our minds. In the next moment, a group of mujahedeen opened up on us from a second story across the street. Separated from the rest of my guys, I crawled along the ditch until I spotted a wall. I leapt up and ran, sliding in next to Cheston Bailon.

"Let's go!" he said.

I was scared. I looked him in the eyes and he nodded. I glanced left and saw Stuart Wilson on the ground laying down fire.

*Fuck it. I am not dying a coward.*

We jumped out and started shooting back in the direction of the gunfire. The tracs, which had been moving behind me, stopped on the street. Probably they started giving us covering fire, but at this point I was totally focused on the building where the gunfire was coming from. I emptied a mag at the window and reloaded as I ran. Someone gave an order to keep pushing forward.

The muj in the building took off. We chased them down toward the river. I lost them and finally had to stop about a block from the water.

We regrouped and went back. I stopped at the building where the initial attack had come from. There was blood and some AK shells on the ground.

I grabbed one of the shells to put with my bag of sand from Chimayo.

I wasn't really thinking of luck at that point, or even the fact that I might have killed the muj who had shot at me. All I was thinking was that I was alive.

And the fact that I had done decently under fire.

Back at the trac, we waited for the ramp to come down. Who was inside but Grant, chomping on something.

*What?*

The back of the vehicle had come up before he could leave, and he'd been stuck there the whole time.

"Want some Cheetos?" he asked, holding out the bag.

"You fucker," I told him. "Yeah."

OUR FIRST FIREFIGHT HAD GONE WELL. WE HAD FOLLOWED OUR TRAINING, CARRIED out our order, and responded the way Marines are supposed to fight.

Our opponents had been a mixed bag. McKenzie, for one, said later that he was surprised at how unorganized and how undisciplined they were. Their bullets had missed quite a bit—while they seemed close to me, the more experienced sergeant thought they were missing by dozens if not a hundred feet. They had attacked haphazardly, and retreated without seeming to have much of a plan beyond getting the hell out of there as fast as they could. That was to be the pattern of most of the engagements over the next few weeks—scattered, brief, disorganized. Our enemy was clearly overmatched as fighters.

To us, the mujahedeen were mostly an anonymous, ill-defined group of terrorists who were just about interchangeable with each other. That's the way I suppose it is in any war; the enemy across from you exists as the enemy, not as an individual. It's not like most soldiers are broadcasting their identity, or flying a distinctive red triplane like the Red Baron in World War I.

BY THE TIME THE OPERATION SWUNG BACK TOWARD HAQLANIYAH, I'D BECOME COMfortable questioning the Iraqis. Every so often, we'd come across a few who spoke English—I remember some engineering students who probably spoke it better than a few Marines. We picked up standard phrases, from the interpreters and the Iraqi National Guardsmen when they were with us, and often just on our own.

After a while you'd see the same people on the streets. One day I approached a few of the men, offering some Marlboro Lights— the cigarettes seemed to be universally loved in Iraq. We started talking, comparing pictures of our families. They joked about affording only one wife—technically their religion permitted two, but they were all far too poor to take advantage of that, assuming it was an advantage.

Shortly later, I had a conversation with an older woman. We talked a little, gesturing mostly, though she had some English. When it was time to leave she got a very serious look on her face.

"I hope you make it back home OK," she told me. "I hope you will live a long life."

# IV.

# LUCKY
# LIMA

## McKENZIE

McKenzie pinned me when I made corporal in Iraq.

Getting promoted from lance corporal to corporal didn't change my life—except for the hundred bucks extra a month, which was definitely welcome. Since it was basically a time-in-grade thing, I can't really say I had to do all that much to achieve the rank, beyond the three-mile run I needed to complete with my bum knee.

No, I was still the machine gunner's bitch in the fireteam. And in combat, rank isn't nearly as important as your role, your knowledge, and what the guys around you trust you with.

Their lives.

You have to earn their respect, whether you have one stripe or a slew of them.

But being a full corporal is significant in the Corps. Unlike the other branches, Marines consider corporals leaders, more the equivalent of an Army sergeant than that service's theoretically equivalent rank. The promotion is a milestone—minor for some, the last important one for others—in the life of an infantry Marine. Call it a graduation to the ranks of the men and women expected to make good decisions for others under fire.

Pinning on the corporal's chevrons—two stripes, as opposed to the lance corporal's one—is an honor and an event. At least personally.

I asked McKenzie to pin me. I respected him not just because of his rank, but because of his experience and knowledge. I looked up to him the way you'd look up to an older cousin.

Of course he pounded the pin in. I ended up bruised and bleeding—more than a little appropriate for Iraq.

To think of him in trouble now . . . it was like the order of the universe had flipped around. Here was a guy who took care of me, who now needed taking care of himself.

## HOME TO THE DAM

The company got a welcome home present when we pulled back into our quarters at Haditha Dam following Outer Banks. The muj mortarmen had obviously taken the time to brush up on their skills and targeting priorities, and launched a barrage of shells at the amtracs.

Most of the guys were just walking—the hell with those bastards.

I ran. The shells were hitting the dam, pretty much on target— the terrorists were getting better.

And in fact, one hit close to the vehicles just *after* we'd all gotten inside. If we'd been a little slower, or the tracs had come in a few minutes later . . .

I had no fear once inside the dam, though. It was massive, solid, and built to withstand a heck of a lot more force than what an explosive round from even a large mortar could put out.

On the other hand, the Russians had designed it and the Iraqis had built it, so you never knew.

We eventually incorporated the muj shelling into our poker games. If they started firing while we were playing cards on the deck outside, the last one to leave the game won the pot.

I always checked out with the first or second. Not only did I know those guys were getting better, but I rarely won at poker. You gotta know when to raise, and when to fold—and when to run for the bunker.

For the rest of April, we mostly did short patrols in the general vicinity of the dam and river. When we had a day "off," we reviewed some of our basic training bits, like first aid or calling for QRF, basically keeping our skills fine-tuned. We also did target work, practicing at distances of twenty-five yards and less. Generally, we're trained to fire at ten times that, but our experience in Barwana made it clear that firefights would take place much closer in Iraq.

Between patrols, we had a few high-value target (HVT) missions—operations that aimed to apprehend a specific person, generally a suspected bombmaker or high-ranking terrorist. These were more directed than patrols, with a specific house or building to search.

Every one of them was scary as shit. Typically, intel would come in—a certain Iraqi in a town was wanted, or a house there was suspected of hiding a weapons cache. Typically, you'd have three squads involved—one going in, one pulling security, the third as a quick reaction force in case something went wrong. I believe we worked with a high-level special operations team on one mission, pulling security for them, but in general we didn't do anything very high speed or Hollywood. When we did apprehend a few folks wanted for questioning, we never really knew what happened to them; we'd hand them off to the intel people or whoever else was in charge, and go on our way.

One of the missions that month involved a twenty-five-mile hike that turned out to be . . . mostly just a hike, since we didn't catch anyone. Another time we marched into a hamlet, went to the targeted house—and were met there by the suspect, who was handed off to the team designated to take him in for questioning. We marched back in the dark.

We were ghosts, entering towns. Eventually the muj started handing out flyers saying we were teaming up with aliens to kidnap people.

No, just us walking long distances in the dark.

Those twenty or so miles back to the dam were among the most beautiful walks I've ever taken—starlit night, nothing around, the temperature cool but not freezing. Almost as if we weren't at war.

Kicking doors in or using Thor was always a last resort, even when we were going after an HVT. I learned that the hard way: on one mission I was first up and knocked on the door without getting an answer. I stepped back and kicked.

And kicked. I went on kicking until my foot was sore. Smith came up, poised to give it a good whack with *his* foot, then reached for the handle and let us in. He gave me the après vous motion as if he were the maître d' at a fancy restaurant.

*Dick move, Smith. Dick move.*

I wised up after that; my foot and leg thanked me.

Unlocked doors were more common than you'd think. There were a couple of times we walked in on a sleeping family and surprised the hell out of them. No one ever fired at us or put up a fight—something that initially surprised me, though I guess when you've woken up to find yourself surrounded by Marines, it doesn't make much sense to do much to annoy them.

Reporters came around, including a few who embedded with us briefly. Where some of the guys had been bemoaning our "bad luck" at the lack of firefights just a week or so before, now the whole thing had turned around. We didn't have bad luck—on the contrary. We were now "Lucky Lima."

We'd been involved in two fairly long operations and a number of smaller ones, patrolled over a dozen cities and villages, and had yet to take a casualty. It wasn't that we were being overly cautious or were given the safest jobs, either. Lima Company was only one of two infantry units in the Marine sector out doing regular ops. We just seemed to be a charmed unit, in harm's way but fortunate enough to be spared the worst consequences.

I didn't pay much attention to the reporters, or to the talk of us being lucky. As far as I was concerned, I had my bag of magic sand and now the shell of the guy who'd tried to kill me, but I wasn't about to add it all up. I certainly didn't think I was anything special, let alone that I had an invincibility card tied to my membership in Lima.

And, frankly, if the fireteam had been tasked to go and sit guard at a quiet, distant base, I would have been more than happy to comply.

Nor could I have told you how the war in general was going. The war for me was broken up into these little vignettes, small moments of actual danger inside hours of adrenaline-surging alerts, themselves encased in far longer hours of total boredom. I didn't get enough sleep. I couldn't have found most of the cities we went to on a map. I would have liked better food, not to mention more alcohol and my girlfriend. I walked miles and miles each day with my best friends around me. Those were the main facts of the war as I knew them.

## OPERATION MATADOR

In the beginning of May, we were tasked to a major operation on the Syrian border. Named Operation Matador, the objective was to clear the area around al Qa'im of insurgents.

Al Qaeda in Mesopotamia had taken effective control of much of the area, using the towns as transit points for insurgents coming into Iraq from Syria. We heard that there would be special operators on the Syrian side helping—they would go on to conduct at least one mission at the start of Matador—but our targets and focus were in Iraq around the Euphrates. The river zigs and zags there, with marshes and farmland bordering both sides.

The plan was to spend five days rooting out the bad guys. On a personal level, that meant stocking extra ammo and as much food as I could carry. But except for the distance from our base, the mission as briefed to us seemed no different from any of the others we'd been on.

The first bad omen came when Command tried putting us into different tracs before we embarked from the dam. It sounds like a trivial thing, but we'd been working with the amphib crews for weeks and had grown to know them. It wasn't just a "these are our friends" thing. By the end of the first week in Iraq, I could tell who was who in my platoon by their silhouette in the dark; now I could do the same with the trac crews. All the guys could. A few probably could tell which vehicle was ours by the sound of the exhaust.

We knew them. We trusted them. That's everything in combat. Changing crews and vehicles was just a mindless command.

So we revolted.

Sergeant Jolly started sounding off first. The other squad leaders joined in. There was enough of a stink that we ended up loading into the vehicles we'd been working with.

Another omen—Grant was switched off from being radioman and put back as a rifleman, though not in our squad. We weren't riding together anymore.

No snacks.

More importantly, we weren't going to be close enough to watch over each other.

The last and most ominous omen: they gave us gas masks and EpiPens, hypodermic setups to be used in case the Syrians had given the insurgents CX gas.

*That* was a new development. That should have told me, should have told all of us, that things were going to be very different this time out. But I don't remember thinking anything but *that's weird.* Or maybe even, *whatever.*

—

**IT WAS FAR.**

Space and time were warped for us. On a map, our destination of al Qa'im base was roughly eighty miles from the dam. Driving on a highway, that might take an hour and a half if you obeyed the speed limit.

But we never went anywhere in a straight line, and we didn't always stick to the roads. Our limits were not speed and rarely time. Danger was the only metric that counted, but that was interpreted by some computation we never had access to. As I remember it, we took something like thirteen hours to get to al Qa'im. That's a long trip if you're sitting in a car; it was interminable in a trac. My legs were numb within an hour.

*Thirteen—is that an actual memory, or a reinterpretation of luck and omens?*

I took an overwatch during the night, sticking my head out the hatch and scanning with my NVGs as we drove. I pulled my gator up and pretended that I could see—the sand and grit kicked up from the other vehicles made it impossible to make anything out, and if it weren't for the gator, I would have suffocated from the sand. Relieved after two hours, I settled back into my spot on the metal bench and gradually willed myself into oblivious sleep.

## AL QA'IM BASE

We went in for breakfast as soon as we arrived at al Qa'im.

The base was crazy—it was a legit base, way more elaborate than our home back at the dam. I was shocked; I thought everybody was living the way we were except at Camp Cupcake. They had air-conditioning and a full-on cafeteria with things like ice cream. We hadn't seen that good a setup since al Asad.

And yet they were near the front line, as those things might be defined in this war. They'd even been attacked, fairly heavily, recently. The difference in the worlds inside and outside the wire was striking.

Lima Company by this point was pretty rough. We were used to sleeping on the hard ground if necessary, eating whatever we could find if hungry. Walking into al Qa'im was like walking into a dream. Not only was there a cafeteria, there was a line—people wanted the food.

No wonder. The warm food was warm, the cold food was cold. And no limits.

There was even steak. We went back and back.

They gave us plywood Quonset huts to rest in. There were no sheets or blankets on the beds, but barbarians don't need them—we threw down our stuff and lay out.

We stayed a little more than twenty-four hours, resting, eating, and being amazed at the place. I played chess with another kid from the platoon, Wes Davids. Davids beat me pretty much every game we played. I'd start out strong, getting an advantage in the opening, but he'd wear me down and outfox me in the end. Marine endurance.

You could just barely see the city of al Qa'im from the camp gate. Our target was farther away, on the other side of the river, as the NCOs told us the next day when we gathered to update our mission plan.

It sounded relatively straightforward. We would drive a few miles to an area on the south side of the river near New Ubaydi. Like just about every smallish city or village in Iraq, there are a few variations of the spelling, which of course is translated from Arabic; Al Ubaidi and Obaidy are the most common. The village, neatly constructed by the government for local workers, was regularly patrolled and considered calm; we wouldn't be stopping there. Instead, we would drive to a point on the river bend a short distance away, where we would cross with the help of pontoon bridges to be built by the Army just before we arrived.

Across the river, we would drive to an agricultural village—smaller, and laid out far more haphazardly than New Ubaydi. We'd clear it, secure any terrorists we captured along with weapons and what not, and then receive further orders. There were several villages and hamlets throughout the area; we expected to clear a good number over the next few days before being ordered to withdraw and go home.

We boarded the tracs and headed out.

Maybe an hour later we arrived at a ridge on the Euphrates where the engineers were to build the bridge. But the bridge wasn't up. The operation was running late, apparently because some of the Army's vehicles carrying the bridging equipment had been held up by mechanical problems.

We sat for a while. The engineers were taking sporadic mortar fire from New Ubaydi. It wasn't accurate but it was annoying, especially for the engineers, who were trying to get on with things as best they could. With no place to go, and possibly seeing the mortars as a threat to the bridge, the engineers, and us, Command decided to clear New Ubaydi.

Hurley was told the city was not actively hostile. Units went on patrols there without running into resistance all the time.

So why was the shelling coming from there?

Jolly pulled out a map and traced the plan of attack for our squad. The map showed a wall around the city. The vehicles would crash through the barrier; we'd dismount, then clear that part of the village. The streets were laid out on an even grid. The buildings on the east and west side of the city mostly shouldered against each other; there was a large, mostly open space in the middle.

About a mile from the village, we stopped for a leaders' recon. I was security for Jolly, so I got out of the trac with him and went over to get a look at our target. I flopped down on my stomach and scoped in on the city. I could see some industrial works and the factory-style housing that dominated the place.

The houses weren't going to be too much of a problem. We were used to dealing with those.

Not too big a place. Typical.

*Except . . .*

Helos flew above. I was used to helos, but these were darting in and out, slamming through the air. As I scoped in, I realized they were hunting targets—and coming under intense fire from the ground.

That was *very* unusual. We'd seen plenty of helicopters flying low over Iraq before, but never ones that had been met with that kind of gunfire. Or *any* gunfire.

A fan of dust suddenly blocked my view. Then the sand around me percolated, as if I'd flopped down on a volcano bed.

*What?*

"Jolly, I think they're shooting at us," I said.

They were. I was more surprised than worried about getting hit. The village was a mile away. No service weapon the insurgents had could hit something at that range. Even my M16 would have been relatively useless; about eight hundred meters was the best area target range you could depend on.

But here these guys were firing—and coming relatively close.

The leader conference concluded. We reboarded the tracs and started down toward the village.

The gunfire ramped up. Then it went into overdrive.

You know those World War II movies where landing craft race toward the sands of Iwo Jima or Normandy? That's what this was like, except in tracked vehicles on sand rather than water.

We came under more concentrated gunfire than anything we'd encountered to this point in the war. And it was damn accurate. Bullets pinged off the front of the trac. The insurgents were firing whatever they could in our direction.

McKenzie, looking at the town from the front hatch of his AAV, watched as a vehicle carrying members of the company we were with reached the outskirts of the town. Six men came out of the back, button-hooking around, three on each side. Almost immediately, all six went down. The rest of the squad sprinted past, continuing on.

He had two instant emotions—one was admiration for the Marines who kept going. The other was a realization that this was not going to be anything like the fights we'd been in.

## GET THE FUCK IN!

"Get ready! Get ready!" yelled Jolly as our trac barreled toward the enemy. "We're going to see heavy contact."

Everyone grabbed whatever extra ammo they could.

"You're going to be behind a wall when the ramp goes down," continued Jolly. "Engage the enemy from behind that wall."

I was right next to the ramp, ready to get out. I lit a cigarette, took a breath, and braced myself as we caromed onwards.

We hit the brakes. The ramp went down. I bolted.

Two steps off the trac, bullets ricocheting off the hull, I looked for the wall Jolly had promised.

Not there. Not anywhere. Jolly had been given bad information.

The only cover was two or three hundred yards away—the yard of a house.

Later on we'd realize that coming in, the tracs had swept south and come through an area where there was no wall or berm, but at that moment, the only thing I thought was *Holy shit. Where the hell am I?*

I took a knee and scoped in, unsure what I was supposed to do. Machine guns began pounding the area, sweeping away from the tracs toward the men jumping out of them.

Old Man Hurley leapt off the turret at the top of the trac.

"Go! Go! Get the fuck in!" he yelled.

I followed him as we ran to the nearest house.

Smith caught up to us, passing us as he usually did. He raced to the door of the house and head-butted it open. Hurley and I went in, followed by the rest of the squad. We didn't clear it so much as consume it, working through with the vicious efficiency of a bulldozer.

The place was unoccupied. We worked through it, got to the roof, and then began working across, rooftop to rooftop, clearing the houses—empty—returning fire.

*Jumping to the next roof. Shoot at the flashes. Go again. Keep momentum.*

The outer ring of houses were empty. That wasn't random. The enemy wanted to engage us inside the city itself, where they would have the advantage of terrain.

Nothing here was random, or like the ops and engagements we'd been in earlier. This was Fallujah—a well-planned and prepared enemy stronghold. We had jumped into an all-out war against a well-fortified and coordinated enemy.

Even in all that, there were moments of something approaching levity.

Norris's team got pinned on the rooftop while I was in the nearby garden with Britten and Smith, trying to decide the next move. Suddenly we heard Norris yell, "Fuck, that round hit the wall next to me. I'm bleeding. Holy shit, does this mean I get a purple heart?"

"Only if you're an officer," answered someone.

I laughed—and at the same time, shot at a silhouette darting in the alleyway.

We started doing what we were trained to do, what we had learned to do by hard practice. We'd go into a house, clear it, get to the roof, and cover the next team of Marines taking the next house. Then we'd jump to the next. We did this all under heavy fire, shooting back as we went.

Where the houses were too far apart, we had to risk the street, bolting to the next structure as machine guns tore up the pavement and nearby structures. We'd reach a house and start the process all over again.

It was like déjà vu, but it wasn't monotonous—you wanted always to move. Stay in one spot and you were dead, an easy target.

Some of the houses were completely benign. Others were set up as strongpoints, but recently abandoned. There'd be weapons, maybe a machine gun and an RPG launcher, along with rounds and rounds of ammo. Jolly found a bicycle fitted out as an IED.

The insurgents fell back as we moved. The civilians were . . . gone for the most part. I didn't see any for quite a while, until finally we came upon a house with some women and kids—light-skinned and green-eyed, not typical Arabs.

*Who the hell are you?*

They said nothing. We'd interpret the mix of fear and defiance in their eyes much later to mean they were probably families of the terrorists who'd come to Iraq to fight us, but at that moment it didn't really register. Nor did it matter. They were unarmed and compliant. We let them be and moved on.

Outside, the roar of the fight was deafening. Some of the guys came across a car outfitted as a suicide vehicle; they piled bombs and explosives into it and blew it in place, showering the area with bricks from a nearby building. A tire flew through the air near where McKenzie stood, a few blocks away.

"Maybe that was a little too much explosives," said someone over the radio.

Time flew by, hours passing in what seemed like minutes. We pushed the rest of the day, generally under fire, until finally we came to a big field about halfway through the town. Air support raged all around. I saw my first triple stack: an A-10A Warthog, one of our Cobra attack helicopters, and an F-16 came in for low-level attacks on insurgents beyond our position. One after the other, the aircraft hit in the same area, unleashing brimstone on the holy warriors trying to send us to hell.

By now it was early afternoon. The insurgents were in full retreat, trying to escape now across the river. The aircraft strafed them as they fled, trying to stop the flow. We were too far away to watch, and had other work to do; there were still plenty of muj around.

The enemy was professional, or at least led by pros. They had backup machine guns, well-laid-out fallback positions. You fired at them and they wouldn't duck. It wasn't that we couldn't handle them; it was just different, urban warfare on a level and of a quality we hadn't encountered earlier. As intense as our sweeps had been, this was something else.

Our M-1 tanks and Light Armored Vehicles—LAV-25s typically equipped with Bushmaster 25 mm chain guns—had come in and were engaging the enemy, who fired back with everything they had. Not particularly logical—even an RPG round bounces off a main battle tank—but a measure of their ferocity nonetheless.

The open field in the center of town became a killing ground. We pulled up to the edge, ahead of the other units in the op, waiting for orders. I was posted up on a rooftop overlooking the field.

I hoped like hell I wasn't going to be ordered to run across it. At least not until the tanks passed through. The math was not particularly favorable: *a few hundred yards divided by a few hundred bullets equals . . .*

I'd already pushed the equation and my luck rushing two hundred yards with rounds landing all around me when we came in; this was going to be a lot harder.

Then things started calming down. Calm's not the right word— the intensity slid down, gunfire dying off, explosions lessening. It wasn't peaceful or entirely quiet, just less noisy, less dreadfully dangerous.

Easier, as long as easy is understood as only a point of comparison.

The day was waning. It was clear we'd won the battle; the last of the insurgents on our flanks were desperate to get away. The squad leaders and Hurley started thinking about where we were going to spend the night.

Then the mother of all shitstorms kicked up two blocks away, louder and more ferocious than anything I'd heard for hours. I held my post, watching to make sure the enemy didn't bring up reinforcements, watching and frustrated that I couldn't do more than that.

## THE SHADOW OF FALLUJAH

We'd all seen the video and news reports on Phantom Fury, the Marine operation to clear Fallujah. The cities and towns we'd been going into over the past few months looked a lot like the ones in those videos. But there was one telling difference: the tactics that the terrorists had used against us were different from those in Fallujah.

Generally, the insurgents tried to blend in, hide themselves among the population. When they did attack, they did so in relatively small numbers. They might plant an IED, ignite it from a distance, and leave before we could respond. They might lob a few mortar shells and move on. A handful of terrorists might try to engage us with rifle fire before fleeing—assuming they had survived.

That had been the general pattern of resistance after the occupation began, certainly in al Anbar Province. The tactics were nearly always those of a guerrilla group vastly outnumbered and outgunned. They might and often did engage and intimidate the locals; they might coerce them into providing shelter and other support; they might even infiltrate the local government and police structure. But they were wary and crafty about taking us on. Pitched battles were unheard of.

That changed at Fallujah, even before Phantom Fury. The history of the resistance there is complicated—alleged contractor atrocities stirred sentiments early on, and a large number of soldiers loyal to Saddam had gone underground there immediately after the war began. A few months before Phantom Fury, the Marines went to Fallujah to apprehend the perpetrators in the contractors' deaths; the operation was bloody and destructive, but by most objective accounts failed to pacify the city. Insurgents fought openly and in significant numbers against the Marines. Once the American forces withdrew, insurgents returned in even greater numbers.

If most operations in Iraq were sweeps, Phantom Fury was a steamroller. The strategy was eons old: block off all avenues of escape, and move from one side to the other, taking out all enemy forces in the process.

Commencing in November 2004, U.S. Marines, along with units from the Air Force and Army, along with some attached special operations troops and British and Iraqi soldiers, cordoned off the town completely. Warned of the impending attack, many civilians had fled. Those who were left were assumed to be at least sympathetic to the resistance, if not actually part of it.

The Marines began moving in. By that point, the mujahedeen controlled the town and had established a network of interconnected strongpoints, a defense-in-depth, to use the technical military term. The insurgents were a smorgasbord of various groups, ranging from al Qaeda recruits to former Iraqi soldiers. The foreign fighters had come from all over the Middle East, Chechnya, and even the Philippines, sponsored or influenced by a hodgepodge of groups and extremist leaders, most prominently bin Laden. They were here with the aim of fighting the infidel.

As disparate as the group was, they were as well-coordinated, prepared, and disciplined as any force American troops had faced since the start of the war.

The Allied forces pushed into the city block by block over a course of weeks. Much of the fighting was at very close quarters. While not hand to hand, it's not an exaggeration to say that the combatants were often within spitting distance of each other. The American forces leveraged technological advantages in various ways—mobility, UAVs, precision-guided munitions, snipers, etc.

The mujahedeen leveraged their own advantages. They prepared numerous ambushes, fortifying select yards and houses, booby-trapping mundane objects, arranging IEDs so they could be used to create traps. One of the deadliest tactics was the use of what were called suicide or death houses. Fighters would hide inside a house, waiting until Marines or other troops entered before showing themselves. These fighters would fight literally to the death, hoping to take as many Americans with them on the way as possible.

There is no direct parallel to Fallujah in Marine Corps history prior to Iraq. The Battle of Hue in Vietnam was surely as bloody and hard fought, lasted longer and was more complicated tactically. Plenty of other operations can be looked at for precedents of individual facets. Overall, the death count among U.S. Marines and even the enemy paled compared to those in earlier battles, especially World War II.

But one of the things that sets Fallujah apart was the sheer religious fanaticism of the people the Marines were fighting. Consider this: many had left homes hundreds and thousands of miles away to come there and die.

You might say the same about us, except that our purpose was not to die at all.

Most of the fighting during Phantom Fury took place over an eleven-day period, but it wasn't until nearly Christmas that the city was fully cleared. Just under a hundred Americans died; more than five and a half times that were wounded. The insurgent toll has never been settled; it was at least one thousand, and possibly twice that. Even with that much carnage, many of the terrorists leaders were able to escape, fanning out to other parts of the province.

They were among the muj we were dealing with at Matador. And while they didn't have as favorable conditions here, they had made their defenses in New Ubaydi as close to Fallujah as they could.

## GOING IN

The firestorm I'd heard earlier had started when First Squad reached the end of their advance line. With the platoons on our flanks delayed for various reasons, Hurley was already preparing to hold our advance and have us go firm for the night. One last house remained to be checked; given how things had been winding down, it looked like it would be a breeze. It was bunched against another, a little on the larger side for our part of Iraq but not exceptional by any means. Squat, with a flat roof and cramped rooms flanking stairs to the roof at the center of the house.

Lance Corporal Collen West went to knock on the door; his hand no sooner touched it than he was shot in both legs.

Corporal Dustin Derga, who was with him, got hit maybe a moment later, wounded in the back.

Marines rallied to the house as gunfire escalated. A lot of 1st Squad was cut up in the initial, chaotic moments of the encounter. Hurley arrived, directing reinforcements and medical help. Goodwin came as well.

After the house was cordoned off, two insurgents attempted to leave through the rear yard. They were shot dead by Richard Cain. (A PFC at the time, Cain made lance corporal before we left.)

That seemed to be the end of it. Two muj—that more or less lined up with what had happened to this point, a heavy machine-gun operator with a helper, holed up in a room or hallway with line of sight on the door and some mobility inside. They'd expended a large number of rounds, saw an opening—or thought they did—as the Marines hit pause, and made a break for it.

Now they were dead.

The house still had to be cleared. Hurley had called 2nd Squad to come over and help do that. By the time they arrived, Goodwin and Camp were already entering the house. Taylor and three of his guys from 2nd Squad—Thomas, Rizvi, and Reynolds—went in a few moments later.

This is Taylor's account:

"Why are we going into a house with insurgents," I thought to myself. "Why not just blow it?" but there was no time for thinking. Thomas cleared the doorway and was closely followed by Reynolds and Rizvi. I entered behind them. There was a small empty room to the right and a kitchen to the left. It had no objects inside and was completely empty.

Staff Sergeant Goodwin and Camp were already in the house and down the hallway. Rizvi and Reynolds stopped. I didn't know why. I pushed past them. On the floor was an RPG round in a pile of burning debris. There were burn marks on the walls and blasted pieces of wall everywhere.

I moved up to Thomas. The hallway was hazy with red smoke. Camp looked down the hall and Goodwin calmly looked at us and said, "Rizvi and Reynolds go upstairs. Taylor, you and Thomas clear the back left room and Camp and I will clear the right one. Is everyone ready? OK, Break."

Thomas and I paused for a split second and then moved. We ran into the back room and cleared our sectors of fire about a hundred times in a split second. The small back room was empty. But then we heard gunfire out in the hall, back on the right where we'd come from.

We stacked on the door. There was no telling whether the shooting was us or them. I counted to three and we turned the corner.

Goodwin and Camp were standing there. In the back doorway was a dead insurgent; another lay in the yard. The one in the yard was wearing dark clothes and was facedown with his arms under his body. The one in the doorway was wearing light yellow clothes and was full of bullet holes.

He wasn't bloody though. The clothes on his chest were shredded and it looked a gooey yellow. There was some red blood but not like in the movies. The bodies looked almost fake. They looked like they were from a wax museum. The man's eyes were open but had a glazed stare like he wasn't really looking at anything.

I kicked him and made sure he was dead.

The other man was clearly dead but was lying in a strange manner. We had all heard about insurgents booby-trapping their bodies and so I told Goodwin I'd get a grappling hook from the engineers, and check the body.

He disagreed at first, saying it wasn't necessary, but I insisted. Better safe than sorry. He told me to go.

I walked back out of the house and up the street a ways, looking for the engineers. I couldn't find them.

When I came back to the house, Gunny Hurley and Thomas were standing outside the front gate.

"I couldn't find the engineers to get a grappling hook," I said.

Hurley looked at me crazily.

"Forget that. Goodwin's inside and we need to get him out."

"I'll go get him." I started around the corner when Gunny grabbed me.

"What the fuck is wrong with you!" he yelled. "Staff Sergeant is *down* inside the house. We need to go in and clear it. There is an insurgent inside with a machine gun."

In the few minutes that Taylor was gone, an insurgent or insurgents hidden somewhere inside had ambushed the Marines checking the house, blasting the interior with a heavy machine gun. Goodwin had been cut down inside.

Taylor's account continues:

I couldn't think of where an insurgent could possibly have been hiding. We had cleared that house. Reynolds and Rizvi looked down at us from the roof.

"Let me go down and clear it," Rizvi yelled. "I can get to Staff Sergeant."

"No, you stay put and cover that roof," Gunny replied.

Camp was stuck in the backyard and couldn't get out because of the wall.

I kept trying to call Scott Bunker to bring his team over. Comm sucked and all I was getting were garbled questions.

Random Marines came out of the houses and we formed a stack to go in, with Gunny in command. Camp made it over the wall and came to join us.

Gunny pointed Hildebrand to the window covering the right room. Dixon was in the front of the stack and I was behind him. Following us in were Erdy, Thomas, and Camp. There may have been others; things were confusing and parts are hard to remember.

We walked in and cleared the corner. We quickly

cleared the kitchen and continued moving down the hall, lead guy firing to keep any enemy back. Dixon got a weapon's jam and stepped aside; I took point.

I continued firing down the hallway into the back room. We made it to the staircase and I looked up. There was no one there.

We were almost at the end of the hall. I could hardly see with my sunglasses on in the darkened house, but I didn't have any other eye protection and the hot brass from my weapon kept hitting me in the face.

Goodwin's feet and ankles lay ahead. He was not moving.

I was just about to assign rooms to clear when suddenly bullets came from out of nowhere. The walls seemed to shred around us. The noise was deafening. I could feel the bullets pass by in the tight confines of the hallway. I could see the tracer rounds pass.

We turned and ran back, diving into the dark kitchen. The room flashed as the tracers flew inches over the tops of our bodies. I tried to squish into the floor and roll over, but I couldn't move. My gear was too bulky. I couldn't roll or squish any further.

I lifted my rifle and began shooting the wall. Thomas did the same. I at least wanted to die trying.

Then as suddenly as the shooting started it stopped. Everyone sprang to their feet and ran for the outside door.

While this was going on, my fireteam and I held a position a street or two away.

We heard bits and pieces and grew more and more frustrated. Somehow we heard that Goodwin had been trapped inside the house. That amped everything for us.

We started agitating to go get him. The reasoning was simple: He's our guy. We're all here, we're all uninjured. We want the mission.

*Maybe Goodwin's still alive!*

*We leave no one behind.*

*We can fuck these guys up.*

I remember thinking that Goodwin was a fighter; he would very likely still be alive.

At some point Britten got on the radio, got Hurley, and told him we wanted to go in. There was a discussion, I think several, basically asking permission for us to assault the house. It was denied.

Smith and I said we should disobey orders and go. We were good at clearing houses; we could get Goodwin out.

What was the worst they could do to us?

Britten, smartly, said that was a terrible idea. Moving to the house without permission meant the Marines around it wouldn't know we were coming, wouldn't necessarily conclude we were Americans when we approached. Even if they didn't shoot at us, we could easily cross up their own operational plan. We could be caught in the crossfire and get our asses shot off.

You can't go Rambo in the middle of any fight, but particularly one in close quarters in an urban environment. Anything we did might, at best, screw up plans that were already in motion that we didn't know about.

So we didn't go. Smith paced like a caged animal, trying to control his impulses. The rest of us sucked it up as best we could.

*What do I do next? What do I need to do?*

*We knew several people were injured. I started to think about Grant. Where was he? Is he down?*

When I'm stressed, I'm quieter, trying to figure out what to do. I was *very* quiet then.

By now it was near dusk or maybe a little beyond. The sky

had turned red, fading to black. I sat back against a wall, my body buzzing. A tank drove up, heading to the house. We heard over the radio that they were going to level the place.

For some reason I looked up and realized the wall we were up against was piled with loose stones.

I jumped up.

"Push on these stones, push on these stones," I yelled. "Or the blast's gonna kill us."

The tank fired. The wall rumbled. A second shot, more rumble—dust and a few small stones fell, but the wall remained more or less intact. As Hurley took stock, we were ordered into a building nearby, covering the area in case the muj tried to reinforce it or otherwise take advantage of the situation.

## BUNKER AND GRANT

Down the street, Bunker's fireteam came up to help clear the building. Their day had been eventful from the moment they stepped out of the trac—Bunker missed a machine-gun barrage by chance when he stopped to ask Taylor where he wanted them.

Luck.

A short time later, the team had been targeted by gunfire from a minaret. Ordinarily, mosques and minarets were off-limits; American troops did not fire on religious structures. But this was clearly being used as a hostile site, and potentially an exception.

Bunker's team called back and got permission to engage. A grenade from a Mark 19 grenade launcher either killed the muj using the minaret or convinced them to move.

Things went slightly easier after that. Before Taylor called them to the death house, they were thinking the day was just about over.

—

THE TANK TOOK OUT LARGE CHUNKS OF THE BUILDING'S WALL. AT LEAST ONE OF the shells set off a propane tank inside the building; it flashed and sent a cyclone of smoke skyward as it or something nearby continued to burn.

There was no way anyone could survive in there. *No way.*

Gunny Hurley lined up an ad hoc group to go in and get Goodwin's body. Bunker and the guys with him joined the line. Taylor joined the line. When he saw Erdy and Camp moving in, he yelled at them to stay back. They'd already been inside and risked enough.

"You can't stop me," answered Erdy.

I'm sure Camp and everybody else in that line felt the same way. Taylor and Hurley let them join.

Hurley decided they'd grenade every crevice of the place as they went in, just to make sure there were no more surprises. Someone passed him a grenade. His rifle had either jammed or been disabled; he dumped it and took out his pistol.

A silent count, then the Marines at the building started tossing grenades.

*Wait a breath—*

*Boom! Boom! Boom!*

Erdy and Bunker went in through one of the holes and reached the hallway. The flames of the fire set by the propane tank gave off just enough light through the ruins for them to get their bearings.

Bunker saw Goodwin lying ahead, half in the doorway, beyond a carpet of spent rounds and a pool of blood.

*No one could have survived those tank rounds.*

Bunker and Erdy got to Goodwin's body. The rest of the Marines moved into the house, clearing different rooms.

A staircase ran to the roof opposite of the room where they crouched. There was a door under the stairs, a cubby families used as a utility closet.

*Better check it, just in case.*

Erdy went to the door. Bunker raised his rifle, covering him.

*Nothing could have survived those tank rounds. But just in case . . .*

The Marines exchanged a glance and then began a silent count. When they reached three, Erdy pulled the door open.

*"Allahu Akbar!"*

Bunker felt his head explode. He was thrown back, thrown down, thrown into turmoil as everything around him percolated with machine-gun bullets.

He found himself on the floor, unable to see out of his right eye.

THE WORDS *"ALLAHU AKBAR"* TRANSLATE SIMPLY AS "GOD IS GREATER." BUT THE phrase has far more meaning than that. It is used in innumerable situations, a way of praising God, a way of saying that one man's fate is in the hands of his Creator, a way of acknowledging God's place in the universe.

And a way of cursing us to hell. It is the phrase used by a maniacal Muslim bent on taking out as many people as he possibly can before being killed in jihad and meeting his Maker.

Which was how it was meant that evening in New Ubaydi.

GUNNY HURLEY WAS A FEW ROOMS AWAY WHEN THE MACHINE GUN BEGAN TEARING through the house. He ducked and rolled and tried squeezing his body into the tiniest space imaginable. At first he couldn't figure out where the bullets were coming from, then he couldn't figure out why he wasn't dead.

There were holes everywhere. The bullets had flown from an odd angle, directly at him, it seemed, but angled oddly. Eyes stinging, choking from the acrid smoke and exhausted gas of the gunfire, Hurley squeezed himself to the floor, then managed to move, stumbling, pushing, running, squeezing into the space beyond the gunfire, out of the building.

It was only later, after he thought about where he had been, and how the bullets had come, that he realized why he hadn't been shot, and where the muj with the machine gun had to be—under the house, hidden in tunnels reached through the door under the stairs, protected by sandbagged walls.

UNABLE TO SEE OUT OF HIS RIGHT EYE, BUNKER TRIED BRINGING HIS GUN UP TO fire. But his arm wouldn't move. He started crawling, pushing with his legs. Erdy got to him in the hall and pulled him along. As they reached the opening, other members of the fireteam spotted them.

"Who the fuck is that?" shouted one.

Bunker was covered in so much blood, the men who'd lived with him for months couldn't recognize him.

They got him out and over to a trac being used as a med station. Erdy stayed with him.

"Dude, I can't see out of my right eye," Bunker said.

It's fine, said Erdy. "You'll be OK."

Bunker knew it was lie, though—the expression on Erdy's face made that clear enough.

I'D BEEN POSTED ON THE ROOF WHEN THIS WAS GOING ON. SOMEONE CAME UP AND relieved me. I went downstairs to look after the inhabitants of the house, who looked pretty shaken up.

Britten, our fireteam leader, barged into the room.

"Stop talking to them," he yelled. "They just took out all of 2nd Squad."

"What?"

"Don't talk to them."

I must have stared at him a moment.

"They just hit an ambush house," said Britten. "All 2nd Squad is dead."

Grant was in 2nd Squad.

I fought the urge to bolt out of the house. I needed to know if it was true, and if it was, I knew I would get him out of whatever he was stuck in. I wouldn't let him die. I wouldn't let it be true.

I could. I solved problems; I always fixed things. This was something I could figure out.

*I have to get him. I made a promise, he made a promise—we would take care of each other.*

But I had my orders. I stayed where I was, carried out the job I was assigned.

WE HEARD BITS AND PIECES OF WHAT WAS GOING ON AT THE HOUSE. WORD GOT TO us that 2nd Squad had gone in, not knowing there were still insurgents inside.

We knew a lot of guys had been hit, and we heard a lot had died. I heard more info, more rumors of dead.

I heard Grant was one of them. I stood around, a pit in my stomach, not knowing what to do.

The house was cordoned off while we waited for an aircraft to bomb it. The bomb missed.

*Fucking pilot.*

They cordoned off the house for the night and waited for another plane.

We moved over to a school. I'd always known that death was a possibility here. I knew always that I could die, that any of my friends could die. But for some reason I didn't know, didn't consider, that there was a possibility that Grant could die.

I knew it in abstract terms—if asked I'd say, *Sure, anyone can be killed. That's war.*

But Grant actually being dead—my best friend in the world gone—there was no way to prepare for that. I felt as if someone had reached inside my body and pulled out my lungs.

The hurt was so complete, I didn't believe it. I couldn't. That's how you deal with great loss—you deny it.

Night fell. The room darkened. I was in a classroom, similar to the places I'd spent so much of my life.

Classrooms had always been good places, places where I could excel with hard work, where effort could be rewarded. Places where you could achieve, have some measure of control.

Not here. Not now. Now the place was an empty hull signifying impotence—my impotence and lack of any power, lack of any chance of redemption or even worth.

I sat down at a desk, spent physically from combat, emotionally drained from the loss of my friend.

Marines staggered in from the fight. Another platoon came in, dirty and battered, having just survived their own ordeal.

Then, there he was, there, with other members of his squad: Grant.

Grant, alive.

I leapt to my feet and hugged him. He hugged me back.

"I can't believe you're here," I told him. "They told us you were dead."

"I'm here. They told us you were dead, too."

"No. I'm alive."

"Me, too," he said. "Me, too."

# V.

# DESOLATION

## McKENZIE

My cell phone kept dropping the connection as I drove. I'd dial back, not get anything, wait a little, then try again. Finally it would go through and he'd answer.

"Remember the pink house," I asked McKenzie. "When we were about to get overrun?"

"Was that Haditha?"

"Haditha was the school."

"I remember that."

"The snipers?"

"Oh, yeah . . ."

"How about the goat you bought?" I asked, searching for a more positive memory. "You cut it up to cook. Who helped?"

The Bailon brothers. It was a great meal.

We just kept talking.

Grant's name came up.

"You guys were like brothers," he said.

"Yeah. We were."

## SUBDUED

Ordinarily, Grant was animated after a firefight or a patrol where shit had happened. Now he was nearly catatonic, sitting in one of the classroom chairs and staring into space. He'd been at the house and seen much of the fight and its results.

I tried to talk to him, without getting much of an answer. After a while, I went to another room with my fireteam. Everyone's mood was sour; McKenzie said later the platoon had suddenly grown many times more serious. There was none of the usual joking, and certainly no smiles. By now, we all had a fairly full picture of what had happened, the amount of loss we'd suffered. There was grief, but there was also fatigue. The company had been in combat for eight hours.

In our experience, the muj didn't fight for eight hours. This was something different—a pitched urban battle of a scale and depth we hadn't encountered. The enemy moved and fought like a regular army, with well-prepared positions and tactics. They had combined arms—mortars coordinating with machine guns and rifles. They wore flak jackets. We had an overwhelming advantage in terms of men and firepower, yet taking the small village had been difficult and costly. Going forward, there would be more of the same.

We knew we were going forward. Quitting would have been inconceivable, not just to our leaders but to us. But we also knew it was going to be just as hard as today.

I'd come to Iraq knowing that people would die, and that some might very well be my friends. I didn't think about that when I did my job. It was only when the fighting stopped that the reality of loss, the possibility of grief, became something real.

Saying the experience hardened us implies that we were soft or at least unrealistic beforehand. We weren't. The battle did something else, something deeper. They say knowledge opens doors. In this case, it closed them, blocking off extraneous bits of consciousness. It sharpened our awareness of what war is by pushing everything else away.

AT SOME POINT THOSE OF US WHO WEREN'T ON WATCH WENT TO SLEEP ON THE floor.

We stayed in the school for another day. Goodwin's body was recovered. He was thirty-three when he died.

Corporal Derga, twenty-four, was critically wounded in the assault; he died the next day. A number of other guys had been wounded, most seriously enough to be medevac'd. By Hurley's count, there had been four separate assaults. At least two insurgents had been killed; more than likely a third was pulverized in the rubble. It's likely one escaped, though we didn't know it at the time.

Gunny Hurley made a point of saying later that those of us who didn't actually go into the house but were posted on overwatch or other duties had played an important role in the operation, even if we would have preferred going in. But I couldn't help feeling that we should have been right there. In the back of your mind, you feel certain you could have been the one to turn the tide—even if objectively you know that's not true.

"Everyone volunteers," said Hurley. "No one gets to pick where they go or what happens."

*True. But.*

Going through the town, we'd found a large number of weapons caches, explosives, and material for IEDs. We also found dozens of hypodermic needles, probably for the methamphetamines used by the enemy fighters to hype themselves up before a fight. This was a common al Qaeda practice, stoking adrenaline and reinforcing the maniacal adherence to their cause and the willingness to die for it.

Excepting Death House, our casualties were light; the enemy's were later put at one hundred forty-four dead, with forty taken prisoner. An unknown number were wounded, and the city was no longer an insurgent stronghold. There were rumors that Abu Musab al-Zarqawi, a leader of al Qaeda in Mesopotamia, had been in the city when we attacked, and a theory that he was in the Death House when the search started. It's possible he was in the city at one point, but unlikely that he remained when the fighting at the house started. In any event, we didn't find him.

Was it a victory?

I guess. But infantrymen in a war like this tended not to make those sorts of calculations. This wasn't the kind of war where you could judge momentum easily from the ground level. In a large set-piece battle—on the Western front in World War II, for example—you know the direction you're moving in, the territory you're gaining, and from that you can make a judgment. But in a war of occupation where you move from one place to another, it's much harder to gauge anything about the wider war. You know what you're dealing with, how bullets are flying at you. You can even count the many explosions going off if you care to. But it's truly hard to put those things into a larger context with the limited information you typically have access to as a grunt.

We didn't feel like we were losing the war, but we also knew we weren't riding the crest of a rout.

With all the shooting I did, I have no idea if I ever killed anyone, either there or elsewhere in the war. I never saw anyone fall, and certainly during Matador it was rare when I was the only one shooting at someone. I saw blood, and it might be reasonable to conclude that out of so many rounds, the odds are high that I did more than wound an enemy. But I don't have direct evidence.

I think I probably did kill some of the muj, there and elsewhere, but I don't care. And I don't care to think about it. I don't want to know. A tally would be meaningless to me.

I knew guys who went and checked the bodies of men they'd killed. I didn't do that.

I didn't need it. More importantly, I wasn't sure how I would feel if I definitely did know. Not so much then, but later on. Now.

I think having dead bodies on my conscience, even those of people who deserved it and had tried to kill me, was something I don't need. I sure didn't need trophies; no one on my fireteam did. All things being equal, at least I don't have that on my conscience.

I've been asked which was more important: fighting to keep myself alive, or fighting to keep my friends alive. I answer quickly: *my guys*. The fireteam, the squad, the company. I felt it was my responsibility to protect them, without hesitation. Those were the important measures of my worth.

Maybe that was because I was an older guy—twenty-five, compared to early twenties or even teens for some of the others—Dixon was nineteen and barely even shaving when he went into Death House. Maybe it came from my family, where I was the only man in the house. Maybe it's just the way I am.

Until working on this book, I'd never really gone back and tried to piece together everything that happened at Death House. I hadn't analyzed everything, gone deep into how it happened, why it happened. Other guys in my company have mapped out every inch of it in their heads, practically every breath.

No two maps are precisely the same, but that's another question. For me, that deep examination is like going down a rabbit hole. I can't find any value in it. It'd be like examining my life cell by cell, analyzing each nucleus, without being able to relate what I found to actual organs, let alone a coherent human life.

I don't mean that self-examination isn't important, or useful. Just that it wasn't important here.

My role was limited. I wasn't the one giving commands. I didn't and can't know everything that went into the various decisions that shaped that day. I wasn't one of the guys going into the house. So certainly I am not anyone who can make a judgment about what happened, beyond saying that the men who were killed and wounded were good Marines, brave Marines, heroes, and my friends.

It was always drilled into my head that hesitation kills in war. It's better to move than to freeze. For that reason, the side of myself that likes to take a long time to contemplate a problem fell to the background while I served. Not that I didn't think through problems or analyze situations, but my default mode became *act* rather than *think. Move or die.*

Marine mode.

That was different for me then, and different for me now. Outside of the Corps, I've always worked with mid- and long-range plans for my life—five years, ten years. In the Marines, I was trained and operated as instantly as possible. That has receded, though I believe much of what the Corps taught me remains an important part of my being and everyday life.

I don't hold myself up as an excellent Marine. I was middling, mediocre. Other guys were heroes. I just tried to do my job as best I could. Serve my country, then move on. My uniform didn't always have the sharpest creases; sunlight didn't bounce off my boots, but I knew my role and I did the task at hand.


**AFTER WE PULLED BACK, COMMAND TOLD US THAT THE INSURGENTS WHO'D KILLED** Goodwin and Derga had been killed overnight in the bombing.

It wasn't until years later that we found out that wasn't true, and that it was likely at least one had managed to escape.

Shocker: the brass lied to us . . . again.

I'm not sure why Command lied. Maybe it was to make us feel somehow better, or maybe to lessen the odds that we would go off and randomly kill people seeking revenge.

It doesn't make me feel better now. I can't say what it did for me at the time.


## BACK TO THE RIVER

With New Ubaydi now secure, we went back to the area of the river crossing where we'd left the Army Engineers and their pontoon bridge project. The road was cratered with the holes from IED explosions; we drove on anyway, hoping there weren't any IEDs or mines left.

Surprise, surprise—the bridge still wasn't done.

No mortar fire, though.

Rather than driving across—which would have been a disaster, since the amphibs were no longer waterproof—Command had the tracs board the Army's pontoon bridging boats. We were ferried across to the other side, moving into a rural farming area. Though it was sparsely settled, we could see a large building in some sort of complex, maybe a mining complex, a short distance away. It seemed the logical approach for an attack, and enough of a threat that we oriented our force protection in that direction.

We took over a four-room house as we waited for further orders. It was around then that Staff Sergeant Kendall Ivy arrived, our replacement for Goodwin. He was a regular-duty Marine assigned to headquarters company, RCT-2, 2nd Division.

"Hey, I know you lost your guy," he told us right off. "I'm originally from Ohio and I volunteered to come out here. Staff Sergeant Goodwin was a good man. I'm not trying to replace him. I have my own way of doing things. I'm sure we'll get along. We're going to do our job. We're not going to do anything heroic. We're going to get out of this thing together."

Perfect speech, given the time and place.

I liked Ivy right away. He wasn't gung ho like Goodwin, but he had that Marine professional attitude: get 'er done, get home. I loved Goodwin, but he was a more-than-ten-foot-tall Marine, the leader you followed but could never really emulate. Ivy seemed more easygoing and accessible.

Both good guys. Just different styles of being great Marines.

Britten and I had to deliver a message to another platoon that afternoon. As we were coming back, what sounded like an 80 mm mortar round came overhead. We jumped into a nearby wadi, expecting that we had fallen into a trap, but no ambushers appeared. We bounded back to the house, unsure whether we'd been targeted by the enemy or even our own guys.

Bounded, in case I haven't explained it, is a specific military tactic. One person watches for the enemy while the other runs a certain distance before taking cover. Then it's the other person's turn. Run-duck. Run-duck. Always be prepared to fire. The problem wasn't that we were targeting someone; we were in enemy territory and couldn't be sure what was going on.

No other rounds came. We treated it as nothing in the end. That was the extent of the excitement that day—a breeze.

The next day we headed back to the tracs, having procured a number of cushions in exchange for some U.S. dollars at the house—the benches in the amtracs were damn hard. I still wasn't quite used to Grant not being in our trac, but there were other things to focus on, more mental practicing as I listened to my tunes, calming my mind so I could do my best when we reached the town we were tasked to clear.

We were told it was going to be a long operation. We expected hell.

Our vehicle, which besides our squad had two engineers, led the way. As we moved toward our target village, I heard an explosion behind us. Our vehicle stopped. Gunny Hurley got out through the hatch, along with the platoon radioman, Roland "Hickory" Ogle, who'd swapped with Grant days before. The rest of us stayed in the trac, peering through the slits and the top hatches, trying to figure out what was going on.

Through the hatch, I could see smoke pluming from a trac behind us.

Hurley's first thought was that the other vehicle had hit a mine—intel had said there was an old minefield in the area, left

over from the first Gulf War years before. Because of that, he ordered us to stay in the amphibs. Meanwhile, Marines from one of
the nearby vehicles and another post we'd just passed ran up to the
burning vehicle.

McKenzie had just passed the area where the trac blew up.
Standing in the top hatchway, he heard a pop, turned around, and
saw smoke starting to billow from the overturned vehicle. He got
the trac driver to stop, then leapt out, telling the others to stay put.

The trac was already on fire by the time he reached it, no more
than fifty feet away. He found Ivy, heavily wounded, half in and half
out of the hatchway. He began pulling him out; as big as McKenzie
was, it took all his strength and he needed help to get him to the
ground. Taking Ivy's legs to help carry him to aid, he felt only jelly,
not the structure of a body you'd expect to feel holding a big man.

The day before, McKenzie had a felt some anger that he'd been
passed over as platoon sergeant, replaced by an outsider. Now he felt
only grief as he carried our dying sergeant away from the roaring
flames. He could hear the screams of the men still trapped inside.

The IED had exploded under the vehicle, igniting its fuel tank
and turning it into a blast furnace. Hurley and others tried getting
the ramp and the crew door open, but couldn't. Finally, Sergeant
Dennis Woullard, a comms guy with the tracs who'd volunteered
to fight with a Lima squad earlier, managed to get the crew hatch
unlatched, despite burning his hands severely on the metal.

Bodies tumbled out. Hurley, pushed back by the flames, heat,
and smoke, screamed into the dark interior, yelling that anyone alive
inside should crawl toward him. He could see the shadows of bodies
inside, four or five men he thought, but there was no way he could
reach them. The heat at the door was enough to push him back.

A faint voice called for help.

"This way!" yelled Hurley.

The shadows moved. Finally, Hurley saw a hand in the smoke
and reached for it. It belonged to one of the crewmen. Hurley

grabbed the hand and with the help of some other nearby Marines, they pulled him to safety.

Camp had been standing in one of the top hatches, pulling security when the trac hit the explosives. Thrown to the floor by the blast, he felt his hands on fire. He jumped up, dazed. He heard Dixon calling to him and dove back to pull him out.

*Camp! Help me!*

Struggling in the mangled, burning interior, Camp moved toward Dixon. Skin fell off his hands as he reached for him.

*Out! Get out!*

Camp yelled to Dixon to push out. As they started to move, another explosion threw them outwards.

Jolly ran up, pulling Camp away from the trac as the fire crescendoed and rounds cooked off. Dixon lay nearby, already among the dead.

WE WAITED IN OUR TRAC FOR MAYBE AS LONG AS TWENTY MINUTES BEFORE THE ramp was dropped. We were ordered over to a house nearby that had just been cleared. The Iraqi family who lived there sat around nervously, obviously apprehensive, not understanding what was going on.

Gunny Hurley came in. He had a small team with him, who took over our watch while he gathered the rest of us in a room.

"Trac was hit. We still have guys in there. The guys who are alive are getting medevac'd out. Don't take it out on the family here—they had nothing to do with it."

He started listing the names of the men they knew were dead. One or two in, he mentioned Grant.

*Grant?*

Jonathan Grant.

*Grant!*

Something got ripped out of my body. Four men died and ten were injured, but at that moment I could hear only one name.

Grant's.

My chest pulled apart. I sank to my knees. Then I lost it. I got up and went into the next room and started hitting things, pounding, breaking them with my hands, destroying everything I could. Tossing furniture. Kicking in everything, the walls, the furniture. Everything.

A sound I'd never made before shot from my throat—an awful, eerie, ferocious wail, a piercing curse against Nature and God and the world, the deepest, shrillest, most mournful cry a human is capable of, so loud it couldn't have come from a person, so awful it couldn't have come from anything on earth. It emptied the universe of feeling; it emptied me.

Grant couldn't be dead. None of us could be dead. We were Lucky Lima.

*Lucky Lima.*


I EXHAUSTED MYSELF, BREAKING THINGS. SPENT, I JOINED THE REST OF THE SQUAD.

Hurley told us we were going back to the base at al Qa'im.

"What?" The question came from me, but it didn't sound like my voice. "What?"

"We're going back."

Not one of us wanted to go back. We wanted—you know what we wanted. We wanted to continue with the mission, do our part to avenge our friends' deaths.

"We have no choice," said Gunny.


## "ALL DEAD"

We walked out to a landing zone they'd set up for a helicopter pickup. The bodies had been removed from the AAV, but smoke still rose from the vehicle. Rounds inside cooked off.

Roy Romero, Grant's cousin in the weapons platoon, came up to me as I walked.

"Hey," he said. "My cousin?"

"He didn't make it," I told him. I could look at him for only a bare moment, feeling I was responsible for his cousin's death.

"OK." He walked away.

The helicopters took us to the base. At that point, I wouldn't have been surprised if an RPG took us down.

It was dark by the time we got back to al Qa'im. They put us up in the same rustic huts we'd used earlier. We dropped our gear, then were ushered over to a "Wizard"—Marine shorthand for head shrinker, aka counselor or psychologist.

There wasn't much to talk about. What do you say?

Back at the huts, we sat around, smoking cigarettes, talking about what had happened. Occasionally we caught disjointed bits of the movie playing on a TV in the room.

Gunny Hurley came back to talk to us.

"I might have to leave you guys soon," he said.

We started telling him it wasn't his fault that this had happened. He stopped us.

"I punched Oliver North."

North—famous as the lieutenant colonel who had helped the contras during the Reagan administration—was now working as a correspondent with Fox News. He'd been at the command post we passed just before the trac blew up. Apparently his crew or he had started filming as they removed guys from the trac. Hurley told him to stop, but North wouldn't.

So he punched him. That at least got him to stop.

I think I cheered when Hurley told us what had happened.

"No, that's bad, that's bad," he said. He gave me the Hurley "what's your malfunction, Marine?" glare.

But whoever it was, famous or not, he deserved it. My gunnery sergeant gives you an order, you snap to it. And hell, filming bodies being taken out of a vehicle?

I'd've punched him, too.

That was a side note to our real trouble with the media. Not long after that, we were ordered to call our families and tell them we were alive, and not say anything else. Not answer any questions, not volunteer any information.

*Huh?*

It turned out that Ellen Knickmeyer, who worked for the *Washington Post* and was covering the operation, had filed a story that accurately reported a squad had been killed or wounded. But it was apparently being misinterpreted by our loved ones back home to mean that the entire platoon was wiped out. We may have been "wiped out" in the sense that we were deeply shaken by the deaths of our friends. But obviously most of us were still alive.

The story had already been published on the web. In the connected world we live in, that meant our families were now grieving our loss.

We each took turns on sat phones. I called Kate. It was around ten p.m. in Iraq; it would have been around midday or so back home.

"I'm calling to tell you I am alive," I said.

"Oh, thank God."

Kate had gotten calls from friends of mine from college, who had seen alerts over the web. She'd been waiting in dread for a government car to pull up to the door.

"Is Grant safe?" she asked.

I hesitated. I was told not to say anything about other Marines.

"No." I cried through my words as I hung up.

## BREAKING POINTS

I went back to the hut and sat on the stoop leading to the door. I lit a cigarette and took some long drags, still in shock.

We found out two days later that the IED had been set up with three explosives detonated by switchblades. The bomb had been arranged so that it would only trigger if a tracked vehicle went over it. I've heard that they found the bombmaker, that he was sixteen, and he had placed the device just before we started the operation.

We'd been the lead vehicle. The other tracs were supposed to follow us, moving in our tracks. So why didn't the IED get us?

Chance? Luck?

If it had been some guy with a trigger, remotely detonating the explosion—that would have made a difference. But this—the way I saw it, I was supposed to die, not Grant. My trac should have been the one destroyed, not my friend's.

I was so crushed by the whole thing I wasn't even able to cry. I just sat in disbelief.

Finally, I made myself move. Numb, but moving. Not yet broken.

Not to be broken.


THEY TOOK US BACK TO THE DAM. I HONESTLY CAN'T REMEMBER NOW WHETHER we drove back in the AAVs or were helicoptered back. Taylor says we flew; Gunny's description makes it seem like we drove. I went to Grant's bunk and bagged his stuff for the family. I took down his pictures of the two kids, his wife. I folded his uniforms. His blanket. I put everything into his seabag and left it on his bed.

That's what happens when you die. Your life goes into a seabag.

We'd lost twelve guys, some dead, some injured. There were rows of seabags on empty racks.

A detail carted them away the next morning.

Back in the States, Kate found herself more anxious than ever. Happy that I was alive, surely, but now even more nervous about what lay ahead.

## GONE

Besides the physical casualties, we lost a few Marines to the accumulated stress; they were quietly rotated back to get a chance to recover. I don't know who they were and I certainly don't hold it against them.

On the contrary. At that time I was wondering myself if and when I would break. Maybe more *when* than *if.*

Different things break different people. Sometimes it just accumulates to the point where it becomes too much.

We had a Marine engineer working with us in New Ubaydi who was always working out and talking tough, your stereotypical muscle head, or at least what people think muscle heads are like. Six-four and jacked.

We started out on one of the streets, pushing in to check for insurgents and weapons stores. He froze at the second house, simply refusing to move. He was paralyzed so badly, he had to be medevac'd out.

He must have recovered, because last I heard, he became a career Marine. Maybe that's the best argument for contemporary treatments of what used to be called battle fatigue; maybe it's a testament to the Corps' ability to find a job for everyone. It's definitely an argument that it's mind over matter that counts in a war—size doesn't matter, nor does gender. The female lieutenant who had worked with us during River Bridge had performed on our level; even the female corporal came through. You can't make snap judgments based on stereotypes.

In the aftermath of Matador, Command reconstituted 2nd Squad with members from some of the other squads, then brought replacements into those squads.

They took Smith from our fireteam and made him a team leader in 2nd Squad; I missed him a lot. His replacement was a kid named Daniel Elbourne. Good Marine, great kid, but I was disappointed losing Smith. We'd had a good working relationship going. We knew how to move around each other in combat. It made sense for the company, though—you didn't want to have a bunch of new guys without a combat-tested leader.

The replacements were all from al Asad, and most if not all hadn't been outside the wire until now. Their uniforms looked new. They didn't have the smell of sweat, sand, and regret that ours had. Coming to our base must've been a real culture shock. We told them we felt sorry for them—no fast-food outlets or fancy coffee here.

We got them up to speed, telling them what to bring on a mission and what not. Simple things—simple to us anyway. The less weight you carry the better. You never have enough ammo. Use your flak jacket for a pillow. Don't eat too many MREs or you'll get constipated. This is how to pop a blister, bandage it, and keep walking.

We told them everything we could think of, all the tips you really want to know but can only get from people who have been in the field. And of course we introduced them to *Sex and the City*.

I moved up to Smith's position as assistant fireteam leader. I think the fireteam and the rest of the squad got closer together following that battle. The new guys, the replacements, probably had a harder time fitting in. Not that it was on purpose; they just didn't share our experiences.

## AND I STEWED, NOT SURE WHY I WAS ALIVE AND NOT GRANT.

The logical side of me said the trac had moved slightly differently in its path. My vehicle missed it for some sort of mechanical reason.

Totally logical.

But the more I insisted on that explanation, the more hollow it felt. I kept coming back to God as an explanation—but that was worse. Grant's death had nothing to do with a Being beyond the sky—because I don't want to believe in a god that is making a decision between me and Grant. No god could decide to keep alive a guy who has no kids and isn't married, while letting a man with two kids and a wife die.

God is fair. God is just.

*This isn't fair. We should both be alive, planning for the day when we're both living side by side in New Mexico, raising our kids, enjoying life.*

I'm pretty social, but I wasn't in the weeks after Matador, not even with my team. I'd grab my own food at dinner, eat by myself. If I had free time, I'd walk around the dam, keeping to myself. At night I'd go out on the deck of the dam and just stare at the stars for hours.

I listened to sad songs, and songs that in some weird way spoke to my desolation. There was this P Diddy song I would listen to. I can't stand it now, even to mention the lyrics or title.

I was cocooning, emotionally at least. Which was pretty easy, because I was with a whole bunch of other guys doing the same thing.

We were confused. We were sad. We couldn't figure out what

anything meant. It was the first time in my life, at least, that I couldn't fix what was wrong.

I'd see Grant everywhere. Walking by, in the squad bay, on the dam. Sometimes there was someone actually there, and my mind turned the person into Grant. And then sometimes it was just a complete mirage.

The first time it happened, someone was walking toward me on the top of the dam. I saw him and my heart jumped.

"Grant!" I shouted.

The Marine came closer and I knew it was someone else, and the elation turned back to pain. I looked away in shame and sorrow.

I didn't say anything out loud after that. I knew intellectually the person I saw would not be Grant, though I couldn't yet get my emotions to catch up.

It took a month before I stopped seeing him.

Looking back objectively, I think I lacked the tools to deal with grief effectively. I'd always been or at least felt in control of my destiny and what I did. I had my training, my intellect, my experiences. But they weren't enough to survive.

What did that leave?

My bag of sand and the shell of the man who'd tried to kill me.

And luck. Which seemed either to have run out for everyone around me, or was fickle beyond belief.

MARK CAMP WAS AWARDED THE SILVER STAR FOR HIS BRAVERY DURING MATADOR. From the official Marine Corps press release recounting his citation:

> During an enemy ambush in New Ubaydi, Iraq, Camp left his covered position to engage the enemy at point-blank range, which allowed an injured Marine to be pulled to

cover. Camp then joined a Marine in a frontal assault of the ambush site, forcing enemy insurgents to change position and allowed the recovery of another injured Marine. Camp's Amphibious Assault Vehicle (AAV) was destroyed by an improvised explosive device May 11, wounding or killing all seventeen passengers. Camp, who was then a lance corporal, attempted to recover Marines from the vehicle but was thrown out of it again by a secondary explosion. Though wounded, Camp managed to return to the vehicle and pulled a Marine to safety.

Sergeant Woullard, the tracker who had helped get the crew hatch open, was also honored with a Silver Star. Woullard had been with us during the initial assault at Death House, where he helped save several lives. He wasn't an official member of our company, but he was certainly one of us. His citation:

The President of the United States of America takes pleasure in presenting the Silver Star to Sergeant Dennis Woullard, Jr., United States Marine Corps Reserve, for conspicuous gallantry and intrepidity in action against the enemy while serving as Radio Chief, First Section, Third Platoon, Company A, Fourth Assault Amphibian Battalion, Regimental Combat Team 2, SECOND Marine Division, II Marine Expeditionary Force (Forward) from 8 to 11 May 2005, during combat operations in support of Operation IRAQI FREEDOM in Iraq. On 8 May 2005, in Al Ubaydi, Iraq, Sergeant Woullard volunteered to assist an infantry squad conduct clearing operations during Operation MATADOR. After clearing several residences without incident, and during a breach of a front door, his team was immediately attacked with heavy machine gun and RPG fire from within. Every member of the team was wounded. Despite his wounds, Sergeant Woullard evacuated two Marines from the residence, and then joined in an assault to recover the remaining trapped Marine. Sergeant Woullard repeatedly exposed himself to heavy fire and assaulted into the house. He rescued the trapped Marine shielding him with his body as he carried him to an Assault Amphibious Vehicle (AAV) where he administered first aid until en route to the battalion. On 11 May 2005, near the Syrian border, Sergeant Woullard's AAV was attacked with an improvised explosive device that killed or injured all 17 Marines on board. Although again wounded and disoriented from the explosion, Sergeant Woullard struggled to the rear of the vehicle and opened the personnel hatch. With complete disregard for his own safety and exposed to the intense heat and exploding ammunition, he repeatedly returned to the burning vehicle to evacuate the severely wounded Marines. By his superior leadership, unrelenting determination, and total dedication to duty, Sergeant Woullard reflected great credit upon himself and upheld the highest traditions of the Marine Corps and the United States Naval Service.

## BACK TO HADITHA

A new captain came to take over command of the platoon—Vincent Knapp. He was a quiet guy, low key. He had known Goodwin and came into our squad bay to talk a little about him, saying how much he had admired him.

"We're going to make it through the rest of this deployment," he told us. "We're going to do our jobs and go home."

Funny thing about officers—he was probably about thirty, but he seemed about eighty. He was hands-on when he needed to be, but for the most part he would step back and let the NCOs do their thing. He knew we knew what we were doing.

Matador had taken a lot out of us, and not only because we were now without a lot of our friends. John Bailon had been away helping to train Iraqi soldiers; when he came back to the dam, he found the unit tighter, sharper professionally, but also much more subdued. The mood had changed. Everyone was dealing with loss in their own way; we were more serious about war, but also more serious about being left alone when the fight ended. A lot of the little joking rituals we'd had—counting off before going out like it was New Year's Eve—fell by the wayside.

We conducted foot patrols out of the dam for a few days, taking it slow. I figured that we had seen the worst of the war, and we would now be given some easier assignments. I guess I thought that since we had just lost a bunch of guys in a few days of fighting, there would be changes. Maybe we'd get better vehicles. Maybe we'd get a new company commander.

Nope.

At the end of May, we joined Operation New Market and went back to Haditha, tasked to take over the school we'd held the very first time we came here.

I knew a little more about it now—it was a technical college. Otherwise, not much was different. The place was still empty, still in a mortar line, still a favorite target for the muj.

I was on the roof doing overwatch when the mortars started trying for us. I went down to my stomach and scanned the nearby road, expecting that if the mortars were coordinated with anything, it would be a vehicle suicide attack, or maybe a ground assault by muj trying to lure us into a trap.

All of a sudden someone kicked my leg.

"What the fuck?" I twisted around and saw a company NCO staring down at me.

"Why aren't you wearing your boot blouses?" he demanded.

"We're taking mortar fire right now."

"Get your fuckin' boot blouses on," he growled before walking away.

For the uninitiated, Marines "blouse" or bind the bottoms of their pants so that insects can't crawl up their legs, securing them with specially made boot bands. It's supposed to be a health thing. On the other hand, if you blouse your boots, you get a lot hotter than you would be if they're loose. And generally in Iraq, we were more concerned about heat exhaustion than bugs.

I generally kept them loose while we were out on patrol since it was so hot. It wasn't correct, but on the other hand, it wasn't the worst infraction in the world.

And worrying about it when we're under fire—inappropriate.

I don't think anyone would have cared about my lack of sartorial splendor if a mortar shell smashed me to smithereens, let alone if taking care of them meant I missed seeing an approaching army of mujahedeen.

I forget if I tucked them in or not. Certainly, I came away with a sharp insight of that NCO's priorities.

There was no ground attack, and the mortaring eventually stopped without hitting us. The insurgents hadn't gotten any better at aiming while we'd been gone.

## YOU'RE *THAT* PLATOON?

When my watch was over, I went down to the classroom we were using as a temporary squad bay and shucked my gear. Our normal combat load was pretty high—heavy plates in our vests to protect against bullets and shrapnel, eight magazines, flash-bang, grenades, K-bar knife, back up mag, water, in my case the spare machine-gun barrel and its ammo. Anyway, it's a load.

I lay down with the other guys and vegged out. That was when FNG Mitchell made his appearance.

Gunny Hurley had managed to avoid any repercussions for his confrontation with Ollie North—North, said Hurley later, had been extremely understanding about it—but he'd irked one of the command sergeants back at the dam. The staff NCO had tried to give us some pointless duty, and Hurley called him on it. As Hurley tells it, the discussion got rather heated and loud. The fallout led eventually to Hurley being sent back for a talk with the "wizard." After he was cleared, he was given an assignment to help another 3/25 company; it was several weeks before he rejoined us—over the ranking NCO's objections. Apparently some people don't like it when a gunny stands up for his people.

In the interim, he was temporarily replaced by a new staff sergeant, FNG Mitchell.

FNG was neither his name nor his actual initials; they were bestowed on him by members of the squad. They stood for "Fuckin' New Guy."

Because, you know. No disrespect intended; it's just the way it is. Or was.

Anyway, some of the guys may already have met him, but this was my first encounter. He strolled in and started bellowing.

"What the @#$#$@#$@#$#@#$@#$@#$!" he shouted when he saw us lolling around in our squad bay. (You can insert your own string of Marine-appropriate curse words there; just let them run about three times as long as you think would be normal.)

"This place looks like a pigsty!" he continued, ranting on the fact that we'd all pretty much doffed our gear in unorganized piles and probably looked and smelled like we hadn't bathed in days—which of course we hadn't.

"I'm sorry," I said. "Who the fuck are you?"

"I'm Staff Sergeant Mitchell. Your new staff sergeant."

"That doesn't explain much."

Probably just before FNG blew the gasket holding his head on his neck, Taylor stepped over and pulled him aside.

"You need to calm down," he told FNG. "These guys have been through a lot of shit. They know how to survive. They've already lost two platoon commanders . . ."

He quickly explained our experiences over the past few weeks.

"This is *that* platoon?" said FNG.

He walked away.


WE LOST ANOTHER MAN IN HADITHA—DAVID WIMBERG, A SERGEANT FROM KEN-tucky. Wimberg was with the command element and a large group of Marines when they were ambushed on a street. He left cover to confront insurgents firing from a house near the Marines. He up-ended the assault but was cut down in the process.

Wimberg was awarded the Silver Star, posthumously, for his bravery. From his commendation:

> In an attempt to eliminate the source of the ambush, Sgt. Wimberg left his covered position, maneuvered through intense small arms fire, and scaled a wall in order to gain access to the courtyard where the source of the fire was originating. Although twice driven back by high volumes of enemy fire, on his third attempt, he opened the gate and allowed his squad to enter. He then provided suppressive fire into insurgent positions in an adjacent house until his fire team was in position. After two failed attempts to breach the front door, and without regard for his own personal safety, Sgt. Wimberg kicked in the door and gained entry to the house. Finding himself face to face with four insurgents armed with AK-47 rifles, Sgt. Wimberg engaged the enemy at close quarters, firing his rifle until he was shot and fell to the ground unconscious. His

heroic actions severely wounded one insurgent, stunned the other enemy fighters and created the momentum needed to break the ambush. Many Marines' lives were saved as a result of Sgt. Wimberg's decisive and selfless actions. By his zealous initiative, courage, and total devotion to duty, Sgt. Wimberg reflected great credit upon himself and upheld the highest traditions of the Marine Corps. . . .

Wimberg was taken for medical care after being critically wounded; he died before reaching an aid station. He was twenty-four.

## BACK TO SWEEPS

A couple of days later—the time span of this whole mission in my memory seems far longer than the official reports say, but we'll go with them—headquarters company rotated into the school and we were assigned to go on sweeps through the city.

These actually felt good. Patrolling, checking houses—it was somehow reassuring to be back doing that.

Although there were moments.

FNG had this habit of coming into a house behind us and dramatically unholstering his pistol—something the Iraqis associated with murders by Saddam's goons. Even though the parallel was unintentional, it didn't relax the inhabitants, which made our job a lot harder. The Iraqis knew we weren't there for tea and cake, but making them more fearful increased everybody's adrenaline.

I was generally in charge of the house searches. I'd go in, talk to the people, calm them down. We had a certain order of things—announce ourselves, secure the family in one place, secure any weapons, start the search. FNG would barge in without announcing himself while they were sitting on the couch, and whip out his gun.

The family were sure they were going to get shot.

*Staff Sergeant, you can't do that. If they think they're going to die. If they have nothing to lose, they may fight us. Then we have to shoot them. Which is not what we want, right? Shooting people is bad and the paperwork you will have to fill out would be even worse.*

I told him that in various ways, all respectful, but he never seemed to get the message.

I have to say, our fireteam was pretty mellow with the Iraqis. Our new member fit right in, really. None of us were Combat Johns. We knew where to check in the house for booby traps, contraband, whatever; we did it as professionally as we could, with as little excitement as possible.

We had made one important change in our procedure when going into houses. Where once we'd go right to the door and knock, standing there like you would knock on a neighbor's door in the U.S. Now we'd check the windows, and sidle up to the door, knocking and announcing ourselves but out of the line of potential fire.

Generally, the male of the house would answer the door. Instead of walking alongside him inside, I would gently grab his shoulder and move him inside. The rest of the team would follow behind, flanking to the other rooms.

The first question was always "Where's your weapon?" We would walk to it—pretty much every Iraqi had an AK, which they were entitled to.

I could deal with that; it was the second or third weapon that was a problem—where would they be hiding that?

The first time I saw a door under a stairway, my heart stopped, remembering what I had heard about the ambush at Death House. We had a procedure now, though. One Marine would open the door while another guy or guys would be ready to fire.

I was always worried about simply touching the door, and could feel myself tensing, even though only for a moment. Once I started moving it, everything just had its own momentum.

We would take turns. We still had our unspoken rule about odds and fairness—everybody took a turn. Even the new guy, once he got acclimated and we were sure we could trust him not to freeze or do something weird.

There was no scientific method to the house choices, and we generally weren't operating on specific intel. Unless we were looking for an HVT where we had a specific person to find, we'd be given a general area to patrol and search; we would work our way down a block house by house. As the day wore on and night approached, the squad would look for the nicest house we could find to go firm in. Nice was usually defined by the presence of a satellite dish for TV.

I'm only half-joking. TVs weren't nearly as important as a location we could easily protect, but once that requirement was met, it tended to rank well ahead of other factors, even swamp coolers, the somewhat outdated but always valued air-conditioning units favored by Iraqis.

I was so tense during the patrols that I slept pretty well, untroubled by nightmares. Those only really started once we went home to the States.

IRAQI TV OFFERED A STRANGE MIX OF SHOWS. THERE WERE LIVE CALL-IN SHOWS of video gamers, something like a Middle East version of Twitch. We would watch a lot of Egyptian music videos at night. I fell in love with an Egyptian singer. I even followed her for a bit on social media after I got back to the States.

I got over that quick.

One night I saw the *Amazing Race*. A popular TV show at the time that featured contests in exotic locations.

One of the contestants cried. "I haven't seen my family in seven days."

I grabbed my boot and threw it at the TV.

## TANKS AND DOGS

One day, the Bailon brothers and McKenzie wanted to get a few photos of themselves with the Navajo flag. I volunteered as their photographer. We went out and took some shots, and ended up near a tank. The gunner introduced himself to us—Julio Chavez. We started BS'in'.

"You have the most awesome job in the world," I told him. "Abrams tank? No one's gonna take that out."

He just laughed. Infantrymen and tankers are two different breeds, but Chavvy was an easygoing guy and we'd often joke a bit if we ran into each other in the chow hall or around the dam. Having a tank crew as friends can always come in handy, right? If you need something blown up, there's nothing better than an M1A1. And as I had joked, those big tanks are next to impervious.

Or so I thought until we were called out June 9.

We were tasked to do a helo operation in the middle of Haqlaniyah; after the insertion we would do some house-to-house searches, looking for a high-value target said to be in the area.

The op order did not look promising. We were supposed to land in a field in the middle of town in the middle of the day—no surprise. All it would take was an RPG from one of the nearby buildings and we were toast.

I was starting to get superstitious by this point, as if my time was coming. But I was a slave to my fate; there was nothing I could do but go along.

The helo ride was quick and noneventful. As we started to descend, though, I heard an explosion below us.

A *big* explosion.

"Get this thing down!" screamed Hurley.

The crew plopped us down and we streamed out of that helicopter, probably the entire platoon setting a new record for leaving an aircraft. My fireteam took a position at a stone wall used for corralling animals, waiting for the attack that was sure to follow.

It took quite a while of waiting in the baking sun before we realized that the explosion had not been the precursor of an attack. Either the force of the helo's downdraft had set off an IED that had been left in the field and forgotten, or the guy with the IEDs detonator had jumped the gun and then took off.

Good luck, rather than bad, since no one had been injured and nothing badly damaged.

We pushed into the residential area, going door to door, looking for our target. We were wrapping up without having found him when there was another loud explosion, this quite a distance off.

*What the hell was that?*

Again, no one targeted us. I figured it was just a random thing.

The tracs met us for pickup. We embarked, driving once more in bone-shaking boredom in the direction of the dam, when we heard yet another explosion.

*They keep trying for me.*

The tracs were almost immediately diverted, driving out to a house overlooking another road about five kilometers from the river. Piling out, the stench of burnt oil and rubber burned my nose.

There was something else in the air—charred meat.

A tank on the road had been hit by a massive IED. Only one person had been injured—my friend Chavez. The mobile company had rushed over, put him into a Humvee, then wheeled in the direction of the dam.

That's when a second IED took them out.

Five Marines had died. There was little left of them when we got there. Body parts and bits of the Humvee littered the road. Nearby, the burnt shell of the tank sat alone, disabled.

We set up security, secured the house, did all the things that by now were absolute rote. We detained a few Iraqi field workers in the area, holding them for questioning as night came on.

I drew a late-night shift pulling watch near the road and the remains. Not long after I took my post, I heard something move in the distance. I scanned with my night vision and saw a pack of dogs approaching, drawn by the prospect of fresh meat.

I fired into the pack.

The dogs howled and whimpered. Some left, some didn't. A few fought over something they'd managed to grab.

A piece of flesh belonging to their fellow pack member, now dead.

I kept firing.

The dog raids continued through the night. Packs of the animals ran wild through the country; they'd occasionally bother us on a night mission, where their barking would alert a town.

*What a weird world I am in. I'm shooting at dogs to keep them away from the body of a friend. And I feel bad when I kill the dogs. But that's better than not killing them.*

## ROES

War is its own reality. It makes its own rules. Still, we try to impose order to do our job, and certainly to survive. We come up with rules to follow.

And others give us rules they *think* we should follow.

One of the most controversial aspects of the Iraq war were the Rules of Engagement, or ROEs, that the military had to follow.

These are basically lists of do's and don'ts that are supposed to guide your actions. They tell you who you can and can't shoot, when, and how; they can be both obvious and subtle.

They also can change, depending on the overall circumstances and time of the war. And the actual reality of the war can bend them in different ways.

For example, before we deployed, we were given ROEs that told us we should never fire warning shots; if we were shooting, it was to kill.

But there were plenty of times when we used warning shots. Working a checkpoint, it was common to fire warning shots at a vehicle in hopes of getting a driver's attention. If that didn't work, the general procedure was to shoot the front of the vehicle with a dummy round—a practice round that was a slug rather than an actual bullet. The round would hit the grille and probably the radiator; usually that got them to stop right away. In a perfect world, the fireteam leader had the practice round set in his weapon and would be in a position to fire.

But conditions weren't always perfect. One day in Haditha, a truck approached us at a high rate of speed. The fireteam leader couldn't get his round ready in time. I ran up and put two real bullets into the grille; the truck stopped quickly, then turned around and retreated.

Right thing to do, or wrong?

It achieved a positive end result—we didn't kill a probably innocent, if negligent, driver.

Was it *technically* the right thing to do? I never tried to decide.

There were times when vehicles were trying to probe our defenses and maybe our procedures. The surprising thing was how many Iraqis were oblivious when behind the wheel, whether because they were focused on the road or something in the cab, or their brains just short-circuited, as if they forgot they were in a war situation. Gives those "don't text and drive" laws a whole new meaning.

## PLAYED OUT

Headquarters realized we were pretty played out from what we'd been through, and some of the seniors would come around and check on us, give us a verbal pat on the back, see if we needed anything. First Sergeant Dan Altieri was always good for some Marine Corps humor, mixing it in with decent advice. Back in the States he'd told us about how important it was to always have a battle buddy with you—even, he implied, in a whore house.

And if you didn't have one in those circumstances, he added, he was always available.

Altieri was a Marine's Marine. He had what sounded like a Brooklyn accent by way of Cleveland; sometimes you'd just crack up listening to him talk.

Captain (later Major) Kei Braun, the battalion executive officer, would come by our squad occasionally to check on the guys from Albuquerque. He'd been with us at Delta Company back in New Mexico and was well-liked by just about everyone. He was a skier, and he had that laid-back style you see on the slopes, someone whose just exudes confidence and makes the slalom look easy. I think guys would have followed him to hell and back if he asked.

I asked him once why we cleared a town and then left it, letting the enemy come back once they knew we were gone.

"We're clearing these towns and we're coming back and we're basically going to the same place, the same houses. We search the same people, you know? And we're not, we're not changing anything. We're playing whack-a-mole. Why don't we stay in the towns?"

His answer was that we just didn't have enough manpower.

And it wasn't the direction we were given from headquarters.

"Well, that's fucking stupid," I answered.

He kind of shrugged, even though I'd been borderline insubordinate. Possibly I was a little more polite, though by that point I doubt it. As a general rule, reservists tended to be a little more direct and somewhat more casual when talking enlisted man to officer.

There was one notable exchange I had with an officer. For some reason I'd been tasked to give the debrief for the entire platoon to an Intel officer. He was young and had a very clean uniform and shiny rifle, a clear sign that he was a REMF.

I started going through it and at one point, used the words "I think."

"You don't *think*," said the officer. "Just say what you saw. I went to college. I am the officer. I'll do the thinking."

"Sir, let me guess," I shot back. "You went to Shit Stain University and got your degree in tinsel-hanging or whatever. I, too, have a fucking degree. I went to fucking Harvard. I know what I saw out there, and I know what I think."

The officer stormed out.

The platoon waited a beat, then burst out laughing.

I tried not to be a dick, but sometimes . . .

The officer was a second lieutenant. Not hard to guess.

Fucking butter bars.

Getting a high-value target could be tricky, but not only because we now had a clear picture of what these guys might be capable of. Generally they would be located in an area of a town or city that hadn't been totally secured. We'd zoom out with the whole squad, knock on the door, secure the house, look for the guy.

We'd have pretty fuzzy pictures with us to make the ID. That was always tricky. Much easier if the orders were to take any male at the house.

I remember we took this guy and walked him to the back of the trac. He looked at us kind of strangely.

"Are you guys part of the Mexican Army?" he asked.

Huh?

I glanced around. The three guys who took him to the vehicle were, in fact, all Latinos.

No idea how he made that connection. We did occasionally speak Spanish around Iraqis, knowing they were far less likely to understand that than English. But as far as I could remember, we hadn't in front of him.

By the time we returned from Haqlaniyah, Operation Teddy Bear had reached its peak. The mail guy called me a "fag" with the latest delivery; I hugged the furry booze transporter even closer.

We took the fresh stash of illicit booze and had a hell of a party, dancing the night away.

The next day, the chaplain came by to see me. He saw all these teddy bear heads scattered on the floor, their body parts hacked beyond recognition.

Our conversation went roughly like this:

"Son, I'm worried about you," he told me, with great sincerity and obvious concern.

"Chaplain, if I talk to you, you can't tell anybody what we talk about in private, right?" He wasn't Catholic, where priests who hear your confession are bound to an oath of silence, but I figured he worked roughly the same way.

"You can confide in me, my son."

"I'm going to show you something."

I got one of the bears that had not yet been dismembered and performed surgery. He visibly relaxed when I produced the bottle.

"Oh, thank God," he said. "I thought you were really messed up."

—

THINKING BACK ABOUT THOSE DAYS WHEN WE GOT BACK, OPERATION TEDDY BEAR, the night we just got crazy with a dance party on the dam—those moments were crazy and insane, but they were diamonds, bright shafts of light amid the darkness. They were moments that had nothing to do with the war. Nothing to do with death.

They were moments of us living outside the black fog that had fallen around us.

# VI.

# WE
# JUST KEEP
# DYING

## McKENZIE

There's not much to see at night driving through western New Mexico. The terrain is desert scrubland, bounded by low hills. In the day, the horizon seems endless; at night, it's more like a dark tunnel created by your headlights. There are buildings every so often, sometimes bunched together near the road. They disappeared in a flash, leaving me in blackness as I tried to get to McKenzie.

The desert in Iraq is nothing like the southwestern U.S. The sand is finer, and looser. The roads are less traveled. There's less evidence of water.

But the darkness is similar at night, deeper because of the war, and then there's the reality that pulling into any sizable settlement meant you were liable to be attacked. Not everybody there wanted to kill us; some, certainly, but most likely the majority were indifferent or even vaguely supportive of us. But they were cowed by those who would plant an IED, and the others who would kill them if they showed any inclination toward either us or the Iraqi government and forces friendly to us.

Yet here I felt the consequences of stopping would be even more dire—stop driving, and McKenzie would die.

Stop talking even, and there was no telling what he would do.

I reminded him of a fight he'd gotten into with one of the Marine snipers on the plane. He laughed. Snipers are pretty elite, generally not folks to be messed with, but McKenzie had no qualms about that. It wasn't just his size, though he was plenty big. It was attitude; he didn't back down for anyone.

The land around me belonged to Native Americans, and if I'd been in another kind of mood, I might have thought about their history here, good and bad; maybe the pueblos south of me, or the Natives who had lived to the north or east for centuries. But in the dark driving for McKenzie, I only thought of him.

Numerous studies record suicide rates among veterans higher than those of the general population. That's saying a lot. Before COVID-19, suicide was the tenth leading cause of death in the United States. The VA estimated in 2018 that half again as many veteran males killed themselves as nonveterans; it also documented higher rates of alcoholism and substance abuse, implying those things are connected by underlying problems. That seems ironic, since military service can give so much purpose to an individual. Countless veterans say joining gave them the tools they needed to succeed in later life.

Post-traumatic stress is undoubtedly a major reason for the suicide rate. But it's too simple to say that PTSD causes suicide. Most times, it doesn't. Most veterans with PTSD don't kill themselves. The majority aren't wild men, either. They're not out of control; they rarely rage, they often don't even express anger or exhibit anything you would point to as abnormal. People with PTSD mostly deal with it quietly, veterans especially. They rely on themselves and a small network of friends.

Or they try to ignore it.

I hunted for another memory, something positive or funny, to get McKenzie to laugh.

"Remember that time—"

I stopped abruptly. The battery in my phone had died.

I pushed harder on the gas. I was still about two hours from Albuquerque.

## HEARTS AND MINDS

We were only a tangential part of Operation New Market. Lima Company records show that, besides having captured a number of weapons caches and disrupted the insurgent network, our presence helped the Civil Affairs Group help the Iraqis recover after an attack by a suicide vehicle on their hospital. Restoring medical services was a tangible "hearts and minds" operation that yielded immediate results as well as long-term benefits. It was literally the exact opposite of what war typically produces—live bodies rather than dead ones.

I don't know if this was directly connected or not, but a female CAG officer gathered intelligence during the operation that led to the apprehension of an insurgent spy at the dam. Whatever the muj hoped to do to us there never came off.

We'd hear what other platoons and companies accomplished entirely by word of mouth, in bits and pieces, when we'd see the guys out on an operation or back at the dam. You'd have a piece here, another piece there. Vague rumors would entwine themselves around facts. We focused on what we had to do—that was the real truth of every day. That focus made it impossible for us to get a full view of everything that even our own company was doing, let alone the others in 3/25.

My myopic view of the war doesn't mean that other Marines were sitting around eating candy and playing cards. While we were in Haditha, Kilo Company and some of Weapons Company were assigned to do a cache sweep on the east side of the Euphrates, leaving around the time we got back at the end of May and lasting a little more than a week. The operation saw them walk across some sixty kilometers, looking for weapons hidden in marsh and the sands as well as the small villages in the area. They found everything from rockets to artillery shells, all of which could have been fashioned into bombs.

TOWARD THE VERY END OF MAY, MAJOR RICARDO CROCKER AND HIS CIVIL AFFAIRS assistant were in a building that came under attack in Haditha. It happened that I was on a rooftop a short distance away, doing point security. I heard an explosion that I couldn't quite place at first; it sounded like a mortar round, though it would have been unusual to have just one round explode. Then someone over the radio explained that it was an RPG, that there had been wounded, and that they were going to be evac'd by helicopter nearby.

I watched the vehicles come over, the helicopter come down, the wounded men fly out. It was only later that I heard that Crocker and his Civil Affairs team had been hit. The grenade that came through the window had been a one in a hundred shot.

Luck, working against us. Crocker died.

He'd been a state trooper back home. There's a stretch of highway in California named after him. I choked up the first time I saw the sign, unprepared for the memory the name evoked.

BACK IN THE STATES, THE BUSH ADMINISTRATION WAS SLOWLY REACHING THE conclusion that its tactics in the occupation weren't working, and that if the U.S. was going to succeed in Iraq, things had to change.

The thing most visible to the American public was the "surge"— the infusion of more troops into the country in 2007. That was on top of a slightly smaller surge or increase in troop strength in 2005.

Less visible, though at least arguably more important, were changes in tactics. Recognizing that many Iraqis no longer saw us as liberators, the administration directed the military to adopt strategies that would alter that.

That's where "hearts and minds" came in. CAG stepped up its efforts. American forces attempted to build working relations with the existing Sunni leaders, prying them away from alliances with the mujahedeen. Many Iraqis hated the al Qaeda bands for any number of reasons: their fanatical interpretation of Islam, their willingness to target and sacrifice civilians, the fact that most came from outside Iraq and didn't particularly care about its people.

This wasn't exactly a secret. We'd often hear fighting between the two groups at night, or even witness it from a distance. In a way, the administration's tactics picked a side, the side it felt would have the most stake in Iraq's future, and therefore the best chance at long-term peace and stability.

All of this is part of classic anti-insurgent strategies, which somehow seemed novel to the media and public at the time.

One of the prerequisites for the strategy to work is stability; you have to provide enough peace in the interim that people can return to normalcy and feel that they will benefit from it. It's a complicated balance, as our next major op, Sword, showed when we went to the city of Hit.

## SWORD

From the moment it was announced, we knew Sword was going to be difficult and different, but also that it might really change the world, or at least our corner of it.

To this point, the operations always followed a basic pattern: we would show up in a city, sweep for a few days, grab some weapons caches and maybe a high-value target or two, and then leave.

The plan for Sword was different. We would go into the city from the south, push north, forcing the insurgents toward a camp near Hit. We'd hold the city for as long as we could, stabilizing it as an occupation force.

There had been a battle there earlier in the war, where Marines withstood seven days of attacks. We called it the Seven Days of Hit, which made it at least semi-famous, if not ominous.

I also knew that by spending a lot of time in the city, we would be making ourselves enticing targets for the insurgents. I had come to understand the relationship of time and luck—the more time you spent somewhere, the more your luck ran out. It was now the end of June—officially, Sword lasted from June 29 to July 4, though our involvement lasted longer.

On the other hand, I knew it was a good strategy to pacify the country. So there was an extra value to doing our jobs. Finally, no more whack-a-mole.

Kilo Company from 3/25 had been holding a base near the city since the beginning of our deployment. They would operate with us on the sweeps, along with tanks, explosives experts, and close-air support. About two hundred Iraqi National Army soldiers would also join the operation—the first time they'd joined a large-scale mission to clear a city. All told, there would be about a thousand men involved in the action.

Hit—also spelled Heet in English, which is how the Iraqis pronounced it—was farther south than any of the places we'd been to at this point in the war. About ninety miles west and slightly to the north of Baghdad, it was within twenty-five miles of Ramadi, the center of muj resistance at the time. Marines had fought a ferocious battle in Ramadi the year before, but the city remained a hot spot; it would not be until some ferocious battles and scattered attacks in 2006 and 2007 that the city could be truly considered pacified.

That lay in the future. We only knew that the Corps had fought tenaciously there without achieving a lasting peace.

Hit is an ancient city. Straddling the Euphrates, it has long played an important role in Iraqi history because of its agriculture, natural resources, and strategic location. In 2005, the population was somewhere over fifty thousand—we'd heard as high as one hundred thousand—making it relatively large by the standards of al Anbar Province.

We started by going back to Camp Cupcake—al Asad. That seemed surreal—we were getting ready for a big op by walking around at a base that had a Baskin-Robbins, air-conditioning, a rec center, video games.

I nearly died when I walked in and saw the sign at the mess hall advertising salsa night.

They also had women. You could smell them before you saw them—soap has an incredibly pleasant and amazingly strong smell when you've been in combat for months.

I missed salsa night, but otherwise took the opportunity to enjoy decent food and rest. After a day or two, we boarded the tracs and drove out near Hit, ready to attack the next day. Sitting in the shade of the vehicles, we gave the new guys advice on what to do when the shit hit the fan in the city.

*When they start firing, just push.*

*Follow us.*

*You'll get into a rhythm as we go.*

*It'll seem like a lot, but you'll get it.*

We checked their medical kits, ammo, gear. Good to go.

Then we sat in the heat and waited.

I listened to my music. An ethnic song from Colombia was heavy in the rotation, a song I'd known all my life, "Los Caminos en la Vida."

The song is basically about what happens in life, the roads or steps in life are where they take you, and where you need to go. Or loosely:

*. . . The steps in life are not what I imagined . . .*

Emotionally speaking, I'd been attached to the song all my life, starting as a child; it was part of being Colombian. The message also resonated.

*Accept what's happening. Ride with the reality around you.*

A guide for war as well as life.

FINALLY, THE ORDER CAME AND WE STARTED IN. AS WE LOADED, NORRIS CAME around and fist bumped.

"See you on the beach, my brother."

As our trac rumbled to the outskirts of the city, Inman, a new guy in the squad, and I went through the top hatch to act as lookouts. There was a tank next to us; other tracs behind. The place hadn't quite woken up yet, the sun still below the horizon.

As we pulled to a stop, I saw a light flash.

*IED!*

"Get the fuck down!"

I grabbed Inman and pushed him down into the vehicle as the concussion blew past.

I took a breath, then grabbed Inman again, pulling him by a strap on his vest.

*"Get up! Get up!"*

We needed to see what was going on and be ready for the attack I suspected would follow.

*"Weapons up! Weapons up!"*

As I poked my head out, I heard the whir of the tank's turret, moving to target whoever had ignited the IED.

*"Get the fuck down, get the fuck down!"*

I jerked poor Inman back into the hull of our vehicle.

*Whoosh! Haruphh.*

The tank fired. The concussion shook the trac hard—had we been up, the shock would have injured us.

The ramp to the trac came down. I grabbed Inman again. He must have felt like a rag doll by now.

*"Go, go, go!"*

I dragged the newbie with me, running from the trac to the first house we were tasked to hit.

"Kick the door in," I yelled to him, already setting myself to cover the interior.

The door flew open. I took a step in, and saw an Iraqi come running toward us.

*No weapon.*

I butt-stroked the Iraqi, knocking him to the ground. Then I kicked him to the side, pushing in further. The rest of the team came in behind me and we started checking the house, unsure if whoever had set off the IED was inside.

Inman wasn't part of our fireteam, but he stayed with us, shanghaied until there was a chance to sort things out. The place turned out to be clean. The Iraqi who'd met me near the door seemed innocent. He was still half-asleep, probably woken by the explosion. His natural reaction was to see what the hell was going on—a reaction that easily could have gotten him killed.

House secure, we set a watch, waiting in the uneasy silence for more light so we could go further into the city.

It turned out our route had been a lucky choice—the IED that went off had been part of a daisy chain. Swap places with the tank, drive a few yards to the right, and we would have been incinerated.


INMAN JOINED HIS FIRETEAM SHORTLY THEREAFTER, NO WORSE FOR WEAR. HE later left the Marines and went to the Air Force, where he became a para-rescue jumper. There he earned a Bronze Star for valor. He's a badass, and a good Marine.

I still feel kind of bad for tossing him around that first mission. He must have thought I was insane.

## HOTEL HIT

The tank had obliterated the house where the insurgent had been. It looked to be a one-off, without a follow-up attack.

Thirty minutes later, we started into the rest of the city. Almost immediately, we started hearing explosions—IEDs going off. Somebody counted an even dozen. I didn't keep track; I'm not sure I even noticed. These were very small, unable to do much damage unless you were very close and relatively unprotected. Had I heard even one of them four months before, I surely would have jumped.

It wasn't just that I could judge how bad or close the bomb was by the sound. I was edging toward a "fuck it" mode—*if I'm going to die, I'm going to die. There's nothing I can do about it.*

Our trac drew up near the street we were to sweep and we unloaded. We hadn't gotten too far when I heard a pop-pop-pop— the distinctive sound of a practice round hitting a vehicle that refused to stop.

A few seconds after that, Marines ahead of me started unloading into the vehicle, which still hadn't stopped.

"Hold fire," yelled Britten.

We took a knee.

It turned out the vehicle was the milk man making his rounds. Wrong place. Wrong time. Wrong thing to do.

Bad luck.

We walked by the body, and started doing house searches.


EVERY TIME WE WENT INTO A HOUSE, I EXPECTED IT WOULD BE A DEATH HOUSE. Time after time, we went in, tense, hopeful, ready to fire, a flinch away from firing.

No ambush.

Two days passed like that. Tense boredom punctuated by extreme anxiety and ruled by general unease. We found a few weapons caches but faced no resistance. At the end of our sweeps, we turned around and occupied an abandoned hotel we nicknamed Hotel Hit, because we're creative that way.

*Welcome to Hotel Hit. You can check in anytime you want, but . . .*

You know the rest.

The building was plain and barely furnished—if I called it austere I'd be describing it as ten times fancier than it really was. It was stifling, hotter and stuffier than the city at large. We'd sweat so much at night that we'd take off our uniforms and they would stand on their own, held up by the salt from our sweat.

I shit you not, they did.

There was a primitive shower—a garden hose that splashed water so hot it could have been used for tea. For the first week we slept on the floors; by the time cots arrived, the salt from our bodies had probably worn little grooves in the concrete.

At twelve stories, though, the hotel had a great view of the city.

We ate MREs for two weeks in Hit; by that point, no one's bowels could move. That wasn't necessarily a bad thing, as the hotel's toilets were out of order and full. For survival's sake, we began buying up food in the markets while out on patrol. The tomatoes were especially delicious—to this day, the best snack I can think of is a fresh tomato with a ton of salt, even if what we get in the States now is a pale shadow of Hit's, at least to my palate's memory.

Those first two weeks or so were quiet. No mortar attacks, no ambushes—it was eerie. The patrols were routine; in the context of Iraq, it was all very easy.

Then it started getting weird.

The city is split in two by the Euphrates. A single bridge connects the two halves. A big pink house on the west bank commanded the bridge. A team of Marine snipers attached to our command were using the house as a post; we relocated there for a few days to provide security as well as watch the bridge and its approaches.

We found a rebar factory nearby, with large wheels of wire. A few of the guys moved them over to use as barriers in the road. Any vehicle that came toward us had to drive a serpentine route, which slowed it down. We could also shut down the passage entirely by using our trac or moving the rebar reels to block it.

The house was cooler than the school, but not by much. We started sleeping on the roof to get some relief. Early one morning, I woke to the sound of a gun firing below. I leapt up in my underwear and grabbed the nearest rifle, running barefoot to the edge of the roof, looking for a target.

I saw a car approaching the wire wheels at a high rate of speed. *What the hell?*

I gritted my teeth and emptied the mag, angry, concerned, and still half asleep.

*It's a vehicle IED. I'm going to die.*

I was irrationally mad, thinking in that instant I was going to be blown up wearing only my shorts and a T-shirt, firing someone else's rifle—not the way I envisioned going out, or would have envisioned going out if I spent the time.

Finally the car pulled to a stop. Its two occupants fell out—injured, but alive.

The Marines on the ground questioned them with the help of an interpreter. They claimed they were on their way to work at a bakery.

"Do you want help?" the interpreter asked.

"No," said the men. They jumped back in the car, turned around, and drove off.

Our guess was that it had been a probe—an attempt by insurgents to test our defenses. But our ROEs didn't allow us to detain them, as they hadn't physically attacked us.

Here's a bigger question: How did a half-dozen Marines firing at a car-sized target no more than seventy-five yards away—and then far less—fail to get a fatal shot in?

Blurry eyes and all, one of us should have been able to take them down. But we didn't.

And for the record, I would never have let them go myself, ROEs be damned.

## IT GETS CRAZY

That day passed without much new. You could tell from the graffiti scrawled on the sides of some of the buildings that insurgents were active here; a boot stomping on an American flag sends a message you don't need an interpreter to read. We moved to another house with better elevation, and made sure that someone with a SAW machine gun would always be on watch. But otherwise the most exciting thing we did was play a pickup soccer game with some of the local kids.

Same thing next day.

Then the mortaring began. We were on foot patrol in the city and I heard them starting to drop, all close together, meaning that it was a skilled attack on exact coordinates. Those coordinates happened to be a school taken over by Kilo Company several blocks from us; the rounds killed several Marines. I saw the plumes go up as they impacted, perfectly spaced. They had to have had coordinates on that place; no way it was just a luck shot.

Not long afterward, a convoy of Iraqi troops and government officials entered the city. On the way in, an unknown SUV somehow managed to join the convoy without being spotted. The interloper followed the government convoy into a school complex where India Company was headquartered.

The SUV got stuck in a patch of mud just inside the camp.

Some Marines went to help get it out; before they reached it, the vehicle blew up.

It was a vehicle IED. Fortunately, none of the Marines were killed in the blast.

The snipers started catching muj planting IEDs around the city. Apparently the insurgents had realized we weren't going away this time, and decided it was better to fight than lay low. For some, it was a fatal decision. I pulled security for some of the snipers a day or two after the mortar attack when a pair of insurgents tried planting a bomb on a street not far from the building where the snipers had set up their hide. It was broad daylight, but obviously the muj felt safe in the city without any troops nearby.

They didn't count on the snipers.

Those guys were good, and quick. One of the Marines shot one of the muj as he stood, then got him a second time as he fell.

That IED never got planted. One that did, though, nearly killed me near the hotel. I was thirty or forty feet away when it went off. It made a deep hole in the road.

Good luck, there. I had my picture taken in the hole it left.

A death trap or a photo op; it was all just a matter of timing.

Even as the insurgent activity ramped up, the townspeople remained outwardly cooperative, even friendly toward us. But they were short on information. We'd ask about an attack or the insurgency, and they'd just kind of shrug. "No Ali Baba, no Ali Baba," they'd tell us, a shorthand best translated here as *I know nothing and I'm saying even less.*

But then they were in as much danger, even more, than we were. Surely anyone seen cooperating with us would have been a marked man or woman.

JULY 4, 2005: WE'RE RESTING IN HOTEL HIT; I'M LOUNGING ON MY PLASTIC COT when all of a sudden a loud boom shook the building.

I dove under the cot, sure that we'd been targeted by a suicide vehicle.

I'm not sure what protection my cot would have provided. The smart thing to do would have been to copy Taylor and run out to the hallway where the walls might provide a bit more hope or at least the illusion of protection.

Another rumble. But the building was intact.

It was a fighter jet pulling low and loud runs overhead. Probably in honor of the holiday. Aviators are a strange bunch.

## PIED PIPERS

As the attacks continued and the tension in the town steadily increased, the Iraqi civilians became more standoffish, clearly worried.

We tried to change things with teddy bears.

They weren't part of Operation Teddy Bear. These were legitimate toys, plush and cuddly, delivered by a charitable organization to be distributed to Iraqi kids.

So we went on a toy patrol. Everyone grabbed a bunch of bears, stuffing them into our vests, belts, straps, basically anywhere they would fit. We hit the road, found our assigned streets, and started walking.

The first kid who got a bear seemed a bit confused, as if he didn't understand that it was a toy. But that didn't last long. Within a few moments, we had a flock of admirers streaming along on patrol with us, each clutching a teddy bear.

We were the new Pied Pipers of Iraq.

Standard operating procedure called for us to double-back while patrolling, to make sure we weren't being followed by insurgents, and to keep our movements at least a little unpredictable. When we turned back midway through the bear patrol, we found some explosives experts working on the street.

"What's going on?" Britten asked.

"There's an IED here," one of the EOD guys explained. They'd already disabled it.

"We just patrolled here," said Britten. It hadn't been more than ten or fifteen minutes, if that. "Why didn't it go off?"

The bomb expert pointed at the kids. Whoever was controlling the IED didn't want to blow up the children along with us.

Luck ran with charity and kindness that day.


THE KIDS IN IRAQ WERE A LOT LIKE KIDS EVERYWHERE—ENERGETIC, INQUISITIVE, curious. They wore Western-style T-shirts and jeans. Occasionally you'd spot an authentic-looking logo, but these weren't designer threads. Even in the areas of the nicer homes—two stories, wrought-iron fences with fancy balustrades—the people were poor compared to Americans. But the children we saw on the streets hadn't yet lost their innocence. They might suck on a firehose of extremist propaganda in a few years and loathe us with psychotic hate, but for now they viewed us as friendly curiosities and potential benefactors.

I picked up enough words and phrases to amuse them, or at least myself. Hurley said later he was always amused at seeing me walking on patrol with a bunch of kids tagging along. He saw it as a hearts-and-minds thing, me putting into practice the strategy Command was now preaching.

It was that, partly. And I do like kids. But it was also protection. The extremists here obviously double-clutched when kids were in the gunsights.


I WAS ON THE HOTEL ROOFTOP A FEW DAYS LATER, DOING OVERWATCH AS A GROUP of other Marines worked down a street not far away. As they neared a mosque, an IED planted within the mosque wall or otherwise on its grounds went off.

A pair of medevac vehicles rushed over.

One of the guys hit was an amazing Navy corpsman named Travis Youngblood. He took shrapnel in the neck and leg, but had the presence of mind to tell the guys who got him how to wrap it up. For a man who'd just taken a pretty serious blow, he was in good spirits, talking and being his usual nice guy, smiling for everyone just like he always did.

"Tell those guys, I'll be back," he told one of our sergeants as he was loaded up for the medevac.

It seemed obvious he was going to lose a leg, but we all felt that he was the sort of man who could somehow deal with that. Corpsmen are our medics; though technically they are sailors, good corpsman are highly valued and become part of the Marine family. Youngblood was absolutely one of us. He had a four-year-old and a pregnant wife back home; it was good that he was going to be with them, maybe even before the baby was born.

We found out later he'd bled out in the hospital a few days later. It seemed more horrible than if he had he passed away on the battlefield. He'd saved so many Marines and helped Iraqis, survived the initial explosion and been in good care when Death finally arrived, far from his family and brothers. The cruel monster Death gives no quarter no matter the good works a man does when he lives. It seemed as if Fate had played an equally mean joke, letting us think a man we all loved would live, only to snuff him and our hopes when there was nothing we could do for him.

The other guy wounded that day was Daniel Foot. He was not only an amazing Marine, he was a walking Purple Heart—he was wounded four or five times without quitting.

Where once the city had seemed pacified, now it was a seriously dangerous place, death lurking everywhere. The days became concentrated units of action, without stop. We were either on patrol or sleeping. There was neither time nor opportunity for diversion.

The hotel had no electricity, so no TV, obviously, and no opportunity to charge even my little music player.

I wasn't surprised when guys got killed now. Of course. That's what's going to happen. That's normal.

I kept thinking I was next.

But I wasn't. I'd sleep, get up, grab some food—there were rumors a chow hall was coming, but it didn't—then go on patrol or pull overwatch. Get back and zone out. Take a watch when it was my turn. Then sleep, and start the cycle all over again.

Two more weeks passed. The attacks continued. The insurgents kept attacking. We killed them, or wounded them, or chased them off. They kept coming.

## THE IRAQI ARMY

The Iraqi National Guards were an asset. They knew where to look for contraband in houses, and what to watch for in vehicles. Even better, they started bringing us food and helped cook, finally providing an alternative to MREs.

In whatever spare moments we had, we taught them how to fight. They were passionate, but very undisciplined, as likely to shoot into the air as at the enemy when engaged.

Sometimes we went beyond the basics. One night we went firm in a house with some Guardsman. Someone started playing some heavy metal music, and the Iraqi got into it. Impromptu instruction in how to head-bang. Somewhere in Iraq today, there's an elite unit of head-bangers searching for a mosh pit.

The Iraqis had a variety of musical tastes, generally preferring things that were fast, maybe so they could dance, which they did freeform and with enthusiasm. Pop and hip hop were favorites.

And, inexplicably, Britney Spears.

We also helped them with their English. Teach them a few choice curse words, and they were friends for life.

Their ROEs were different from ours. They had no problem going into mosques—ordinarily off limits to us. One day on patrol they went into a mosque suspected of sheltering the insurgents. They next thing we knew, they were chasing a guy with a rifle out of the building. Before any of us got there, the Iraqis cornered him under a tree. He raised his gun but didn't get a chance to fire—they shot him dead.

Still, they were a mixed bag as fighters. Taylor worked with a group that was excellent. But others . . .

Toward the end of our stay in Hit, Batchelder and I were separated from the rest of the squad while leading six Iraqi National Guardsmen on patrol. We kept going, trying not to betray our nervousness, hoping the whole time we wouldn't end up in a firefight. Having spent just a little time with them, we figured that if we did, two would run, two would shoot but miss what they were shooting at, and the last two would end up shooting themselves.

We were lucky that day—we didn't see anything suspicious, and we eventually got back with the rest of the squad. Still, no matter what Taylor or anyone said, I always preferred a single Marine to a half-dozen Iraqis.

We did admire their sidearms. In contrast to their well-worn AK-47s, the Iraqi government had issued them brand-new Glocks. We tried a few times to trade, but found no takers.

I didn't carry a pistol myself. As the smallest man on the fireteam and one of the smaller Marines in the company, I was occasionally tasked to go into a tunnel or narrow hole somewhere. Gunny would lend me his Beretta, and off I'd go.

Not quite that enthusiastically.

We were in a refinery—the location is a blur now, but it was probably in or near Hit—where we came across a building that had collapsed. The wreckage had formed a cavern, a perfect hiding place for a cache of guns or explosives.

Or muj hiding from us.

I stripped my armor, took Hurley's Beretta and a flashlight, then held my breath as I squeezed into the small space under a collapsed floor.

Why no armor?

Wearing it would make it harder to squeeze into the space and make it easier to get snagged. Besides, I figured I'd be shot in the face, where armor wasn't going to help.

I started down, squeezing in like a mole between dangling concrete and pieces of pipe and lumber. Damp air and pulverized concrete filled my lungs.

*We should have a machine that does this.*

*Whatever the hell is down here, let's just leave it.*

I slithered onward. Dirt fell off the "roof" above. I kept going, crawling and squeezing. By this point I'd lost tons of weight—I was probably down to one thirty. Even so, it was a tight squeeze until I hit an open pocket. That was worse—plenty of space for someone hiding in the shadows at the edges.

I played the light around, pretty fitfully.

Just debris. Battered pieces of what had once been a place where dozens of people worked.

I found another little crevice and poked forward again. I started hoping that, given all this trouble, I'd find something worth my while—but not so worth my while that I got shot in the process.

A weapons cache. A store of money socked away by one of Saddam's minions.

But there was nothing, just this sweaty Marine squinting through the darkness. I can't remember ever being so happy to come to a dead end.

Later on in Hit, I was lowered into a pit from an unfinished irrigation or water diversion project. Beretta in my pocket, I clung to a rope as the other team members lowered me. Once on the bottom, I started crawling through the narrow tunnels, flashlight showing the way.

Under other circumstances, it would have been an opportunity to joke about wandering through the sewers of a famous city like Paris or New York. But nothing about the empty, lightless tunnel evoked humor.

I worked my way down to a cavern that opened octopus-like into a number of tributaries, all dry. I picked the largest, deepest one and began moving down it, able to stand. But it was so deep and had so many twists that I had to stop after a while, worried that I would lose my way back.

All I found when I went into tunnels was a lot of fear.

## BURGER KINGS

We were pulled out of Hit on July 21 or thereabouts. Told we were done, we packed up and got ready to go back to the dam. As we gathered our gear, a convoy of trucks appeared with air conditioners for the hotel.

Large, commercial air conditioners, which had to be gotten to the top of the roof somehow.

*We need you men to help get these air conditioners set up.*

Haul them up eight stories to the top of the building, to cool off our replacements?

Excuses were found and we avoided the work detail. I'm sure our replacements were far more motivated to get the ACs in place—assuming electricity or at least some good-sized generators followed.

We didn't take the direct route back to our camp at the dam. Instead, Gunny Hurley or someone in Command directed a detour that afforded us six hours at al Asad.

First stop off the tracs—Burger King. Rarely has a fast-food burger tasted so good.

Food, cigarettes, skin magazines such as *FHM* and *Maxim*—we restocked in the base stores.

A staff sergeant came up to me and one of the other Marines who was walking with me while we were shopping.

"Who the hell are you?" he asked. "You look like shit."

"Lima, Three twenty-five," I told him.

"Oh," he said, a note of recognition and pity in his voice. He walked away.

We were famous by then.

I THINK THERE'S A CULTURE IN THE MILITARY THAT ERRONEOUSLY EQUATES UNIform discipline with discipline in combat. Let me be clear: discipline in combat is essential. It saves lives. It gets the job done. And uniform discipline, especially for young guys, does have value— until you face combat. Then the measure of everything is different.

Until a unit goes into combat, you really can't tell if they have true combat discipline, so you need a proxy, and I suppose uniforms are as good as any. But buttoning your shirt and blousing your boots are not substitutes for pushing into gunfire, or making your rounds count when suddenly attacked. Spit-shining a shoe doesn't mean you'll bond properly under fire. Goodwin's dress was hardly a drill instructor's dream—the American flag bandanna tucked over his nose wasn't exactly government issue. But there was no better Marine in combat.

A certain level of good hygiene is absolutely necessary, even at the front. You can't have a bunch of young dudes sitting around stinky and smelly, breeding the crud. But I saw how being overly fastidious could become an obsession, a substitute for what really counted. And it wasn't a coincidence that this tended to happen when we came across senior enlisted inside the wire, decently removed from steady combat. I don't know if the NCOs and officers were bored there, secretly jealous that they weren't seeing action, or what.

My unbloused boots during the mortar attack were an obvious exception. That one totally defies explanation.

But I realized something during our short stay at al Asad—what could anyone do to us if our uniforms were out of order? Confine us to base?

That's a laugh. Maybe we could make the next salsa night.

I understand there were complaints to our command. I have no firsthand knowledge, but my suspicion is that they were met with, at most, a shrug.

BS about uniforms was annoying. More serious, and related to our own command, was the fact that it was nearly impossible to get special permission to go home for a family emergency. Guys' parents and grandparents died, babies were born—ordinarily the Corps makes an allowance for that, shipping the Marine home for a short visit. That wasn't happening for us.

I don't think there was much grousing until we heard that one of our leaders went home that month to attend his daughter's high school graduation.

*Graduation? If he can go for that, why can't I go for a funeral?*

A good question, not quite satisfactorily answered by the insignia on the particular individual's uniform. I'd say the move cost him quite a bit of respect among his men.

## CYKLA

There were so many operations and patrols, and so much variation on them, that inevitably everyone in the company had very different experiences. You might be in a squad that did overwatch ten blocks from a firefight and remember it completely differently. You wouldn't necessarily know the details until things quieted down or even until much later, days after you returned when you ran into a friend who told you what happened.

On July 28, Lima was tagged for a one-day mission to a town named Cykla (we pronounced it "Sick-la"), about twenty-five kilometers from the dam. Depending on who was talking about it, the tiny village was either not considered a high threat, or was viewed as a halfway point for insurgents traveling further into Iraq. Either way, it had not been swept in a long time. The op was a quick hit to clear it out; it didn't figure to be a major op, certainly not compared to Sword or Matador.

Batchelder and I were sick that day, wiped out with a stomach flu, and didn't go. Among those who did was my friend John Bailon.

His squad was working on a "cordon and knock"—the area was blocked off as Marines went house to house, knocking on doors and then searching. They'd gone into one house and begun searching it. John drew the assignment to watch the occupants.

The first things John noticed were the belligerent expressions on the faces of several males in the house. Ordinarily, they would avoid eye contact. These guys didn't.

But what put him on edge was an older woman, sitting by herself in the corner of the living room, tears draining her eyes. He finally passed it off, telling himself she didn't like the fact that they were going through her things; he wouldn't either.

Later he'd interpret it differently—she knew what was going to happen.

The squad cleared the house and started for the next, a largish building that looked as if it hadn't been completed when the war started. His squad leader, Andre Williams, started toward the door then stopped, realizing that one of the team members was still in the back of the other house. He sent John to fetch him.

John had taken two or three steps when he heard what sounded like a large explosion. He turned back to see Williams falling under automatic rifle fire from inside the house. He ran over and pulled Williams back, checking his wounds as a gunfight erupted around them.

Williams was covered with blood, his body shaking from shock. By the time John checked for a pulse, the sergeant was already dead.

John still had Williams's head in his hands when grenades began exploding around him. Miraculously, the grenades wounded several guys but didn't kill anyone—years later they'd joke they must have been "Chinese grenades," which typically are packed with less explosives than Western grenades.

One of our tanks came up and put five rounds into the structure, turning it into a pile of rubble. When the Marines went in, they found a blood trail out into the yard.

Chris Lyons was one of the men who started following the trail. He and another Marine followed it around the back to a small building, about the size of a chicken coop or an outhouse. Lyons started for the door, then was hit by gunfire from inside. Marines rallied over; they emptied their magazines at the insurgent but he kept shooting until finally he was out of bullets and then blood. He bled out, fighting to the last. Corporal Jeff Hunter is said to have had to resort to his Kbar to take him down.

Years later, Hunter married Lyons's widow. That's how close our families became because of the war.

He'd been hit, conservatively speaking, a dozen times. How had he kept going?

A search found vials of adrenaline and some sort of drug—probably meth—in the building he'd run out of.

I knew both guys pretty well. Lyons was liberal—very liberal, and not just for a Marine. We'd play chess and talk politics sometimes, long, philosophical but adamant discussions. Mostly, though, we just hung out, trying to enjoy our limbo of ease before diving back into the real war.

Williams had a daughter. A few weeks before he'd recorded a video for her birthday, and drew her some pictures because he couldn't buy any sort of present.

A lot of us knew Williams pretty well. He was Norris's best friend; he'd come in all the time and hang with us. He'd been practically a member of their squad.

Norris took it pretty hard. I felt terrible for him. It was a mirror, I guess, of how I'd suffered when Grant died.

AL QAEDA IN MESOPOTAMIA HAD APPARENTLY BEEN USING THE HOUSE AS A HEAD-quarters; the search after the fight recovered a laptop and other materials.

It was during that same operation that Gunny Hurley got hurt, though not by direct enemy fire.

Under fire, though. The squad Gray Hair was with had started taking gunfire from a tower. Rather than assaulting it—not a good idea—a plane had been called in to neutralize it. The Marines nearby had to extract back under fire to keep a safe distance between them and the expected bomb blast. Hurley, the last man back, was running in the field to the rest of the squad when he suddenly fell forward.

"I'm all right!" he screamed, along with some other choice words. He scrambled, stumbled, and limped to the perimeter the squad had set up just in time to avoid the bomb blast.

Gunny had torn up his leg falling into a hole in the field. His ankle was sprained and his knee was pretty badly damaged—eventually it would have to be replaced—but Hurley being Hurley, he declined to be sent back home. Instead, he hobbled on a crutch over the next few weeks, even going out on a mission until he realized he was more a liability than an asset when hobbling around.

Before returning to the dam, the Lima guys were woken in the

early morning to detour to Barwana, where a team of special operators had trapped fifteen insurgents in a school. The specop unit—
one of the ones that doesn't officially exist, I believe—didn't have
enough people to take them, so our platoon's 2nd Squad came in,
set up a cordon, and then waited while the building was destroyed
by a tank and aircraft.

Good mission, right? Fifteen insurgents killed; their base destroyed. Except, the higher ups wanted to know *why* a school was
destroyed. Taylor, whose squad had been there, tried to explain the
circumstances.

Not good enough. Command needed proof that it had been
used by the insurgency.

As it happened, the specop team had video. But they wouldn't
release it to us, supposedly because it was top secret. And since they
weren't the ones who were there when the building was blown up,
it wasn't their problem.

Taylor's squad had to go back and pull out evidence of the insurgents' cache of weapons from the rubble. Not a popular mission.

They did get what they needed, and the questions stopped.

## BANK ROBBERS

Grant's death and those of the rest of the company had affected me
deeply. I can't say that I had gotten over them—I still mourn them
every day—but I was starting to feel more like myself, more out of
the deep fog that had descended since Matador. I think the rest of
us were, too.

We were talking with each other more. Our chemistry wasn't
what it had been—the humor was darker, our moods were darker.
In some ways, though, we were tighter, having gone through that
together.

One day at the dam we started talking about what we would do when we got back to the States. One of the squad's machine gunners, Adam Griffin I think it was, talked about taking his money and making a Halloween theme park.

My first reaction was, no, don't do that—you're going to waste your money. I tried to give him advice—spend it on yourself—but he wasn't listening. Money had nothing to do with what he wanted out of life, and my advice wasn't on point. Wisely, he insisted, what he was going to do was make people happy.

There's an antidote to misery.

He followed through on his dream, creating a Halloween park. I don't know what it took for him to do it, how successful it was, or really anything but this: it fulfilled an ambition that became important after what we were going through.

Gradually, we got around to sharing more of ourselves. McKenzie and the Bailon brothers would all talk about the "Rez"—the reservation—and about how they might start a business when they got home. They also talked a lot about the mountains. They loved talking about the mountains. Listening to them, you fell in love with the mountains, too.

Then somehow the talk got into weirder shit.

"Why can't we be bank robbers when we get back?" someone asked. "We know how to do it."

A company of Marine bank robbers. Well, it hadn't been done, at least not since the Civil War.

We laid out an entire plan with elaborate steps, from distracting the cops to the getaway.

I listened for a while, then made an observation.

"What trips you up isn't the bank robbing," I pointed out. "It's the money tracing."

"This is why you need to be part of this," answered one of my would-be co-conspirators. "You know how to wash the money."

"What makes you think I know how to wash the money?"

"You're Colombian."

"But—"

"You went to Harvard. You can figure it out."

Maybe I could have, maybe I couldn't have. We had serious—or at least long—conversations about our possible outlaw life. It was a bizarre release from the reality of where we were.

For the record: it was all play. To the best of my knowledge, no one in Lima ever robbed a bank.

# VII.

# THE WORST ROAD IN IRAQ

## McKENZIE

I still don't know how I managed to figure out where McKenzie lived—he hadn't given me his address. Maybe it was in an old email or one of the Bailon brothers had told me, or maybe it was divine inspiration. Whatever. I showed up at his apartment, a one-room studio in a converted motel. The place was dark.

I began pounding on the door. It was well past midnight.

No answer.

I kept pounding.

Nothing.

Fuck it.

*Thunder!*

I kicked the door. I broke the lock and the door swung open.

McKenzie lay on the floor a few feet away.

Shit!

I jumped over to him. The place reeked of alcohol.

"McKenzie!"

I grabbed him, afraid he was dead.

He groaned.

Alive, at least. Thank God.

I went and closed the door, then lay down next to him on the floor. We talked for a while, not about anything very specific, not about PTSD or the war in particular, just wandering talk, the way friends who haven't seen each other in a while talk.

His voice dropped off. He fell asleep. I lay on the floor, staring at the ceiling, thinking of Iraq, drifting.

"This doesn't make me gay," McKenzie mumbled, waking.

"Yes, it does, buddy, yes it does," I deadpanned.

He gave a half-laugh. Better than nothing.

We talked a little more. Finally he got up and went to his bed. I stuffed myself into his couch.

The next morning, someone from a veterans group that had been trying to help him came with some groceries. We sat and talked—still nothing deep, nothing revelatory, just random sort of talk, the sort of normal, nonimportant stuff we would have said to each back at the barracks.

Bullshit, basically.

We drank and bullshitted the rest of that day. On Sunday, I took him to a pancake place and had breakfast. Finally he started opening up, talking about how his marriage had busted, how far down the black hole he felt he'd fallen. In the meantime, I'd called some friends who worked for a congressman on the VA oversight committee. They managed to arrange for him to be admitted that day.

We drove out there after breakfast. I parked across the street from the hospital, and asked if he wanted me to walk him in.

"I gotta do this on my own."

McKenzie reached for the door handle. I took a deep breath, and watched him walk across to the hospital, hopeful that he would finally find some help.

## SHORT-TIMERS

It was August when I started thinking about time, and how that played into our equation of war and luck. I figured they wouldn't keep us here beyond October, due to the way the activation system worked. We would stay in the war zone for six months, max, and only six months. There was a reason we had landed in Kuwait March 1 rather than February 28. We'd be out by October 1.

I worked it backwards, counting the time we'd need to stage out. We had roughly six weeks left.

So where once time had been infinite, now I saw an end to it.

The end I saw wasn't relief. It was far more fatalistic. It meant not that I was going home, but that I would die before it came.

And I just didn't care. I wasn't sure how I would die, but I knew it would happen. I can't say that I was blasé about death—I still experienced fear, and I certainly didn't *want* to die, or let one of my brothers die. But emotion had been walled off by fatalism. I was powerless against the large danger of war, and small dangers no longer bothered me.

You might say there are no small dangers in war, and you'd be right. But having seen how random death could be, I had decided unconsciously that there was no sense getting worked up about my fate.

I believe other guys thought the same way. It expressed itself in different ways. Taylor shrugged off being shot at by our own guys. We couldn't change fate, so we just played through.

I smoked a lot of cigarettes. On the one hand, I guess, I should have been more concerned about my lungs. On the other hand, we sucked in so much spent diesel fumes while riding in the back of the tracs that the cigarettes couldn't have done much harm. Maybe they even neutralized it.

## QUICKSTRIKE

### AUGUST 1, 2005

We'd been out for a few days on a combat patrol and had just climbed out of the AAVs when suddenly the NCOs ordered us back into the vehicles. There was trouble in Haditha; we needed to get down there quickly.

We found out a little more as the tracs rumbled down the east side of the Euphrates, heading to secure the bridgehead into the city. Marine snipers were missing in the city. At least one was believed to have been captured. The routes in and out of the city had to be closed to prevent the insurgents from leaving and an operation could be mounted to recover the missing men.

A GROUP OF SNIPERS HAD BEEN WORKING IN AN AREA AT THE EDGE OF TOWN. ON August 1, two three-man teams went out together to set up for a mission around two in the morning. At some point they were ambushed; when they failed to check in on time, a QRF team found five of the six dead, their guns and some gear missing. The sixth man was reported to have been taken away in what was described as a local taxi.

Because of the circumstance, no one knew then, or later, exactly what happened. Maybe they were fed bad intelligence; maybe insurgents had been tracking their moves. A group called Ansar al Sunna posted credit for the ambush on the web shortly after their bodies were found. Independently, the Associated Press reported that men who claimed to be part of Ansar al Sunna showed up in a market in Jazeera on the north side of the city with helmets, flak vests, and other gear from the Marines, taking credit for the kill.

Ansar al Sunna was believed to be a splinter of a larger organization formed in 2001 by Sunni militants in the Kurdish areas of Iraq and linked by American intelligence sources with al Qaeda in Mesopotamia. Following the American invasion, some of the members apparently sought refuge in Iran, returning with new strength and organization during the opposition. They were active in the Sunni Triangle of Iraq, which included areas where we operated and some cities a little farther east. Later, they were reported in Syria, operating against the Syrian government.

Like many of the insurgents we were fighting, Ansar al Sunna's exact lineage and composition were opaque, and probably confusing even to its members. Its claim of killing the snipers was never definitively verified, or at least hasn't been publicly.

Whoever did the killing, they were clearly the enemy. We didn't care what they called themselves or who they thought they answered to.

## VISIONS OF DISASTER

The city was buzzing by the time we arrived. There were helicopters and fixed-wing aircraft overhead. Sporadic gunfire resounded from the narrow streets of houses near the river. While there are always ways to get across a river, the bridge was the only easy passage from west to east near the city center; the closest other bridge was about two miles south.

We pulled up to a house on the eastern bank overlooking the bridge approach. The house appeared empty; it had probably been cleared by another unit before we got there.

We were barely inside when we started getting lit up. Machine guns, rifles—the bullets just kept coming. Insurgents had taken over a palm grove on the other side of the water, on a direct line to the house. We began firing back, taking turns at the front windows.

Then the mortars started. The first round wasn't particularly close, nor was the next one.

Far right, far left.

Then, a little closer left. Closer right.

Homing in on us. You didn't have to be trained as a mortarman to understand we were the target, and they were working to get us.

More rounds, still far enough away not to worry about, but definitely closer.

Then they stopped.

There was a short quiet before the small arms fire from the palm grove stoked up, and the whole cycle repeated, the muj apparently having relocated to nearby positions. I took my turn and sighted on some flashes in the grove, looking for something solid to hit. I saw a flash and I fired, taking my time with each shot, hoping to hit the bastard rather than the trees and ground around him. But given the distance—I'd guess at least twelve hundred meters—it's debatable how accurate my shots were.

This went on for about five hours, the Iraqi attack gradually picking up steam. The intervals shortened, the enemy's aim tightened. As I was relieved from my post at the window to catch a breather, I looked up at the roof of the house. It was tin.

I went to the back of the room and lit a cigarette as the mortars stoked up. These were the closest salvos yet.

*Range good. Just need a very slight correction.*

Britten came back and looked at me.

"They're bracketing us," I told him.

"What do you mean?" asked the fireteam leader.

"They're dropping rounds all around us to get us on target. If you listen closely, you can tell that they're getting closer with each shot."

*Just a matter of time.*

I started doing the mortar adjustments in my head as each shell landed. Fifty yards, twenty yards.

A round hit the trac we'd been in. It was ten yards from the house.

*Fuck.*

I stepped back to the window. There were so many flashes now targeting was easy; I ran through my mag very quickly, then gave my place to someone else on the squad and went back to reload.

Britten gestured at the tin roof. "Will this hold up?" he asked. "Nope," I told him.

Britten stared blankly. The rest of my fireteam, which had rotated back with me, listened silently. There was nothing we could do, nowhere to run.

I lit a cigarette and waited, unsure which was coming first—my turn at the window, or the mortar shell through the thin roof.

Halfway through my cigarette, a tank pulled up near our house and fired a round into the palm grove.

The muj went quiet. It was as if a switch had been flicked.

Luck ran heavy in my direction that day.

AS IT GOT DARKER, ANOTHER GROUP OF MARINES CAME DOWN RIVER IN A RIVERINE boat, a rigid-hulled craft you might think of as a fishing boat with a bit of armor and machine guns fore and aft. We couldn't quite see them because of the bends in the river and the growing darkness, but we could hear them taking fire. The boat answered with its mini-guns and probably everything else on board.

Whoever was shooting at them either died or decided engaging Marines in their natural environment was a very bad idea.

Things calmed down for good after that.

Another unit came to take our place and we relocated to a building near where the snipers had been ambushed. By now other Marines were pushing into the city, scattering the insurgents. Lima held its positions, waiting for new orders.

I have in general a very high opinion of all Marines, but especially snipers, and especially these snipers. Taylor told us later he'd watch one of the guys hit an enemy at 2,200 meters—that's shy of the best recorded shot by Carlos Hathcock, the legendary Marine sniper in the Vietnam War, but only just. These men were incredibly good at their jobs.

So it just seemed to make no sense that they could have been ambushed, let alone that they wouldn't survive an ambush. I know what they say about underestimating your enemy—*don't*—but it seemed incomprehensible then, and even now, that these Marines had been cornered and killed.

Normally, six Marines can hold out pretty well against a force two or three times its size. And those are just your everyday Marines, assuming there is such a thing. Snipers?

Hell. They could take on a division and come out on top.

Where the hell was their QRF—the quick reaction force that is supposed to be available when shit like this happens?

What the hell was our battalion leadership thinking?

I'm not assigning blame. I'm telling you what I thought, and I'd guess what most other Marines with me were thinking at the time.

*How in God's name could this happen?*


AFTER ROUGHLY A DAY'S WORTH OF WAITING, WE GOT A NEW BRIEF: TOMORROW WE would push into the city via the main road. Command had adapted an operation already planned—Quickstrike—moving up the timing because of the death of the snipers.

As soon as we heard the plan, we knew there was a problem—we were going down a path sure to be staked out and planted with mines or other traps.

"That can't happen," some of us said. "That's going to be an IED alley."

The enemy would have had at least two days to prepare for us. They'd seen where we were, knew we'd be coming for them, and once we started to move on that road, we'd be obvious and easy targets. The area in front of the city was open and easily observed from the cluster of houses we were to sweep.

Our platoon leaders told us they'd communicated those same concerns up the chain of command. A long-range surveillance unit had been on overwatch for the past two days, observing the road. No one had laid out any IEDs.

"Too dangerous," we insisted loudly.

But that was it. We had no say.

Later that day, I sat back to smoke a cigarette. Lance Corporal Nick Bloem was nearby.

"You know, tomorrow's going to be my birthday," he told me.

As soon as he said that, it came to me.

*This guy is going to die.*

It was just bad luck. Bad juju, as some of the Louisiana trackers would say. At that point I was so fatalistic, there seemed no other conclusion.

Square jaw, all-American kid. Good-natured. Squared away Marine, always with a half-smile on his face. No reason he should die in such an obvious trap on such an obvious day to live.

But he would.

I didn't say any of that to him. "Happy birthday, man," I told him instead.

---

## AUGUST 3

We moved out August 3. By now, we knew that the missing sniper's body had been found, dumped by the muj in the market. We knew the killers were still out there, waiting for us.

For the first time in Iraq, I said a little prayer when I got up in the morning. It wasn't anything fancy. I made the sign of the cross as all Catholics are taught when young.

*"God protect me. I'm going in."*

It wasn't so much a plea for safety as an acknowledgment that I was going to die, and that my fate was beyond my control. I'd run out of time. Our luck was gone. If the snipers could be killed, any Marine could be killed.

In those moments of despair, did some hope remain? Maybe that was what the prayer was about—maybe unconsciously I thought I could escape by pleading to God. I'd been taught as a little boy that He could save anyone, that He wanted to save us all. Here was His chance to save me, and my chance as well.

Faith sets deep roots, remaining when hope and even fear have been shorn. I'd never been very religious at all, and this was the very first time I prayed in Iraq, so interpret it as you wish. I only know what I did, not my motivation.

What I was feeling about our fate wasn't just emotion; there was logic behind it. The insurgents were hemmed in. Even if they weren't fanatics—and experience showed they were—there'd be nothing for them to do but fight.

I pulled on my gear and walked out to the trac. So did everybody else. I nodded to a few of the guys I passed. Their expressions mirrored mine. Probably their thoughts did as well.

*Good-bye. Good-bye.*

*So long.*

*Last time I'll see you here, one way or the other.*

Thoughts, rather than words—not because saying these out loud would be too intense or morose, but because there was no sense saying them out loud.

I was one of the last to get into the trac. I sat next to the ramp, lit a cigarette, and waited. The AAV clawed forward, clanking loudly, spewing diesel exhaust through the interior. We bumped along ferociously, the road as uneven as any we'd been on. I could hear the other tracs moving behind us, a mechanical drone of engines and thick treads against the earth. The sound pounded my ears and armor; I tried my best to think only of my cigarette.

We still had a bit farther to go to get to the city proper when our vehicle jerked to a halt. I leaned against my gear and the thin armored side of the trac, listening to the second vehicle come up nearby, then take our place as the lead. Why we stopped or switched places, whether it was on purpose or a fluke, I don't know.

*This ain't a race.*

I pulled out another cigarette and lit it.

*We gonna move, or what?*

Our trac began moving again as my cigarette burned down. I stabbed it out and released the spent filter.

At that moment there was a loud explosion outside, followed by a sickening pop, another of those sounds you can only know if you've heard it, the sound of an entire AAV's air supply being sucked out of its interior, the sound of men dying in an instant's breath.

McKenzie had been looking out his hatch for IEDs when a white flash pulled his attention from the side of the road to the trac ahead. He felt the wave of a blast push past.

He yelled down to the corpsman inside and they got out quickly, running toward the vehicle.

They stopped maybe two hundred feet away, feeling the heat from the blasted vehicle.

"No way anybody survived that, Sarge," said the corpsman.

Our trac stopped. The ramp started to go down.

"Get to the nearest house," one of the sergeants shouted.

I was the first out. I glanced over my shoulder as I ran. The amtrac that had passed us was upside down.

Charred.

*Go to the house.*

I got to the house. I kicked in the door. A teenage boy came at me.

*No weapon!*

I grabbed him by the neck and threw him to the ground.

His father came down behind him. I tossed him aside and continued in, gun raised, finger twitching.

The family was there—I waved my gun at them, made sure they weren't armed, had them sit.

The rest of the fireteam came right behind me. Britten, on the fireteam's radio, got an order for us to hold at the house. I was already moving to the roof, charging up the stairs.

*Clear!*

I was practically right over the AAV. I could see the vehicle on its top, completely blown apart.

*Who was in it?*

I cried a little. Not like when Grant died, not anything you would recognize as a cry. No tears. A quick sob, nothing more.

I made sure no one saw me.

I blew a wad of air out of my lungs, shouldered my weapon.

*This is it. This really is it.*

*Time's up.*

I stood tense, not knowing how I was going to die, just that I was.

The rest of the units with us were clearing the nearby houses, holding the area; leadership was below, shouting directions.

*Hold this house. Wait for the attack.*

We waited for what seemed like forever. The squad leaders went on a leader recon.

"We're continuing with the mission," Britten related. "Push into the city."

ELEVEN MARINES—THE ENTIRE 1ST SQUAD OF 3RD PLATOON, EXCEPT FOR MARINE Lance Corporal Travis Williams, died in the trac. A translator and two vehicle crewmen were also killed; only the driver survived.

Williams survived because he hadn't been in the trac; he was the platoon radio man and his commander had pulled him out just before we kicked off to ride with him so he had comms.

He's been haunted ever since.

## BETTER WAYS

There were other ways to take that settlement. We could have dismounted and gone in from any number of directions, avoiding the main route; we'd done that before. We might have been hit by that IED regardless, but that would have taken out two guys, not sixteen.

The commander who ordered us down that road never explained to us why he made a decision that even a PFC knew was dumb. Interviewed for a documentary years after the war, he said that he was under pressure to get into the town quickly. He said that we were traveling with a unit of the Iraqi Guard, and that their vehicles couldn't travel in the soft sand. Because of that, he had to keep us on the road.

I don't remember any Iraqi Guard with us. I don't remember seeing any of them in the videos and pictures I've seen since of the attack. Maybe I missed them.

The commander told the documentary interviewer that he had contacted a unit that had "eyes on" the roadway and was told that it was clear, and had been clear for the past twenty-four hours. He implied that other patrols had been over that same area.

We all knew that IEDs were often planted days before they were used, with the terrorists waiting to attack for maximum effect. We were the first unit to sweep that area in force, and it was obvious that we were coming, given how long we'd waited outside.

Whatever.

Many different things could have been done. At the end of the day, there shouldn't be any argument that it would have been better if they had.

## PATIENCE AS A FLEETING VIRTUE

We spent the rest of the day clearing houses in the city, looking for insurgents, caches of weapons, and IEDs.

I had a lot less patience on house searches that day and those that followed, especially when it was obvious that we were not getting the full story. We knocked on the door of one house—at this point I can't remember when, but I think it was the first day we were there—and were greeted by the owner, an Iraqi in his thirties.

Not unusual, except that right away he went off to wash his hands.

A dead giveaway that he knew we could swab him for explosives.

I sat on a bed and waited. When he came back, I had my interpreter ask him about the bookcase that had been moved in one of the rooms.

The man feigned ignorance. I pointed at the line of dust on the floor—something no Iraqi woman would tolerate for very long. Clearly, the bookcase had been moved very recently.

"I want you to ask him what's behind this," I told the terp.

He did. "Nothing" was the answer.

"Ask him again," I said. "And this time, tell him that if I pull it away and something comes at me, it's the last time he sees his family. Be harsh."

The Iraqi insisted there was nothing there.

For some reason, I had a baton in my hand—to this day I don't remember why. Whether I'd been issued it earlier or I found it along the way, I've forgotten.

What I do remember clearly is this: I raise it and put it in his face. "If there's something there, you are fucking dead."

I had him pull away the bookcase. There was a panel.

The Iraqi started crying even before we opened it. Sure enough, there was a little space in the wall where he had stored like a shit-ton of AK-47 rounds.

I don't mean one or two magazines' worth. I mean enough to outfit at least a squad.

Now, the Iraqis were allowed to have one AK-47 and some rounds, but he had way more.

The Iraqi wet himself while we waited for Captain Knapp to arrive. The man claimed he wasn't an insurgent. He claimed he was on our side.

*Right.*

Knapp took over. The man was taken off for questioning by whatever unit was in charge of dealing with suspected insurgents— and later inexplicably released. I have no idea what sort of explanation he gave for having all that ammo. Probably it was bullshit, but it wasn't my call.

I wasn't mad when I found out they'd let him go. By that point, I figured of course upper command would screw up.


SOMETIME THAT SAME DAY, I SAW WHAT LOOKED LIKE A SOUP CAN IN THE MIDDLE of the road. I stopped, spotted it through my scope, looking for wires, looking for anything that made it something other than just a can. I widened my view, scoping around for a sign of an IED nearby. The guys controlling IEDs often put these out as markers— they'd watch the can and wait until we were close to it, then ignite the buried or hidden bomb.

Then something inside me took over.

*Fuck it!*

I ran and kicked the damn thing. I didn't care if this was how and where I died. I just kicked the damn can as hard as I could, anger and sorrow propelling it across the dust.

I kept running. Nothing blew.

I kept going. Not surprised at being alive, not caring about being alive, not thinking about anything, just running. My moves were automatic, baked into my body and brain by training and experience. I was just a machine now, running toward my death. Not wishing for it, but not wanting to avoid it either. Because I couldn't.

*Next house.*

Mentally, I was so done with all this shit. So done with trying to figure out who was going to kill me. So done with wondering how I'd get food that day. So done with knowing how to slam the magazine into my rifle while running. So done with luck, and war.

And that was liberation. Relief. Acceptance. For some reason, dying here was just fine with me.

*You're going to die here, but you're not going to go out like a little bitch. You're going to just fight until you're done. That's it.*

Not dying like a scared little dog was the best I could do. It felt like a real achievement.

AS MAD AS I WAS ABOUT THE DEATHS OF GRANT AND THE OTHERS, A THREAD OF decency remained within me and the rest of the fireteam. We had less patience, but didn't snap, at least not completely. I still felt some empathy for the people whose houses I entered. The teenage kid who'd run at me in the first house—I grabbed him hard and threw him down, not because I wanted to hurt him, but because I didn't want the guys behind me to be hurt. Fear and some degree of rationality governed my actions, despite my anger.

By the next day, I could look in the faces of the Iraqis and realize that most of them were just caught in the middle. They just wanted peace, too.

Still, it frustrated the hell out of me. An IED goes off in front of your house, and you claim you saw nothing?

Right.

There is something that keeps most of us from becoming animals. It held here.

Maybe in this case it was our training, and the fear of being punished, but I'm not so sure.

Some credit goes to our leaders—I personally had some good ones. Being a reservist—having spent so much time among civilians—probably helped my unit as well. But I think it ran deeper, a basic humanity that humans feel for others, and that can't be completely stomped out even in the worst circumstances.

Or, fortunately, was never fully stomped out in me or the rest of the squad.

Words I'd read from Nietzsche in school came back to me several times after we lost our second trac; they were a reminder and a warning:

*When hunting monsters, be sure not to become one.*

I recited those lines a few times after the second track blew. But I'd forgotten the rest of the quote, though now it seems even more poignant:

*When you stare into the abyss, the abyss stares back.*

WHEN YOU START ACCEPTING DEATH, IT AFFECTS YOUR MENTALITY. I KNEW THAT things were fucked up and that the war was fucked up. But to the extent that I thought about these things—which was limited—I wanted to leave the war with my ethics intact.

Maybe in my case it was the memory of Grant. He had been such a good human being—I honestly think he would have been disappointed in me if I started beating the shit out of people.

Whatever the reason, it wasn't just me. Everyone in the company lost friends, a lot of them, and come close to dying themselves. No one took it out on civilians. Maybe there was a time or two where someone got a little handy, but there were no war crimes. Maybe some of us wanted to get revenge and wipe out people, but we didn't.

We remained good Marines. Good human beings.

Hurting, but good in our hearts in spite of everything.

## WE DID THIS FOR DAYS. HOW MANY?

I could have been there two days. I could have been there three weeks. My brain has lost the ability to divide what happened there into days or weeks; everything is jumbled together, with a vague reference point to steer by. News reports later said we killed seventy-five insurgents and captured seventeen; I have no idea if those numbers are right. I can't remember anyone giving us the tally at the time.

What I do remember is the monotony of the days, searching, patrolling, knowing my time was up but not really caring.

Intel directed us to an industrial-style building where there was supposed to be a weapons cache. We blew open the locked steel doors and went in like we were SEAL Team 6.

*Hell House!*

*I'm going to get blown up and this is over.*

It was empty.

I didn't talk much to the locals. I didn't care anymore. They didn't care about me, so why should I care about them?

Military Command didn't care about us either. How long had we been talking about the AAVs? How long had we been saying we needed better armor to go into these towns and villages?

Did Donald Rumsfeld care about us? Not if he wasn't giving me proper equipment.

I decided the hell with everyone, except my fireteam, except my squad, except my company. Nobody cared about us and that was just the way it was.

I'd been disillusioned before we started the operation. Now I was beyond that. Even our own command didn't seem to really care—we'd told them about that road, about the obvious dangers. Every single one of us had told them. But no, they insisted. They knew better.

The snipers, the route—you put all of these things together, and you see a pattern of something other than competent decision making from the guys making decisions. It's tough to follow leaders when you don't trust their judgment.

But follow we did.

# VIII.

# DEAD
# MAN
# WALKING

## McKENZIE

The thing about McKenzie is that I knew he had PTSD. What I couldn't figure out was why. Yes, we'd seen combat—plenty of it. But there had been no one single event that stood out for me, no suddenly horrific moment out of the blue. He'd never been hit in the head, that either of us knew about anyway, so a brain injury wasn't involved. And as bad as combat had been, it didn't seem like something that would cause a trauma.

Now I know that's ridiculous. He'd seen over a dozen friends die. He'd seen people shot, buildings blown up, IEDs rip through vehicles. He'd smelled bodies burning, seen mangled remains.

But back then, I thought, why did it affect him? Why not me?

It turned out it did.

## STILL AT IT

And yet, for all my despair, for all the missions we kept slogging through, for all the premonitions . . . I didn't die.

I have no explanation for that. It makes no sense. Clearly, I was out of luck. Clearly, time had squeezed down.

I knew I wasn't dead but should be, and so nothing made sense.

If you can imagine a human being walking through the motions, that's what I was doing.

Finally they pulled us out of Haditha and took us back to the dam.

I think Command must have realized a lot of us were at the breaking point. We chilled out for a couple of days, walking around in numbness.

After Grant died, I'd spent days wandering around in my mind, trying to make sense of the war and his loss. I didn't do that now. I didn't think about anything. I was the ultimate stoic, aware I was going to die, accepting it as a fact, just ready.

I listened to my music. Read. Turned off the constant flow of thoughts habitually running through my brain. I sat in a cocoon of white noise filtered by the songs on my iPod knockoff.

Then Command decided to send us out on more patrols.

We did our jobs, but we just weren't feeling it, to be honest.

While I knew in my heart that I was going to get smoked, I didn't want someone else to get smoked because of me, so I certainly paid attention to what I was doing. I followed my training, our unwritten procedures. I was wary; I was professional. I just wasn't enthused.

The overall theme was the same—look for bad guys. The variation came in how the missions were actually carried out. One day we were dropped off by boats in the middle of a marsh. From there we snuck into town, checking areas where we thought insurgents might be gathering and looking for possible mortar sites. Another time we staked out a road junction in the middle of the desert, digging into the side of a wadi and hiding there for five days, living off the water and rations we'd humped in. Our goal was to find someone setting an IED ambush, but no one came.

Stupid stuff kept happening—or *almost* happening.

One of the platoons was accused by villagers near Haditha of unnecessarily shooting a civilian, a war crime. Investigators were called in, and our platoon was assigned to provide them security.

Not a problem—except that a time and place were agreed on for the investigators to meet with people in the village. Word of this "appointment" could hardly be kept secret in the village, and so any insurgent still in the area—and we knew there were plenty—had days to set up IEDs and an ambush.

We lost our minds when the investigators told us.

*How could you tell them when and where we were going to show up? Are you fucking stupid? This is a straight-up ambush.*

That's how the "discussion" in the briefing area went, except there were a lot more adjectives flying around.

It made no difference; we were going.

But not in tracs. We now had seven-ton trucks to ferry around in. The thin armor had been replaced by slats and canvas.

They were higher off the ground, after all.

They thought they'd be more survivable. I have no idea if that would have proved true or not. I suspect that some of the reason may have been political—the news media had picked up on our disaster, and any new strikes on a trac where a lot of men died would surely raise a storm of questions. Those questions would undoubtedly extend up and down the chain of command, ruining careers.

Too bad those questions hadn't been raised a lot earlier.

And really, would it have been better if a truck full of Marines blew up?

From what I'd seen, though, anything would have been better than dying in a trac. They were chugging coffins.

We piled into the truck and drove out through the desert.

"Fuck the war," I muttered as we bumped along in the back.

"Fuck this war," echoed Wilson.

"Fuck the war," said a few others.

All of a sudden, the truck stopped.

"Comms down," said one of our leaders—it might have been Hurley, maybe Knapp. "We gotta go back. We can't go on without comms."

I broke out laughing for the first time since August 3. Orders are orders, but a good leader finds a way.

The investigation went on without us. The platoon was eventually cleared.

SENDING TROOPS INTO AN EASY AMBUSH SITUATION WAS NEVER A GOOD MOVE, BUT doing that with a month or less of time left on the deployment struck us all as especially reckless. Realistically, there should be no difference between the thirtieth day after you've deployed and a point two weeks before you're going home.

But psychologically, those are very different times. As our activation wound down, we felt like we were just about to go home. We saw the finish line ahead, and felt that any deaths now would be doubly cruel. It was as if a thirsty man crawled across a desert for days toward a water hole, only to be stopped a foot or two away.

Being done in by fate or luck was one thing, but to be dealt that hand by our commanders would have been far worse. After everything that had happened, how could anyone be so cruelly foolish?

Certainly, we would have done our jobs, and protected the investigators. We would always do our jobs. But just as certainly, our collective mental state would not have been ideal.

## CHEERING MORBID DEATH

Not that it was necessarily ideal.

Back at the dam, a team had been brought in to try counterfire when the Iraqis mortared us. The squad would be sitting outside when the shells started to land. Our mortar team would rush to set up. We'd start cheering as they began plunking rounds back.

There's nothing more ridiculously blasé and maybe morbid than sitting on a balcony, smoking cigarettes and drinking illegal hootch, as shells fall all around you.

*Whatever. We're going to get it no matter what. So who cares?*

The weeks went on. We kept doing patrols. McKenzie thought later that everyone had begun acting kinder to each other, more aware that life is a fragile thing. Taylor thought Hurley had become more approachable, and while inappropriately easygoing, had a lighter touch now.

I'm not sure those impressions were universal, but there certainly weren't many conflicts within the company by then. We'd all been through so much together that we were a family.

Hurley had gotten rid of his cane but was still hobbling around and largely confined to working at the base—he'd only come down to see us at Quickstrike after the trac was taken out, and had to leave soon afterward, realizing he was in no shape to run with us, let alone lead a mission. Just having him around, though, was a plus. His aura as a leader had only been enhanced by everything he'd been through with us.

While we had been out on Quickstrike, someone had managed to place IEDs in the dam complex. The explosives were disarmed; we heard later that they had been placed by two Iraqi policemen. Security was increased but it was hard to think of even the dam as a safe place. So if even our base wasn't safe—fuck it.

*Just fuck it.*

I started paying close attention to the calendar, calculating how many patrols we could possibly go on, understanding how they were assigning us, crossing things off in my head.

As August trudged on, hope began to seep back into my consciousness. If nothing crazy happened, maybe those of us who were still alive might make it back.

Maybe I wasn't going to die.

Maybe.

HURRICANE KATRINA HIT THE U.S. AT THE END OF AUGUST. LOUISIANA SUSTAINED AN enormous amount of damage. That distressed the AAV crews particularly; they couldn't get news about their homes and their loved ones. They were helpless here, halfway across the world, while their towns were flooded. The grim news reports that followed were as devastating as any of the battles.

I caught one of the trac crewmen, Sergeant Woullard, in the computer room. "What's going on?" I asked.

"I have no home. It's gone," said Woullard.

He sat there defeated, utterly lost. The man who had saved so many, lost it all.

They couldn't even go home. We had stopped using the tracs by now, but Command wouldn't clear them to leave early.

Those last few weeks are just a slur of images, jumbled memories stored haphazardly in my brain. Back home, the families were told that we weren't doing dangerous sweeps anymore. But that was a crock. The company kept going out, returning to the train station in Haditha and even going back to Hit. At the train station, the insurgents tried hitting the weapons platoon with a suicide vehicle; only the driver's quick reflexes and demolition derby tactics saved them from disaster. Several guys were wounded during the action, including Foot, who got what I believe was his fourth Purple Heart.

In Hit, the muj tried a suicide vehicle attack and gunfight. It was a pale replay of action there earlier—we got through without major casualties—but it was still nerve-racking and dangerous.

Then there was the twenty-five-mile slog through the desert in the middle of the day with Iraqi National Guard.

That was a very warm walk. The temperature was 110 at least. You couldn't call it a wild-goose chase, since we weren't chasing anything. Just another pleasant summer stroll in the sandbox to show the muj we could go anywhere we wanted.

My boots were worn out by then. So worn out, in fact, that I had to get new ones. Which was a shame, because I really wanted the old ones as trophies, something to remember Iraq by. But in order to get the new ones, I had to turn in the old ones.

With our departure date approaching, a lot of us started coming back to life. Conversation picked up.

A lot of my friends were wondering if they'd ever be normal again.

We knew about PTSD. Guys talked about whether that would affect how they raised their kids; they wondered if the ailment might somehow be passed on to their children.

I talked with Cheston and John Bailon about death, trying to understand their perspective as Navajo. They were as unsettled as anyone in the unit. They talked about purification rituals, about taboos involving the dead. It seemed even more difficult for them to sort war out than for the rest of us.

McKenzie had almost completely shut down, not talking to anyone really.

In our off time, we wondered about what was going on back home. We had no consistent internet connection or steady source of news; vague rumors and heartfelt wishes stood in for actual information.

Going home was more and more a possibility, so plans for the future became more serious. A few guys talked about going in on a vacation home. The bank robbery idea hadn't totally died. I was starting to come around on it myself.

My original plan had been to go back to New Mexico. With Grant having died, New Mexico had lost its appeal. Kate and I had a brief phone conversation about our own future. It was brief—I don't ordinarily like talking much on the phone, phone time was limited, and the circumstances made it that much more awkward.

"I don't feel the same about New Mexico anymore," I told her. We'd talked vaguely about her moving there when I was back. "If you have a good job in Arizona, I'll just move there."

That was about it. I really didn't know how to talk about my emotions. I had never talked about them in depth with anyone, not even with her.

I'd say that was common in the squad and probably within the entire company. We'd talk, but our grief and our feelings of loss were never mentioned. It was obvious what had happened, obvious that there were guys missing. Everyone felt bad about having lost them. Everyone had a close friend who was gone.

Why talk about the obvious? Why pick at the scabs?

Talking about feelings would have seemed out of place.

I CAME ACROSS CHESTON ONE DAY, STARING OUT AT THE LAKE BEHIND THE DAM. I sat down next to him, quiet for a moment.

"What you need," I told him after we'd sat quietly for a bit, "is a life song."

He glanced at me, pulled out of the reverie he'd sunk into.

"Mine is '(Sittin' On) The Dock of the Bay,'" I explained, mentioning the Otis Redding song, which I had on my device. "When I hear it, it gets me thinking everything's going to be OK."

I played it for him. He nodded. Then we went back to sitting in silence.

## LAST PATROL

Every town in Iraq was the same in a different way. From a distance, yellow-brown houses shouldering each other, cramped streets and alleys, green palms near the river or other water source.

Up close, there were infinite variations. An elevated market area in Haqlaniyah. Different-colored tiles on roofs in Baghdadi. A front yard turned into a parking lot, a driveway and garage that could have fit into suburban New Mexico.

Danger and death sat everywhere, inside an abandoned house, below a dirt highway, in a placid field along the river. Yet running through these places were children and friendly if frightened people, warmhearted Iraqis who would welcome us into their houses as guests, who would share a cigarette and good advice: be careful, and make it home intact.

The human mind wants to sort things into strict categories. Read any website for travelers and you'll be told about the neighborhoods, where not to go, where not to linger after dark. But no such categories could be carved for al Anbar Province; every place was dangerous. Most mixed ease and evil together unpredictably. We had sharpened our senses to see the signs of impending trouble, yet even then it came down to luck. Bad decisions killed many of my friends, but not all deaths in Iraq could be blamed on errors. More than half of a year here gone, and the only true thing I knew was what I had arrived with: war sucks, people die.

No, that's not quite right. I'd come to know a lot more than that. Grief, especially.

Camaraderie as well. Brotherhood. The men I served with were truly my brothers. Even the most casual relationships had been deepened by shared experiences of stress, horror, and triumph.

THE LAST WEEK OF SEPTEMBER, WE GOT READY TO GO ON PATROL. WE'D GOTTEN into a pattern where each squad was taking a patrol a day; mathematically, this was going to be our last patrol before leaving.

It was a foot patrol along the western side of the Euphrates to Little Haditha Dam Village, the small settlement used by the dam workers. There were two stated purposes: show ourselves, and look for possible mortar locations—in military jargon, a presence patrol and a POS hunt, POS being an abbreviation for "point of origin search" but pronounced more like poo-z, drawing out the "o" sound like "pooh" because . . . because that was how we pronounced it.

All this time at the dam, and we still hadn't found the guys firing the mortars at us.

We patrolled for a few miles, walked through the town, and went back. As we passed under the archway that led to the entrance, a thought popped into my head:

*We're going to get shot by the Azerbaijan soldiers who'd taken up posts at the dam to provide security.*

They were a trigger-happy bunch.

*This is it. Some nineteen-year-old Azerbaijani is going to put a bullet through my noggin.*

I kept walking. None of the guards fired.

We passed the AAVs, walked through the armory, trudged up the four flights, and we were in the hootch.

I let out a huge sigh of relief, something I'd been holding in for months.

I sat on my rack and just . . . just . . . just realized that I had survived.

Barring anything crazy. Which would have been completely routine in Iraq.

NOTHING DID.

A few days before we were scheduled to leave, Hurley passed the word that taking war booty or souvenirs back from Iraq was not something we were allowed to do. A large portion of the company gathered together on the dam and on a signal hurled pistols gathered variously in our travels into the water.

The pistols hadn't been kept as souvenirs. We'd all seen the footage of what happened to the American contract workers in Fallujah, and heard stories of other atrocities. Nobody wanted to be tortured to death; by the same token, they wanted to spare their families the burden of knowing that they died by their own hands. Ideally, the pistols were loaded with one bullet, meant to be a last good-bye.

We were past that now.

We started catching up with members of the other companies in 3/25 those last few days. The Delta Company guys from New Mexico, who'd been assigned to India and Kilo, came back and we caught up, swapping stories and that sort of thing. It was cathartic to see our old friends.

There was more apprehension than people realized about going home. Still, most people wanted to get back to the States.

The Corps was offering bonuses for people willing to stay in country. They had a pitch: *If you would like to extend your stay, we can make it worth your while.*

Not those exact words, but that was the gist. You'd have thought they were selling vacation timeshares. Except the prize was a small bonus, a two-week leave, and an assignment to return to Iraq.

I thought about it for maybe a minute before deciding, no. But a few guys did take the offer. Maybe because they felt they weren't ready to go home.

The booze supply line shut down. We'd long since run through our cigars.

I packed my seabag and threw it on the bed.

Memory hit me hard: it looked exactly the way Grant's had when I'd packed it for him after he died.

We made room for the new unit rotating in. We took them through some of the nearby neighborhoods, brain-dumping info on them. Meanwhile, we sorted through the usual rumors about how we were getting out of the country: helicopters, vehicles. Hell, maybe they'd land a jumbo jet in the desert and we'd launch out of here on that.

Someone suggested we patrol all the way on foot to al Asad.

"Don't give Command any ideas," I told him, only half joking. "With this bunch, you can never judge how bad an idea they may implement."

In the end, we took helicopters, flying out the way we came in. The landscape looked a lot different now. The same colors, the same geography, the same little villages and hamlets and swamps and desert, endless desert.

But very different.

Bigger. A real place with actual people. A place with blood soaking into the sand. A place that smelled of half-burned fuel and incinerated bodies.

I'd arrived at the dam with notions of adventure and derring-do. Now I knew what war was.

You could feel the tension release as the helicopter banked away.

"Watch us get hit by an RPG," I muttered.

I was finished with luck; morbid pessimism had become my shield against the reality of the world.

IX.

# BACK
# TO
# ME

## McKENZIE

McKenzie and I came to the Marines from far different back-grounds, with far different perspectives. Some of those differences hurt him especially. I would imagine, as one of the senior NCOs of the unit, he had full-blown survivor's guilt. If I felt responsible for Grant's death, he must have felt doubly responsible for all the men who were serving below him.

There was something else cultural. The Navajo nation has dif-ferent attitudes toward death than those I was raised with. Marines would talk about who died, celebrate their memory at memorial services, try to touch them, at least symbolically, one last time. But for McKenzie, death was like a poison. It had to be purged and avoided, lest it infect everyone. There was just no way he could reconcile the two understandings.

On top of that, he came home to a world where he was no longer a guy in charge but an anonymous cog. That alone would have torn away at him.

Add the fact that his marriage was pressured and he didn't have a supportive household around him, that he was coming back with really no time to decompress—it's a wonder he made it at all. Maybe that speaks to not only his inner core, but to some of the skills he honed as a Marine.

What was my story?

I was lucky to have Kate, and my mom and sisters. I was lucky to not need to get a job right away. Moving to Arizona gave me a fresh start, and kept me busy, taking my mind off of what I'd been through, occupying me with new experiences as well as tasks I could handle.

But I still drank more than I should have, a lot of times. I smoked like crazy. And ultimately, I didn't escape the effects of the war, or PTSD. It's just that it played out in socially acceptable ways.

It seemed like I was doing the right thing. I had worked to achieve bigger and better things all my life. When I got back, I worked even harder.

I advanced through a political career. I achieved. I did whatever it took to get ahead, then did more. I kept moving forward.

And yet, I lost the connection between what those things really meant and who I was.

I don't know that I consciously thought, "get elected to X position and the nightmares will stop," or "win this election by five percent and you will never jump at a loud noise again." It was a more subtle tradeoff. I don't think guys with PTSD—and I'll include myself—drink themselves blind because they are consciously planning to forget; it just feels natural to numb yourself. It feels good, in a perverse way.

I haven't lost my ambition to do things to help people. I still want to—just as I don't mind having a beer or a bourbon with someone. But I'm conscious of the damage the war did, and more careful to judge how to go about repairing it.

## TOUCHING DOWN

We landed at al Asad and stayed there for about five days. We were just living life. Eating tons of chow-hall food, relaxing in air-conditioned quarters, watching movies and playing the video game Halo, still relatively new at the time.

Halo was tough—we'd sign up as a fireteam and go online against groups of players there. They'd kick our asses.

I don't like losing. That pissed me off.

"Dude," Britten would tell me. "These guys have been playing together for six or seven months. Chill."

It was weird seeing other Marines at the base. Honestly, it was hard to look at them as *Marines*. They were all young and smiling and happy, wearing clean uniforms, carrying shiny rifles—that was crazy.

They hadn't seen combat. They weren't us.

Most of the men we saw were air wingers and people supporting them, and indirectly us. They had an important role in the war but there was a difference measured in burgers, ice cream, and latte.

Not that I should criticize. I got addicted to Starbucks shots while I was there.

Less welcome than unlimited fast food and good coffee were the pitches from firms trying to sell things—big things—to young Marines who would probably be coming home to rather large amounts of cash, at least for them.

*Buy this car and pay no sales tax. Low interest rates!*

Except the rates weren't actually that low.

*Want a Cuban cigar?*

It's fake, but you can buy as many as you want.

*Why not buy some Dinars, Iraqi money? It's cheap now; hold on to it and come back in a year or so, and it'll be worth a fortune.*

Right. Take a look outside the wire and tell me how much change you expect to see in a year. Or a decade.

Night watch was interesting. Not interesting as in dangerous, just . . . illuminating.

We took turns pulling security in our own hut area. For the first time, we could hear people's nightmares. We were letting our guard down and things were creeping into our dreams.

Me as a kid, flaunting my Mexican ranch-country upbringing.

My mom,
Elisa Gallego,
and me in 2005.
*Courtesy of my sister,
Alejandra Gallego.*

You gotta get vax'd if you want to fight. With my fellow Marines, (LEFT TO RIGHT) Gilbert Miera, me, Jonathan Grant, and Cheston Bailon.
*Courtesy of Lima Company. At end of the deployment, most of the survivors of Lima shared our photos, in effect binding all our memories together as we had our lives. We share these photos back and forth to this day. Photos credited to Lima come from that common pool.*

Phillip Jolly and Andrew Britten on patrol. We tend to think of Iraq as a desert, and much of it is. But many of our operations brought us to cities along the Euphrates, lush with plant life. *Courtesy of Lima.*

Part of my squad, standing above Haditha Dam, which we called home during our deployment. (TOP ROW) Peter Batchelder, Brent McKitrick, Gerald Norris, Andrew Britten, me, Cody Inman, Phillip Jolly. (BOTTOM ROW) Gilbert Miera, Chris "Doc" Robinson (our corpsman), Nicholas Hawkey, Patrick Griffin.
*Courtesy of Lima.*

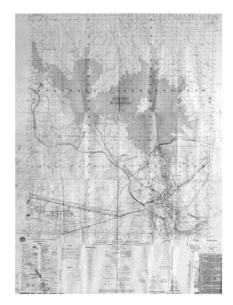

Our main area of operations in al Anbar Province. Haditha Dam is at the bottom right-hand corner of the lake; most of our early missions were along the Euphrates. Today the map hangs in my den at home.

On patrol, early in our deployment.
*Courtesy of Lima.*

Batchelder and me in the market area of Hit. Daily life went on despite the war. The fact that there were many people in the streets was actually a comforting sign; the terrorists were less likely to attack. *Courtesy of Lima.*

Sitting in a trac with Stuart Wilson and a combat engineer named Eisenstein assigned to us for the mission. *Courtesy of Lima.*

Marine Corp's AAVP-7A1s, generally known to us as amtracs or just plain tracs, were our main mode of transportation in-theater. *Courtesy of Lima.*

CH-53s got us to the battlefield faster, but I was always leery—an infantryman wants to be on the ground where he can fight, not in the air where he's a target.
*Courtesy of Lima.*

Hookahs provided a different take on smoking, thanks to the Iraqi National Guardsmen, who encouraged me to try. I can't say I really enjoyed the experience, though it wasn't quite as hair-raising as the photo makes it seem.
*Courtesy of Lima.*

Andrew Taylor deserves the highest medal possible for obtaining an immense case of cigars for the men. Between the smokes and the fruits of Operation Teddy Bear, the dam was a bit of heaven . . . for a night or two. *Courtesy of Sergeant James McCauley.*

(BELOW) Aside from fatigue, thirst was a constant companion while patrolling. Water bottles were nearly as important as rifles. Andrew Taylor (SECOND FROM LEFT), Sajjad Rizvi, and Aaron Reynolds sit in the middle of some of the "replacement" Marines who joined us toward the end of our deployment. *Courtesy of Lima.*

(ABOVE) You learn things quickly in combat. Among the most important—take advantage of any opportunity to rest you get. Here we catch a few minutes in waiting for the amtracs to arrive. *Courtesy of Lima.*

Signs would warn Iraqis that they had to stop at our checkpoints. Not everyone paid attention, to our dismay and, on a few occasions, their destruction.
*Courtesy of Lima.*

Not the most artistic graffiti, but it did tell us what a few of the locals thought of us.
*Courtesy of Lima.*

Part of a haul seized during one of our sweeps. Possessing an AK rifle was generally allowed and didn't mean that the owner was an insurgent. Machine guns and grenade launchers were a different story. *Courtesy of Lima.*

Men detained for questioning during an operation in one of the towns east of the Euphrates. At the far right is a child's tricycle; terrorists regularly mixed with civilians, complicating efforts to keep the latter safe. *Courtesy of Lima.*

Hell House in New Ubaydi near al Qa'im. The photo was taken by Sergeant Andrew Taylor after the ambush but before the house's final destruction. Anthony Goodwin died inside the building May 8; Dustin Derga died soon afterwards from his wounds. Their deaths were a turning point for our platoon. *Courtesy of Andrew Taylor.*

Dark smoke billows from a blast of captured armament in Haqlaniyah. While the demolitions experts always handled the tricky stuff, often captured arms or isolated IEDs would be destroyed by whatever means were expedient—a tank's big gun, in this case. *Courtesy of Lima.*

(ABOVE) Heading back after a day in the desert. *Courtesy of Sergeant James McCauley.*

(LEFT) Looking out on Haditha from the school building we occupied. Fortunately, the hole in the window occurred before I got there. *Courtesy of Lima.*

Patrolling on the northern side of the river during Operation Matador. *Courtesy of Lima.*

The deadly explosion on the road to Haditha, August 3, 2005, the worst IED attack of the war. *Public domain, credited to Sergeant James McCauley.*

One of the services for our fallen brothers after the August IED attack.
*Courtesy of Lima.*

(LEFT) A detail from the same service. Helmet, bayonet, empty boots—there is no more mournful a symbol than the Soldier's Cross. *Courtesy of Sergeant James McCauley.*

Our platoon at the end of our deployment in the fall of 2005. *Courtesy of Sergeant James McCauley.*

(ABOVE) Vice President Cheney pins a Purple Heart on Daniel Foot during a ceremony after we returned to the States. To be honest, I didn't go to the ceremony—as much as I liked Foot and the other Marines honored, I didn't feel like listening to Cheney BS about a war he didn't fight himself.

*Courtesy of Lima.*

(LEFT) Goodwin's grave at Arlington, with his favorite smokes and drinks left by Corps brothers. Semper Fi.

My son. From the day he was born in 2017, he has brought me strength, humility, and love. I am proud to say I am a father, Marine, and Congressman.

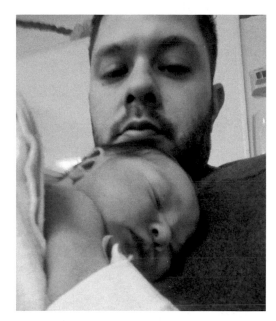

The Gallego family today—Michael, me, and Sydney. *Courtesy of Lauren Comini.*

## THE SERGEANT MAJOR OF THE MARINE CORPS

4 August 2020

To the Marines and Sailors of 3rd Battalion, 25th Marines,

Fifteen years have passed since the warfighters of 3rd Battalion, 25th Marines responded to our Nation's call to fight the Iraqi insurgency. The Battalion's fight in Haditha was the single deadliest deployment for a Marine battalion since that of the Beirut Barracks bombing in 1983.

Today, we remember these Marines and Sailors who proudly self-sacrificed their personal commitments and went forward to push the cause of freedom. They were emblematic of the citizen soldiers who serve as beacons o the community by living the Marine Corps' story of daily service to family, community, and nation.

We honor the Lima Company Marines and Sailors that paid the ultima sacrifice in the preservation of freedom for future generations and live lives worthy of their sacrifice. Mission First, Marines Always!

Semper Fidelis,

TROY E. BLACK
19th Sergeant Major of the Marine Corps

On the fifteenth anniversary of the Haditha attack, the Sergeant Major of the Marine Corps (the highest-ranking enlisted Marine) honored the service of Lima Company, noting that ours was "the single deadliest deployment for a Marine battalion since that of the Beirut Barracks bombing in 1983."

People would yell orders to others, call names—the names of the dead.

A few guys wet their beds. One even ended up sleep walking and peeing on someone's head.

That happened on one of my watches. He was the only guy I woke up during our stay. I got him over to the toilets and got everything cleaned up as best I could. I don't think anybody else knew.

All this made me wonder: *What am I doing in my sleep?*

Fortunately, I never woke to a wet bed. If I talked in my sleep, no one on watch ever let on.

We flew to Kuwait and transferred to a civilian airport. For the first time, we didn't have our own security. We had our guns, but they weren't loaded and we didn't have live ammo. If you want to make a Marine feel impotent, take away his bullets.

I happened to be sitting with Major Braun at the front of the bus taking us over to the airport. As we drove, both of us spotted a car parked on the side of the roadway.

*Suicide vehicle!*

I gripped the seat and held my breath as we passed.

"You felt that, huh?" said the major when we were beyond the vehicle.

"If I had a piece of coal in my ass," I told him, "it'd be a diamond right now."


FOR YEARS, THAT SENSATION—A COMBINATION OF READINESS, FEAR, ANTICIPATION, exasperation—would recur any time I saw anything that would have been a threat in Iraq. It can still surface now, unexpectedly summoned by my subconscious mind for whatever reasons it's privy to. It's a reaction ordered by a part of my brain and body I no longer have control over.

—

I'M GUESSING EVERYONE IN THE COMPANY SLEPT PRETTY WELL ON THE PLANE. I know I did. By the time we landed in Shannon, Ireland, to refuel, everyone was rested and ready to check out the airport facilities.

The bars, basically.

But as we touched down, word came back that only E-6s, or staff sergeants, and above would be able to get off the plane.

That order was quickly changed. The officers decided everyone could get off and have exactly one beer during the two hours we'd be on the ground.

I guess none of us were good at math, because it's doubtful there was any beer left in Ireland when we got back on the airplane. The two hundred or so Marines of Lima Company drank as quickly as the two bartenders on duty could pour.

The first beer never touched my lips, flying directly to my gullet. The second was phenomenal, the coldest, sweetest brew I'd ever had.

Every emotion was on display in that terminal during that layover. Elation, grief, happiness, sorrow—between the alcohol and the release from combat, we were all flooded with feelings we hadn't dealt with in months.

Did we get sloshy drunk? It depends on your definition of sloshy.

After we took off, one of the snipers flying with us made some sort of remark that McKenzie took offense to; he said something back that they disagreed with, and within moments McKenzie and the snipers were taking swings at each other. A couple of guys interceded, probably saving the snipers' lives. They may have been the cream of the crop, but they were no match for McKenzie.

The plane flew on.

When I got off the plane in North Carolina, I realized I'd left my RayBan sunglasses in the terminal. I'd worn them through the entire war, during the worst times, always careful to keep them from harm . . . only to lose them in the easiest of places to watch your stuff.

We were back in the States, but far from home, still technically on active duty. We went to Camp Lejeune to deal with paperwork for a few days. That gave us a lot of time to train . . . on drinking.

We hit the strip clubs, pizza parlors, and bars. I'd lost some thirty-five pounds in Iraq. I probably gained half of it back that week. One night we all went out for drinks. My friends got me drunk—not hard to do at that point—and they took me to a tattoo parlor.

For some reason, the place was closed. So I never got a tattoo. A good thing, because I probably would have ended up a walking cliché—"Mom" on one arm, a Marine bulldog on the other.

My left knee had gradually gotten worse during the deployment. It had become legendary among my platoon. Marines would ask to see it wondering how I could still hump. I was taking non-prescription painkillers like candy. With time to myself now, I went to see the doc.

He grimaced.

"You're going to have to get that fixed." The cartilage between my tibia and femur was now gone, and the bones were fusing with the knee cap. I hobbled out of there, feeling even worse than I had when I'd come in. But I soon cheered up—once I was past the stress of combat, I was certain it would take care of itself.

Wishful thinking like that rarely works. Neither did the prescription painkillers I tried after my knee operation before hearing horror stories about guys getting addicted. Rehab was a bitch, but at least I don't hobble around like an old man.

Not yet, anyway.

AT LEJEUNE, THEY MADE US GO THROUGH A PROGRAM DESIGNED TO HELP US TRANsition to civilian life. It started with lessons in how to write a résumé and progressed to dealing with family issues. None of it went very deep.

*Don't get mad if your wife got fatter. That happens.*
Followed by:
*Don't get mad if your wife got skinnier. That happens.*
And inevitably:
*Don't get mad if your wife looks the same. That happens.*

Not that issues weren't there—they certainly were. Stress over family situations is epidemic among fighters back from the front. But the program came no closer to giving us tools to deal with problems than Rumsfeld had come to giving us adequate armor.

They did mention PTSD, but fairly obliquely:

*If you need any help, you know, somebody to talk to, make sure to reach out to your battle buddy. The VA is there to help . . .*

Oddly, I think the idea that a lot of servicepeople *would* experience PTSD from the occupation hadn't really taken hold. I associated it with the Vietnam era, not ours, and I'm guessing a lot of other guys did as well.

We had a few celebs say hello and welcome us back. The "biggest" was Vice President Dick Cheney.

I'm not sure what he said. I blew it off and didn't go. I can't remember how I worked that, but I was damn glad I did.

Why?

This asshole pushed us into a war that we didn't need and then didn't get us the armor that we did need. My tour in Iraq had made it clear that he really didn't care about the guys on the line doing all the actual fighting and most of the dying.

It wasn't just that my cynicism had grown; my understanding of reality did as well. And the reality was this: not only was the war a mistake, but they had no real plan for it. They had no real plan for the occupation. They didn't know how to stabilize the country. They just kept sending guys out to die in lieu of a plan. Young boys dying for old men's folly.

I was bitter, but it was an earned bitterness. I learned to see the war now in terms of my guys keeping me alive, instead of the glorified ideas of saving the world, protecting the United States against bad guys, or even nation building.

Nation building: in the beginning I would make an effort to talk to Iraqis, even play with the kids. By the end, that was gone. I wasn't going to be mean to the Iraqis; I just didn't care. I didn't believe in nation building. The important thing was surviving.

AS A CONGRESSMAN, I SERVE WITH CHENEY'S DAUGHTER. WE'VE NEVER TALKED about the war, or her father's role in it. There's no value in it. And once you start down that road, what are you going to say, anyway? Nothing of value.

My thoughts on war have evolved since Iraq, but my knowledge of its reality has stayed stubbornly fixed. The reality of war is that the guys on the line quickly come to think of it as simply: Stay alive, keep your friends alive. Try and keep some level of sanity, dignity, and humanity.

As for the rest of us, we have a duty not just to understand the ugliness of war, but to think of its context, implications, and effects on those who fight it. If your country goes to war, make sure it goes for the right reasons—actually preserving freedom, protecting our country, liberating people from a horrible situation. Equally important, make sure the men and women actually fighting have the equipment they need to do that successfully.

## THE PLANS GOD HAS

After we'd spent a few days in North Carolina, the Corps organized our trip home. The guys from Ohio were given buses. That didn't seem all that great, until we heard the stories about how people lined up on the highways and streets to welcome them home.

I've seen the video footage of their rides and some of the news pieces. The outpouring of emotions was stupendous.

The media had done a number of stories on 3/25 after Matador, talking to families and others in the community. Deep-felt grief mixed with patriotism and pride. People appreciated the sacrifices and difficulties we'd been through, even if they'd been given only a small glimpse.

Let me recognize, though, that news stories can't fully communicate the grief of those who lost family members—mothers who had to find a way to push on without their husbands, parents who would miss their sons and their families at the holidays. The hoopla has to fade, and at some point the only thing left is loss—opportunities gone, love missed.

Those of us from New Mexico were hearing the stories of our brothers' celebratory homecoming while we contemplated the ping-pong connections we had to navigate to get across the country. They made us a little jealous, knowing we weren't going to get that sort of reception—there weren't enough of us, and a lot of people in New Mexico didn't realize we had been assigned to 3/25. We weren't big news for the local media.

I for one didn't feel like I was a conquering hero, returning home. I certainly wasn't a hero. And I hadn't conquered anything, not really.

I'd fought and been lucky. Being alive when my best friend had died was my prize.

Which isn't to say we didn't have our moments. The flight attendant on the last leg to Albuquerque gave me her phone number. I never used it, but it's the thought that counts.

Thinking about my homecoming while I'd been in Iraq, I'd pictured happy scenes—crying, kidding, hugging Kate and my mom. Instead, walking into the auditorium of our training center, I felt a bit stunned. I genuinely missed Kate and Mom and the rest of my family, but it didn't feel like I was coming home.

For one thing, Grant wasn't there. I'd always imagined walking through that door with my best friend next to me.

And I wasn't the person who'd left New Mexico. I didn't know all the changes that I'd gone through, what they might lead to, what they cut off, but I did know I was a very different man than I'd been a year before.

I slept-walked through our hugs and kisses; I stood in a static fuzz during a brief memorial service for our fallen. I went to Kate's parents' house where I was temporarily staying, had dinner with the family, then went out gambling.

I played roulette with my numbers—7, 11, 3, 25, and 20—variations on my birthday, my unit, and the number of times I escaped death.

Maybe I had some luck left after all. I won two thousand dollars before cashing out.

## GOD'S CHOICES

Kate and my mom had to go back to work the next day, my mom to California and Kate to Arizona. I had to report back to our training center in a few days, but otherwise had nothing really pressing, so I decided to visit Grant.

I put some things in the car and drove up to the Santa Fe Memorial Veterans National Cemetery, roughly an hour by car. It's a classic military cemetery, with rows of simple markers over veterans' tombs. Somber, but very correct.

I stopped at a motel first, getting a room. On the way out, I stopped in the gift shop and grabbed a pack of Skittles for him.

His grave was fresh, the stone bright white, chiseled letters crisp. I dropped to my knees and told him I was sorry. So very sorry.

It was the first time I'd talked to him in months. I'd never had a chance to say good-bye. I apologized for that. And for not bringing him back.

"If I could have switched places, I would have," I said. "I promise I'll be a good man, and make my life worth living."

*It's fine, Ruben. Everything's fine.*

I felt his hug. Heard his laugh. Because of course he would laugh. Of course he would tell me to go on.

I left the Skittles with him and walked back to the car.

THE NEXT DAY, I DROVE PAST THE MOUNTAINS WHERE WE USED TO TRAIN, REMEMbering how Grant pushed to get me in shape. Every word of encouragement, every mocking joke, every "Come on, Marine."

I heard them all again. They were still echoing somewhere in my consciousness as I drove up the road to the sanctuary at Chimayo to return the sand I'd taken with me to Iraq. It had helped me get through seven months of hell; now it was someone else's turn to trust its luck.

The roads narrowed as I drove. The day had grown quiet. The threads of thoughts trampling through my head disintegrated; only the immediate present remained.

Inside the sanctuary building, I knelt and bowed my head to pray.

I asked for forgiveness. I don't know why; I just felt I needed to. I had an overwhelming sense of guilt—*Why am I the one who lived?*

I emptied the dirt back into the small hole that is said to refill itself, hoping that the sand I added from Iraq wouldn't break the spell.

*There must be a God for all of this to have happened, for me to have survived so many times. And yet, how could that make sense? How could I have been chosen? And what god would allow Grant and the others, whose lives were so much more valuable than mine, to die while keeping me alive?*

It was and remains my knotted conundrum, questions that can never be answered in this life, not by me.

"Thank you," I told God or whatever spirits controlled the site and had parceled out luck to me. "I am going to make my own luck now."

## A MARINE APPROACH TO POLITICS

There was nothing for me in New Mexico now but the ghosts of plans that should have been. My job was gone, Kate was in Arizona, and I saw no reason to stay.

We were still going to live together, still imagined a future together. That hadn't changed. So the logical thing was to move to Phoenix.

I lazed around for a few days. A friend of mine who was a Navy veteran recommended I join American Legion Post 41. I think he thought sooner or later I'd need some sort of help, and there was a good network of people there. I'm sure I didn't think I'd need help, but I'm a social guy, and being with people with similar backgrounds and interests appealed to me. Besides, it was a nice place to hang out and get to know people.

Post 41 had been started years before by Latinos who felt shut out of other posts dominated by whites; it included a lot of guys who worked for the city and in general had experience dealing with veterans' issues by referring guys to different services and possible jobs.

A couple suggested job possibilities and offered to help with interviews, but the truth is I didn't feel like working quite yet. I did a few job interviews, but my situation and résumé confused prospective employers.

*You went to Harvard?*

Yes.

*You joined the Marine Corps and went to Iraq?*
Yes.
*But you're not an officer?*
No.

I couldn't blame them—it was unusual. Maybe they figured I did something wrong and was made an enlisted guy as punishment.

I applied to a bank management program, thinking maybe I would work my way up into management. Somehow the fact that I didn't have a finance or business degree trumped my actual education and experience. I told them I could take finance classes at night, but that didn't make an impression. Neither did my leadership experience in the fireteam in Iraq. You'd think getting shot at would prepare you for banking, at least on the retail side, but apparently not.

I was still a Marine, still part of the Reserves. I'd given some thought to re-upping, but a succession of just petty little incidents turned me off to remaining. I joined a unit in Arizona and did my time as a bulk fueler—I had to accept whatever MOS or job was available—and worked as a reservist until August. Because of their specialty—they take care of airbases—the guys in the unit had never received full infantry training, let alone had any combat experience. So I held informal classes and workshops, brain-dumping some of my experiences on them.

They weren't the only ones. In 2006, I heard Bravo One Two Five—my old New England unit—had been activated and would be heading to Iraq shortly. Just as we had, they were training at 29 Palms, about a two-and-a-half-hour drive from my home in Arizona. I threw a lot of my old gear—tourniquets, webbing, bullet magazines—into the car and headed over.

I told them some of what we'd encountered, and gave them the gear, explaining why things were valuable. Like the H&K magazine boxes I donated, which tended to jam far less than the standard issue. We talked about the interpreters, missions, hell houses, and the like.

We went to a bar, and of course there was a bar fight with some of the other patrons. Some things are mandatory before seeing combat.

THERE WERE SOME FUN TIMES–OR AT LEAST INTERESTING ONES. A MARINE FRIEND of mine wanted to move to Connecticut to go to school, and I offered to drive with him there. Along the way we stopped in New York City—the second time in my life I'd ever been there. We went to a bar and drank for a while. I lost track of him for a bit; when he came back, he told me he'd befriended a guy who knew about an after-hours strip club we had to check out.

"I don't know," I said. "Sounds sketchy."

"We have to go. It's legit. And I gave the guy my wallet."

"What! Where is he?"

The guy was waiting outside. He was a big Italian-looking fellow, obviously a local, and definitely a fast talker. I stopped him mid-pitch.

"Why do you need our wallets?" I demanded.

The guy gave a story about wanting to make sure we weren't narcs.

"Give him back his wallet," I said.

"I have a phone call," said our erstwhile guide to the slimy side of New York.

Before we could grab him, the guy turned and took off. I started running for him but tripped; when I looked up, he was gone, and so was my friend's wallet.

I ended up driving him to the Groton area and helping him get settled. A few years later I returned to the area, where he was still going to school.

"Let's go get a drink," I said, suggesting a nearby bar I'd passed.

"Can't. I'm banned from there."

I named another.

"Can't go in there either."

"What about—"

"Nope."

It turned out he was banned from just about every place in town. I'm not sure what you have to do to get banned in a place where they deal with submariners all the time, but whatever it was, he did it.

Marines.

## A REAL JOB

Before the war, I'd still hoped to eventually work for the State Department. Now, though, that career didn't seem enticing.

I was so mad about the war, I didn't particularly want to work for the government. And I was tired of moving around. My life fit into two seabags in the back of my beat-up 1998 Jeep Cherokee.

I found a job with a marketing and advertising firm in March 2006 by sheer chance. I was volunteering at a charity event as a waiter. I started talking with the brother of a friend of Kate's named Joe Yuhas. He'd just started the agency's branch in Phoenix.

They were new and young, and wanted someone who could help with Hispanic and Latino cultural issues. My background with political campaigns—which they wanted to get involved with—helped, though I didn't want to be in politics. That ended up being the agreement—I would do some political work for them, but I would do other things.

Some of the simplest things can mess you up in advertising, or at least make the work less effective, if you are not fully aware of the culture you're pitching to. For example, you wouldn't want to inadvertently diss the idea of a large, extended family with an audience that puts a heavy value on that. Inversely, you would want to celebrate things that have a positive connotation—that big family with all the uncles and aunts and grandparents and kids, say— when you are selling a product.

Common sense if you've grown up in a certain milieu, odd maybe if you haven't.

We were sitting in a meeting one day about pitching a specific salsa.

"Better than your mom's salsa," said one of the creatives.

"Never say that," I told them. "That's an insult. It'll turn people off to the product."

Easy stuff. And they paid me.

My next job was working for a city councilman.

The agency was helping a candidate for council running against the daughter of a popular congressman. She had more money, name recognition, and I think everyone in the city assumed she was going to walk into the job.

Everyone except him and me.

He had a huge family with a lot of young adults who wanted to help. I organized them into fireteams and laid out our plan of attack. It's too hot to walk door to door in Arizona in the middle of the summer when it gets to 115 degrees; you're exhausted very quickly. But that is also the most effective way to win a race. So I had each team organize around a vehicle, with a driver—vehicle commander—and three guys or gals. They'd jump out and hit doors, then come back for water and air-conditioning.

Meanwhile, the vehicle commander would relay data back— who was home, what sort of reception we were getting, etc. I could use that information to refine our approach and follow-ups. Our small, disciplined teams were able to adapt quickly to changing circumstances.

Politics meets Marine organization—hard to beat.

The other campaign relied strictly on mail and TV. They didn't have contact with the actual voters. We won what was considered one of the biggest upsets in the city's history.

My candidate was grateful, but he had a problem. Being a city council member in Arizona's largest city (and the sixth biggest in the U.S.) is a very serious job; he needed a staff, and someone to run it.

"Want to be chief of staff?" he asked.

It didn't take much persuasion. I didn't know what chief of staff was, but I was sure I could figure it out. I left the PR agency and went to work for the government.

When I got to New Mexico, I stopped using the last name, Marinelarena, I'd been given at birth. Part of the reason was that I felt like I was starting new, erasing or at least stepping away from the past.

The bigger reason was that I didn't want to be associated with my father, even symbolically. I was ashamed of his crimes, and angry at him for abandoning us.

I didn't want to hold on to the ghosts of my past, but I also wanted to honor the people who had supported me as I grew—my mom, my maternal grandparents. So I chose Gallego, my mother's maiden name. I waited until I was done with Marine service so it wouldn't be too complicated, but once my time was up, I filed in court and officially became a Gallego.

A few years later, political opponents would try to make an issue of the name change. I'd been pretty upfront about it though, and whatever political capital they hoped to gain didn't pan out for them.

## WOUNDS OF WAR

When I first got back, I had a temper.

I'd never lost my cool before the war. Now I did, snapping and yelling at people for little reason. Especially for people not taking things seriously—projects or deadlines. It continued for several years. Later on, I yelled at a staffer for not doing something for a councilmember. She started arguing with me—I yelled back and slammed my hand on a table.

It became a story in the newspaper.

Humorous under other circumstances, I guess. Politically motivated, maybe. But serious enough that I ended up being investigated for harassment—not sexual harassment, just plain old harassment. I was cleared.

Still, to me, things were different. I shouldn't be, and am not, a guy who loses his cool.

It shouldn't bother me that other people don't take things seriously. Or it can bother me—it does bother me—but not to the point where I lose my cool.

But after the war, everything was serious to me. And people not being serious bothered me immensely.

The problem was me. After six months of having a real achievement—surviving every day—coming back to "normal" life was disorienting. The goals were nebulous, the relationships far less intense, and therefore less meaningful.

I hated cars that were too close on the road. Trash on the side of the highway made me nervous. A car following me too close might make me miss a stop or accelerate off a ramp at the last moment.

I always wanted to be the driver, though. Sitting on the passenger side of a car gave me too much time to look around and see threats. Driving close to a curb would unnerve me; I expected IEDs to go off. If I had to be a passenger, I would try anything to distract myself—read on my phone, anything to not pay attention.

But it was impossible not to pay attention.

What else?

I was drinking a lot. When I was busy, I was fine. After work, I would always go out and have a drink.

I couldn't stay in the same place for very long—a chair, the house. When I went out to a restaurant, I could only spend a small amount of time there.

Stay too long in one place, and you're going to get mortared.

I'd check out the place, just to know where the enemy might come from.

And I had dreams. Different bits of the war coming at me. I don't remember most—probably a good thing.

When I first got back, Kate found me on the patio of our apartment staring out.

"What are you doing?" she asked.

"I'm on my watch."

I was sleeping.

It weirded her out—how could it not? She took me inside and put me back to bed.

I had to buy a gun. I was so used to having my rifle around me, that when they took it away from me, it was like losing a limb. I bought a 9 mm pistol. I didn't get it to do anything but to feel whole. I can't even say I was scared to be unarmed—I was unsettled but not scared.

Other guys from Lima went through some similar things. I didn't keep in touch with everyone. I wasn't that active then on social media. But I did remain close with the Bailon brothers. And McKenzie, when he started reaching out, calling to talk and clearly distressed. Friendships with some of the other guys were more slow simmering. Hurley would spend vacations in Arizona. Taylor, when I was back east for vacations. Norris—man, what a Las Vegas wedding he had. Others, when they were in town or we saw each other on Facebook.

I got real busy in my job. When I was really busy, things seemed better. As long as I was focused on things, not brooding about the past, I was a lot better—or maybe I just presented a lot better.

People have different addictions. My addiction was work, which I equated with success.

Part of me was always that way. That's how I got into Harvard. But now it was in overdrive.

## FROM STAFF TO STATE HOUSE

Public service doesn't actually pay that much, but I hadn't been making huge money at the PR firm, and the council job paid more. I also knew that I didn't want to be a political consultant—let's face it, you end up working for a lot of politicians who, candidly, are dopes.

There was something else. I felt like I was falling behind. I wasn't far along a career path. I wasn't earning what a Harvard grad should.

I'm describing my feelings, not necessarily external realities.

A lot of the people I'd gone to college with were well advanced in careers. I was still more or less kicking around, with no real direction. Getting into government seemed more like a focus and possible growth path than the PR firm.

City government proved to be a whole new challenge, with plenty of new things to learn. My curiosity was stoked, and stoked me in turn. At the same time, we had a chance to actually impact people's lives in a very real way. Zoning issues. Making sure trash got picked up.

Trivial, unless it's your garbage and it's been a month since it was hauled away.

For a twenty-seven-year-old, it was a heady challenge. I loved it all. I could see results, rather than helping people get into positions where they could get results.

Or not get results. We *are* talking about politics.

One of the coolest things I did was help a community that had been neglected establish a citizens' crime watch after a young woman was shot by a gang member. The only opposition to that came from the local gangs, who tried to intimidate us by following us around and training cameras on us.

*Cameras. Really?*

*Come on, boys. You're going to have to go further than that.*

Maybe even if they'd been guns, the threat wouldn't have seemed too dire. Since I'd gotten home, no crisis here was really a crisis to me. It frustrated Kate. It would sound to her as if I were blowing off her concerns, or her bad day. I didn't do it with intent; I just had a different context now. Stuck in a traffic jam for hours? That was nothing compared to watching a trac burn.

I WAS CHIEF OF STAFF FOR TWO YEARS. BEYOND MY EVERYDAY JOB HELPING MY councilmember, I spent time trying to encourage people to run against the established old guard in the city and the state. Like a lot of younger people, I felt we needed new energy, new ways of seeing and doing things.

One day, trying to persuade a prospective candidate to run for state representative in a particularly difficult area, the candidate turned to me and said, "Why don't you run?"

*Good question.*

I thought about it, and decided he was right. I should run.

So I did. I had to quit my job to avoid conflicts of interest, which meant giving up my pay. That took some security away. But it also raised the stakes and made me work harder.

Had that come from being in the service? Probably not originally, but the intensity of being "all in" on something with high stakes was pretty familiar. The Marines had honed that. I wasn't sleeping with my boots on and my rifle nearby, but I was thinking about the election 24/7. And pushing myself every second.

There was plenty to think about. My name recognition was close to zero, and I had no money for a campaign. The district was heavily Democratic—so much so that the primary was the real challenge. Many voters not only didn't realize how important the primary was, they didn't know that there was one.

I attacked it like a military operation. I set objectives, knocked them off one by one.

I began with fundraising. By the time of the primary, I had raised more money for state representative than anyone except the Arizona speaker of the house. I organized a door-to-door campaign similar to the one I'd used for the councilman. We digitized our tracking and information system, giving us instant information to help guide the effort. Instant intel that we could operationalize, something missing from the battlefield in Iraq.

We knew we were doing very well when my opponent recruited other candidates to join the race. The idea was to dilute my support. (Two representatives would be selected from the district, and voters could choose two on their ballot.) You couldn't vote for me twice, so everyone who voted for me and then added another name to the ballot, was effectively voting against me.

It didn't work. We went door-to-door. I talked to people. We signed up eight thousand new voters. I came in first in the district.

I WAS IMPATIENT. MY FIRST REACTION ON GETTING TO THE STATE HOUSE AND SEEing how things ran . . .

*This is fucked up.*

As a Marine grunt, I couldn't do anything to effect change. If I'd been in command, in leadership, I might have made some small differences. But I'd seen good leaders—Hurley came immediately to mind—who while they made a big difference to us, had no real effect on the overall system, let alone the shape of the war.

I wasn't in the Marines now. I wasn't just a grunt. I worked my way to a leadership position by my second term.

I made mistakes. I was way too rough around the edges, bruising egos on the way. I could've, and should've, done better. But we did get some things done.

The Democrats were in the minority and had little chance to get most of their bills passed. Nonetheless, some of our ideas made it into law. I'm most proud of a measure that gave all veterans in-state tuition to state schools, which was passed with the help of GOP members of the House. We think that more than nine thousand veterans have used the program, moving to Arizona and immediately getting tuition to go to school. I imagine most of them are still Arizona residents and contributing to our economy and tax base.

Probably voting against me, but who cares.

The other big accomplishment was Medicaid expansion. We had a huge budget deficit at the time—something that accepting the Medicaid expansion and Obamacare would help solve.

It took a bit of chicanery to get it done. Not quite on the level of Operation Teddy Bear, but in that direction. First, though, I had to convince my fellow Democrats not to go out and blast the GOP as negotiations bogged down. Their criticisms were right—but going public so forcefully would have killed any possibility of an agreement. One caucus meeting grew so heated I had to throw myself in front of the door to keep members from rushing out and talking to the media.

I managed to calm down the caucus by explaining the situation. The Republican House majority was opposed to the measure—but some Republicans would in fact vote for it, if we could arrange for a vote. Meanwhile the governor, though also a Republican, was in favor—but couldn't get past the speaker of the house.

Knowing that she couldn't get him to bring the measure up or a majority of her party's representatives to override him on the floor, she hatched a plan to detour around him with our votes. This was possible due to a quirk in state law and the legislature rules, which would allow us to form a quorum and appoint a temporary speaker during a special session. All the governor had to do was call that special session when the speaker and most Republicans were out of town; we'd meet, ram the vote through, and adjourn.

The key was getting them to leave town. Which wouldn't happen if they knew what was up.

So we hid out. In twos and threes, members hid in the darkened halls of the lower capitol, or snuck away and went firm nearby. Figuring we had all gone home, the Republicans did as well.

The governor called for the session, we showed up, took over, and passed the legislation. She signed it, and then we left.

The GOP cried foul, and tried a number of maneuvers to overturn the bill. They failed. Many of their constituents were saved by the better medical care the law provided, and the budget was filed without the extreme cuts that would have been the only alternative. A number of hospitals would have closed if the measure hadn't passed. Four hundred thousand people got coverage who wouldn't have had it.

## SEVEN-YEAR ITCH

Kate and I had been together for almost seven years when I asked her to marry me.

What was I waiting for? I'd been so focused on my career, and still unsettled from the war.

For so many reasons, marriage made a lot of sense. I value stability; marriage promises it. We were both approaching thirty. We were used to each other; we got along well. We'd both made a number of personal sacrifices that demonstrate love—she waited for me while I was in Iraq, afraid for me every day. She'd endured my nightmares, my blank spots, my irrational fears on the road and in restaurants.

And I loved her. And she loved me. So it made perfect, logical sense. It was the next thing to do.

So I decided to propose. But of course I decided I had to go the extra mile.

We were both attending the 2008 Democratic Convention as volunteers for the Obama campaign. I was in charge of the Obama delegates on the floor. I got some of the volunteers and staffers to add a second sign on the back of their Obama signs with the words *"Will You Marry Me?"*

After Hillary Clinton gave her speech, I signaled the team to switch from the regular signs to the special ones. Kate turned around just in time to see the signs.

I pulled out the ring.

"Will you marry me?" I asked.

"Yes! Of course!"

Call it kitschy and lame—I have. But it felt romantic at the time.

We got married in 2010. We were busy, and I'm a procrastinator.

It was a rooftop wedding. Great crowd, great music, lovely bride—everyone had a great time.

Then we went back to the life we'd known, both of us very busy. I was working my way up in government. She got accepted to an MBA program. We kept growing career-wise, but maybe not emotionally.

I became more and more insular and closed, even with her. I had plenty of friends and acquaintances, work contacts and the like, but the truth was I really didn't have very deep relationships with anyone.

Kate shocked me after she graduated business school by saying she wanted to run for city council. Not that I was going to stand in her way, but it seemed like a very different direction than she had started to take with the MBA.

Outsiders saw us as the ultimate political power couple. In fact, her decision caused a heck of a lot of political mayhem and complications for me. It wasn't a give-me election. She was a white Jewish woman running in a traditionally black area. Unknown, and not a member of the political old-line.

She won.

I knew she would. That's Kate.

# ELEVEN IS MY FAVORITE NUMBER

## McKENZIE

I tried to convince McKenzie to move to Arizona, closer to me, where maybe I could help him better, more consistently. I found housing for him, but understandably he wanted to stay closer to his family.

He had a horrible time for many years.

I did, too. It was strange. I was achieving, moving up politically, yet feeling more and more . . . unbalanced I guess is the word. I cut contact with a lot of people from Lima. I couldn't be much help to McKenzie anymore because I was going through my own black period. It was as if I was in my own quicksand.

In retrospect, I must have realized I couldn't take care of him and myself. I had to save myself first—kind of like what they say on airplanes—fix your own oxygen mask first.

I stopped talking to him because I was close to breaking myself. I needed to stop my own slide, and so I cut him and the other guys from Lima off.

## CONGRESS

I made the decision to run for Congress not more than ten minutes after the incumbent announced that he wasn't running.

I'd never thought about running for Congress before, but now I was in election mode.

The incumbent's announcement was relatively late in the election cycle—less than six months before a possible primary. I think the timing was meant to help a specific candidate who was in the state senate. On the other hand, the shortened time frame helped me as well, since it meant there wouldn't be a lot of other opponents. I could focus my efforts.

Why run? I'd never really given much thought to becoming a congressman, but it was the obvious next step in a political career, the next rung in the ladder I'd climbed. Political analysts would look at it and say, *of course*.

Not that it would be an easy climb. There was not a lot of overlap between my representative district and the congressional district; maybe about a quarter of my area was in the congressional district, so there were a lot of voters who really didn't know me.

In war, hesitation kills. The same in politics. I started raising money right away and assembling a campaign team. I resigned my leadership position—you should have seen the stunned faces in the caucus room—and within an hour or two I headed to D.C. to talk to unions and other potential backers. I called every friend I had and asked for their help. My immediate goal was more defense than offense—I knew the outgoing incumbent would back my opponent, and was likely to pressure people to support her. By heading this off as best I could, I hoped to at least neutralize his efforts. I wanted people not to help my opponent, even if they wouldn't help me. Neutrality would make things more even, and in that way benefit me.

Back in Arizona, my campaign canvassing flew into high gear.

It helped that my opponent, though she was a county supervisor, hadn't faced a difficult campaign in quite a while, and her election operation had ossified.

A poll in June, about two months from the primary, showed me ahead.

My opponent tried to go negative. One of the big issues was my vote in favor of allowing hunters to use standard-sized magazines rather than ones limited to five rounds—not popular in the heavily Democratic and progressive city area. Another was my support for adding automobiles to the law allowing people to defend their own homes if attacked; it was meant to help a person in the rare case he or she shot someone trying to carjack them.

My opponent painted me as a blood-thirsty, gun-happy crazy man.

Didn't work.

And so I won.

Congress was exciting, frustrating, and a learning experience. It took me a while to learn that you can get things done, you can have an influence—even as a junior member—but you have to accept that you often won't get credit for what you get done.

Measures are folded into larger bills that don't have your name attached, at least not prominently. And you have to work through your committee and caucus. The Armed Services committee, which I sit on, is a great committee, but it passes basically one bill per year, and that's the big defense budget. So if you want to do anything related to the services, it will go into that one big bill, where basically no one sees it. You don't get credit for passing the defense budget. Nobody gets to own it.

The rancor and over-the-top vicious partisanship that's so much a part of national politics these days didn't really affect me that much. The good thing about being from Arizona is that I was already used to everyone being hyper partisan and divisive. I realized I wasn't going to change that. Members are just stuck in their ways, I guess.

Still, my biggest disappointment is how much of a scam some things are, and how people just play along. For example, when Paul Ryan was Speaker, he would often say things like, "Oh, don't worry, we're going to work on XYZ issue eventually." The press would play along, saying he's going to take it up. But then—well look at DACA, the Deferred Action for Childhood Arrivals—a policy that *could* give children born to undocumented immigrants a way to gain citizenship. There are over a million people potentially affected. Congress has a responsibility to do something for those people, rather than leaving them in, at best, a gray area short of citizenship. For all his good words, Ryan never took any concrete steps to fix DACA. I doubt he ever had any intention of doing so.

That's just one example. There are many issues where leaders in Congress say, "we're going to take care of that." The media quotes them and the public believes something is going to be done, but no, nothing happens.

And the attitude among too many of my colleagues is, yeah, we know, but who cares?

That hypocrisy is one reason that government moves so slowly. Then, as time drags on, frustration multiplies. People with real problems grow disillusioned. The situation festers; the problem is viewed as unsolvable. It's a terrible, unproductive cycle.

## TONGO TONGO AND IRAN

My experiences as a Marine rarely come into play in Congress. But they do give me a perspective.

In 2017, a Special Forces unit was badly mauled in an ambush in Niger. The first reports were very sketchy, but it was obvious to me that there were numerous problems not only with the mission but with what the Army was saying about it.

Briefly put, the Americans were working with a Nigerien force fighting against Islamic militants known as the Islamic State in the Greater Sahara, an ISIS-affiliated or ISIS-inspired group whose ultimate goal is to impose an extreme Islamic state on the area.

An A Team of Army Special Forces troops working with a Nigerien force of about thirty-five were sent to apprehend a militant leader in the area of Tiloa in western Niger. After failing to locate the militants, the unit started back for its base. New intelligence arrived, and the mission changed; the Americans and Nigerien troops went to a new area near the Mali border, apparently in hopes that they would find the leader nearby. They discovered a hastily abandoned camp. After destroying it, they once more began returning to base.

On the morning of October 4, they arrived at the village of Tongo Tongo, where they stopped to rest and meet with the local leader. The local leader seems to have been working with the militants; instead of the brief stop the Americans intended, they were delayed by the leader and then ambushed shortly after leaving the village.

Four Americans died; two others were wounded. The Nigeriens suffered thirteen casualties, including five dead.

There were numerous problems with the initial accounts, which basically blamed the SF troops for not being trained properly. That in itself is questionable—we're talking about a unit with the highest training level in the Army. The initial reports omitted the fact that the SF troops were not provided with adequate intelligence or the proper firepower and that the SF commander had objected to the meeting with the leader—who had purposely delayed them as part of the ambush plan.

Even without knowing the entire details of the operation, any soldier or Marine familiar with recent combat operations would wonder where their Quick Reaction Force was at the time, and why, given the distances involved, the mission was conducted on the ground rather than by helicopter.

When I heard the initial reports, I knew what we were being told was bullshit. I could tell there hadn't been adequate communications for the Green Berets, and surmised that the weapons and vehicles were not substantial enough for a mission in that hostile an area—and that's just for starters. It brought me back to my service in Iraq.

I was angry with the generals, but even angrier with my congressional colleagues on the Armed Services Committee, who barely took the matter seriously. No one asked the obvious questions about the mission, the intelligence, the poor preparation by Command, and so on.

The administration's official spokespeople were full of BS. And when Donald Trump told the family that one of the men who had been killed "knew what he signed up for," my head nearly exploded.

The soldier signed up for crappy intelligence, poor support, and finger-pointing after obviously flawed decision-making by those above him?

I grilled the generals when they appeared at our hearing.

*Where were the right weapons, the armor, the QRF?*

The answers were . . . inadequate. But at least someone in Congress asked the questions.

The closest I've come to having to vote on something related to war came during discussions on the Iran nuclear deal. To be clear: only the Senate votes on treaties under the Constitution. But in this case, a law passed prior to the agreement gave the House as well as the Senate the right to object to any agreement reached on Iran's nuclear arms program.

As a practical matter, the agreement could only have been blocked with great difficulty and overwhelming numbers. Still, the vote was at least symbolic and would influence public opinion.

Pro-Israel and veterans' groups visited my office often, pushing for me to oppose the measure. I think many of them thought I'd be anti-deal because I'd been an infantryman.

But I'd come to exactly the opposite conclusion. While the agreement fell far short of ideal, and I certainly didn't trust the Iranians, I felt it was the best chance to prevent war.

They brought a veteran in who had been hit by an IED in Iran. He shoved pictures of his wounds in my face.

I don't know what the intention of that was. Was I supposed

to feel guilty that I'd "only" watched numerous friends die, and therefore I would vote against the agreement?

If anything, the Iraq war is a tremendous argument *against* war with Iran, something the agreement was designed to prevent. But they were arguing that the agreement should not be approved. And they were trying to use my service as some sort of lever to get my support.

I was so mad I got up and left the office. I started walking down Capitol Hill and didn't stop until I got to Arlington Cemetery.

I saw my friends buried there, and talked to a few.

Eventually, I went back to work. I voted for the agreement.

I loved being a Marine; I hated the administration of the Corps. The line Marine was a great fighter. Then you had these shithead leaders who didn't do anything.

I still loved America then, and I still love it now. What I hate is the fakeness—the "rah-rah support the troops" BS slogans that don't accompany the will or the money to get them the tools they need.

It's a fake patriotism.

My job as a congressman now is not to be patriotic; it's to ask the tough questions, get the tough answers, and then vote as my conscience dictates. That's true on every issue, but especially the military and war, where lives depend on it.

## PTSD AND "SUCCESS"

Despite being in Congress, despite having a political career that I'm sure others would be envious of, I was still stuck emotionally in a darker space. It wasn't a deep depression but more a hollowness, as if something inside had gone missing or died. The fact that it was vague and really undefined didn't make it any less real.

I knew I had some sort of hangover from the war. At times

I even admitted to myself that I might have some kind of low-level PTSD. I sill drank more than I should. Smoked more than I should. Lost my temper more than I should.

Why didn't I have control over these things?

I had nightmares. I thought about my dead friends. I wondered why I was alive. I couldn't seem to find anything to cheer me up.

I freaked when cars drew too close. I sat in the safest chair in the restaurant or room. I saw danger in shadows constantly. Ten years after the war, my fears remained real.

Yet I was successful. Very successful.

PTSD?

That disorder ruined lives and pushed people to suicide. It was dire, extreme.

Not like what I experienced. What was my problem?

Whenever I had any doubts, I could always come back to the idea of success. I had climbed the ladder of respect and achievement, with accomplishments that were hailed in news stories and applauded by colleagues.

That did not happen if you had PTSD.

The drive to achieve success in life had very early roots. I could trace them to the night I slept on the floor in the apartment my mother had gotten south of Chicago after my father left. Lying there at fourteen I could honestly say that my life sucked—and that I was not going to stand for that.

The idea that I might not be able to succeed troubled me deeply. I was smart, I could plan, I could work hard . . . But what if I failed? What if I worked hard, and didn't get anywhere? What if I weren't successful?

Work hard and get nothing? That was a terrible, unacceptable thought.

As a young teenager, I had flicked despair away and replaced it with anger. I knew I was smarter than most of my classmates, but I was starting ten or fifteen paces behind them. That wasn't fair.

The world wasn't fair. It was the world that was at fault, not me.

Anger was a strong motivator. If the world wasn't fair, I would succeed in spite of it. If there were obstacles, I would overcome them. I was going to plan, work hard to fulfill that plan, and I was going to succeed. That mixture of emotion and intellect—and probably teenage hormones—motivated me through my high school years, at Harvard, even in the Marines. Working through it was socially acceptable. People call it drive.

Yet, for all of that, I was off-kilter. I had all of these things that the outside world called success, yet inside I felt like I had nothing.

It was only around 2017, some twelve years after the war, that I started realizing how deep and empty that hole was. Lightning didn't strike me from above. There was no parting of the clouds, or even a more prosaic moment of recognition brought on by some telltale incident that brought me to self-realization.

I was having arguments with my wife, and I didn't really understand why. We'd had disagreements before but these were just—pointless. They didn't make sense. They were the sort of arguments that you walk away from saying to yourself, why am I feeling this way?

The emptiness and pointless anger gradually increased. Then came a new pressure: the pending birth of my son.

Starting a family raises the stakes for every relationship, and I can't say the disagreements that Kate and I had were unusual. Trying to figure out how we would handle life and work with a baby on-board—what couple hasn't experienced some sort of frustration over those problems?

Yet, they seemed incredibly intense. Maybe because I sensed there was something deeper at play—maybe because I couldn't explain to myself why I was so mad all the time, and why I felt like I had done nothing with my life, I arranged to see a therapist.

Honestly, I thought he would focus me back on my marriage.

He wasn't a marriage counselor, but he did specialize in those sorts of issues from the husband's perspective. The root of my problem, I thought, was probably related to my relationship with my father. That's where the anxiety was. And the counselor would help me figure a way past it.

I wanted to be a good father. I knew my father had been a poor father at least partly because he'd been raised by a poor dad. I wanted to break that cycle.

But our sessions quickly became mostly about the war. Every time we talked, I brought it up. What I'd experienced, the loss of my friends, the constant danger. It didn't take long for the therapist to point out that Iraq was still affecting me. Paranoia in public places, extreme outbursts, feelings of emptiness and despair, unchecked grief—eventually even I had to recognize and admit that, yes, his diagnosis of PTSD did fit.

When you go into a place and the first thing you do is line up your egresses—yeah, that's probably a sign of post-traumatic stress.

You drink to excess—possibly self-medicating for PTSD.

You wake up shaking in the middle of the night because of dreams about your friends dying—could be PTSD.

A general malaise—feeling of worthlessness, unease about everything, light depression—it still hurts to use that word, even in the informal, nondiagnostic sense—and just emptiness—certainly in the realm of PTSD.

Debilitating paranoia about driving too close to the side of the road or being in a crowded place—not necessarily PTSD, but certainly not a sign of perfect mental health.

In my mind, PTSD was this horribly massive ailment, something that took you down—like what McKenzie was suffering. On my worst day, I wasn't him.

Most people with PTSD aren't. They're not in dramatic crisis.

But that doesn't mean they don't suffer from it. It doesn't mean that the decisions they make unconsciously are related to the trauma they experienced years and even decades before.

What I didn't know about PTSD could fill libraries. I didn't realize that researchers believe there is a physical component to it, and that the changes in your nervous and hormonal systems, along with your brain, may alter the way you think. Nor did I know that PTSD could express itself in ways that had nothing to do with trauma itself.

I may have been offered medication during our early session, or maybe the suggestion was there, but I did not and have not taken any. I try to stay away from pharmaceuticals in general. Which is not to say that they don't help people, or that they aren't necessary in specific cases. But I've heard so many horror stories about addictions and side effects, that I think it's better to exist without them if you can.

The counselor gradually helped me understand that extreme cases are not the norm. Given all the deaths we had witnessed, the battles we had been in—I suppose he could have made an argument that *not* having PTSD would have been extreme.

"But I'm so successful," I told him.

Not those words, exactly. But, come on—I was a congressman.

He was patient. Achievements don't mean you don't have an ailment. Being a congressman doesn't keep you from getting the flu.

"What would make you happy?" he asked.

The question stunned me—I didn't have an answer. I hadn't actually considered that. I was chasing things, but not actually enjoying what I caught or achieved.

We talked for a bit more.

"What am I chasing here?" I finally asked.

*A reason to be alive.*

Because I didn't think I deserved to be.

## THE FOREVER FAILURE

I realize that there is great irony in this—a man achieves goals that the rest of the world envies, and yet feels as if he shouldn't even exist.

I also realize that what I am saying can sound perilously close to whining, to complaining about good fortune. The fourteen-year-old kid with tears in his eyes because he had no bed to sleep in every night would be amazed to see me today.

To be clear, I'm not looking for sympathy, or even understanding. I'm trying to translate what are really untranslatable feelings into words.

I'm too much of a control freak to commit suicide, but it was only when I reached this point in my life that I began to truly understand the void McKenzie had been fighting. I had a black hole in the middle of my chest that sucked enthusiasm and energy from every cell in my body. It wasn't the opposite of happiness; it was more a negation of any real emotion, as if my arteries and veins had been torn out at night and replaced with wires and printed circuits.

I kept coming back to this: no matter what I achieved in life, I was already and forever a failure. I had let my best friend die.

My best possible friend, and a number of other men whom I'd been close to, men I should have protected. I'd failed them all.

And if their deaths were beyond my control—that's the sane argument—wasn't that worse?

Because in that case, what right did I have to survive?

God hadn't singled me out. God is fair and just. No god of any religion would choose a man without a family to live when others with families, better men, existed to take his place. It wasn't fair.

Luck?

I'd seen that was an illusion.

That was the mental part. Deeper down, biologically, my body had adapted to the stresses that were no longer relevant in the world I returned to after Iraq. The violence of the war, the days of keeping every part of my body on high alert—all of that physical stuff commanded the pathways of control in my body. Whatever chemistry was involved compounded the emotions of loss, embedding trauma and its after affects in my brain.

Since leaving the war, I'd unconsciously tried to re-create a world that aligned with the world of war. That was a formula for disaster. Or emptiness.

So what should I do?

One thing, obviously, was to recognize what was going on.

I began reexamining my motivations. I realized life isn't a series of boxes to be checked off. A congressman is certainly an important job, but being elected isn't a fulfillment or "success" in and of itself. They don't hand you a jar of happiness when you walk through the door, as impressive as those doors may be.

I started consciously trying to do things that would make me happy. It sounds a little silly, even ridiculously easy, but it was like learning a new way to walk. Rather than feeling obligated to do A, B, and C because they were "required" to take the next step on the ladder, I focused on doing X, Y, and Z because I wanted to do them.

On the job, for example. Veterans issues are important to me, since I am a veteran and know how so many men and women are currently being shortchanged by the system. I want to help them. I want to do that regardless of what others in Congress think. Focusing my energies there was something I did because I wanted to, not because leadership asked.

Native American issues are also important to me. My district does not have a large number of Native Americans, but some of my closest friends, McKenzie and the Bailon brothers, are Navajo. I care about them, and by extension, I care about their issues. Helping them, directly and indirectly, made me happy.

This may not translate into huge, immediate changes. As chairman of a subcommittee on Native American issues, I realized that I had to focus on things that could be done, like improving internet access on reservations. That doesn't seem massive, but it means people can be educated better, people can get jobs and work, people will be more informed about what is going on not only locally but in the country and world in general. Real lives are affected.

Making it easier for Native American veterans—there are a large number—to get help from the VA. Getting running water to places where, believe it or not, it is still nonexistent—those are seemingly small goals with massive impacts. And there are similar issues, for Latinos, who make up a large part of my district, for poor kids and all my constituents, not to mention the rest of America.

I want to help them not because it will help my next election, but because it's what I want to do.

Maybe it's a difference invisible to the outside world. But it's critical to me.

My shift in my personal thinking—cut out the extraneous, don't try and do everything, focus on importance rather than checking boxes—may seem more like common sense than a radical life change. Maybe in the grand scheme of things, it is. But it's helped me do my job better. And made me feel happier at the same time. And I think it's helped other people.

My son, too. Focusing on him, being a great dad—yeah, that makes me happier than anything else in the world.

I'm trying to live my life, not justify my life.

I still have a weird relationship with God. I don't like to think I'm living in a world where He chose me to live rather than Grant.

But if God isn't the one making the choices, it's a scarier world.

I'm not sure if I believe in an eternal life. Sometimes I don't even believe in God.

I come back to Him. I deal with the randomness. I don't pretend to understand it, or God.

## DIAGNOSED

PTSD is not a diagnosis handed out lightly in the VA system. It took roughly three years and a lot of examinations before I was officially "rated" as having the ailment. Some of that delay was due to the fact that I had started dealing with it with my own private therapist, but not all. One of the examiners in my case told me, almost in so many words, that I could not possibly have PTSD since I was successful.

*Only crazy people have PTSD.*

It was surprising to see that VA people had that attitude. And the problems aren't all with the agency. As McKenzie's case shows, the process of being certified eligible for care can be needlessly prolonged by problems originating in the military rather than the VA. We had seen combat years before when McKenzie tried to get help—yet our records had not been updated to include that fact.

*Years.*

How many other people had been discouraged from seeking treatment or help in that time? How many other units and men and women are dealing with the same problems?

Rhetorical questions.

The VA has changed its procedures, making it easier for veterans who lack the proper paperwork. It's at least a step in the right direction.

—

I THINK OF PTSD AS A WEIRD, SYMBIOTIC THING INSIDE ME. LIKE MOST PARASITES, it's generally bad. But it also can help me in unexpected ways—on some level, it helped push me to become a congressman. If you asked fourteen-year-old Ruben if he would be happy being a congressman, having a family, being all that I am—he would have been ecstatic.

It drove and drives other people to very different places. Maybe I was close to following that path, and got lucky. Maybe that's the final piece of luck connected with Iraq.

I don't claim to be "cured." As I understand it, you don't get a "cure." You adapt as best you can in ways that are useful to you and those around you.

Think of it this way: You get the flu or a stomach virus. Your body fights it off. You feel better. Your body, though, has altered its biological systems in the fight. Most of those alterations, time-tested through millennia of evolution, are good—the production of antibodies that fight the disease the next time it comes around. But some of the other products of the disease—maybe a weaker heart, impaired lungs, a tear in your stomach lining—will affect you for a long time, possibly the rest of your life. And while you have biologically adapted to dealing with the disease, you make behavioral or mental adaptations as well: resting more, maybe, or avoiding the restaurant where you got food poisoning.

Not the most perfect metaphor, I know.

One of my most important strategies for dealing with my life now involves simple questions:

*Is what I am doing going to make me happy?*

*What thing on the day's agenda is the thing I should do because I value it, not because it is something to be checked off?*

Simple questions in the abstract; quite often difficult ones in the reality of the moment.

The things that will make me happy are not exotic. I'm not looking to own a yacht or the Hope Diamond. I want a stable family life; I want a very loving and close relationship with my son. I want to help my constituents. I want to look out for veterans and for Native Americans. I want America to live up to its ideals.

I want to look at being a congressman as a job, not my entire identity. I want to do things for the right reasons.

The most concrete example of how my thinking has changed came when Arizona's Senate seat opened last year. Prior to having gone through therapy, I would have immediately and without thought declared I was going to run for the seat—even though I had never to that moment ever considered becoming a senator.

Of course I'd run. Another step on the ladder.

That time, things were different. When people started to ask whether I'd run, I consciously took time to think.

*How will this affect my son?*

*What will this do to the most important relationships in my life?*

*How does being a senator help me do those important things? How will it affect my happiness, and that of our family?*

The answers, then at least, added up to *No, don't run.* So I didn't.

It's possible that under different circumstances, the answer might be different. But for then, and for now, I'm happy being a congressman.

And yes, I would have won, even if the odds were against me. Especially then. I'm still a Marine.


I HAD NO PLAN TO ANNOUNCE TO THE PUBLIC THAT I HAD PTSD. BUT WHEN TALKING to veterans about the syndrome, I would always urge them to seek help. And since I know that male veterans are especially reluctant to talk about it or admit they have the problem, I'd often mention that I, too, had been diagnosed with it.

Eventually, I guess, word of that got around. One day a reporter called and told me that she was doing a story about PTSD, and asked point-blank if I had it. It would have been silly to lie, and lying never entered my mind.

"Yes," I said matter-of-factly. And like that, I went public.

It wasn't a hit piece; it was about members of Congress who were in the war. I answered the questions as best I could, explaining what I'd been through. The reaction in my district has been fairly supportive. It mostly doesn't come up, but maybe my example has helped some people get help. And if it's helped change the image of PTSD from people who are rage-aholic crazy men sitting alone in their home, so much the better.

As for a reaction in Congress—nil. Everybody pretty much just cares about themselves, and the heck with everyone else.

Admittedly, there's still a lot of stigma attached to PTSD. You could argue that I've put myself in a bad light by admitting that I have it. But I feel obliged to be honest about who I am and what I've experienced.

Maybe that's another effect of having changed my life.

Part of the reason I wanted to work on this book was to come to some sort of terms with my service in Iraq. I wanted to honor my friends, honor the Marines, put the war into some sort of perspective for others, and more importantly myself.

It has been harder than I thought. The brain stores its memories very deeply. Sometimes all we can access are the emotions rather than the facts they're attached to. We relive the horror without knowing exactly what we're horrified of. We flinch without being able to say why.

One night a few months after we started, I woke to find myself combat-loading my M16. I was sleeping, of course, and didn't have a gun; it's been years since I held that weapon for real. But my fingers danced around as quickly and carefully as they had in the AAV going to battle.

I've teared up and cried at times recounting the stories. I'm not ashamed of that. They're honest tears. If anything, I owe the dead far more tears than I've shed.

## BREAKUP

Kate and I had a lot of disagreements about how we thought we should handle not only raising our son, but also on the direction of our lives. Eventually we both came to the point where we realized we had grown apart from each other in many ways.

My time in Iraq meant that we spent a lot of time apart early in our relationship, but I don't think that hurt the relationship. Iraq hurt me, and I think that hurt the relationship. I came back a different person, and what in effect became an addiction to career didn't help our marriage. I spent energy in places that didn't help build our relationship; by the time I realized that, it was too late.

We'd been able to coast along despite the differences for years, but having a son changed things. They got real. I couldn't walk away from the issues that I had buried or tried to ignore. Our careers in politics, my job, her job, had helped us skate past the problems; now they forced us to face them.

You can deny a lot of things in a relationship, but when a kid comes along, it's go time. I didn't want to be bitter and end up taking it out on my son. I'd seen bad marriages—my parents had one—and what the effects are. I didn't want that for my child.

Neither did Kate. We separated when she was still a few months from giving birth.

I WAS IN WASHINGTON IN THE WINTER OF 2017 WHEN KATE CALLED ME FROM Arizona.

She was starting labor.

I managed to get on the last flight to Phoenix out of Baltimore later that evening and reached the hospital while she was still in labor. A few more hours passed; I fell asleep in the waiting room until a nurse woke me up and took me in to meet my son.

*Michael Grant Gallego.*

It was an enormous moment. Surreal.

And then I had to go to work.

Later that day, I held him again with my shirt off, giving him the skin-to-skin contact I'd been taught was important in parenting class. We talked for about an hour—he's very precocious.

I told him he was named for his grandfather and my best friend, Grant. I told him about Grant, and said he would grow up to be a good man just like Grant. I told him I loved him, and that I felt more responsible for him than I felt for anyone in the world, even myself.

## TIES THAT BIND

Cutting myself off from friends, I thought I could isolate myself from the war and its effects. But that was the wrong approach. I'm not one of those people who lives constantly in the past, or bemoans the present and wants to return somehow to the "good old days." Nor do I want to rub my nose in the horror. I'm someone who moves forward, attacks the future; it's just to do that effectively, I have to understand and deal with the past.

And part of that means not rejecting people simply because they remind me of the war.

I check in with Lima Marines a lot through text and social media. A few I see and talk to fairly regularly—Taylor, for example, lives in the Virginia area, not that far from D.C., so it's easy to drop by for dinner or something with him and his family. But most I don't have the chance to do more than give a "like" to on Facebook.

Most of Lima, while dealing with the loss of their friends, has gotten on with things and are doing well. A lot of them find ways to give back to the community at large—still serving in a way, though no longer in the Marines. Just one example: The Bailon brothers have gotten involved with the Pat Tillman Foundation and helped raise money for its various initiatives. (Pat Tillman left the National Football League to become a U.S. Army Ranger. Killed in action, his family and friends established the foundation to assist veterans looking to further their education and leadership skills.)

The Bailons' plans are bigger than that; they hope to eventually start a school and community center for Navajo children modeled after the highly successful Harlem Children's Zone headed by Geoffrey Canada.

Everybody deals with loss and grief and injury differently. For a while, Scott Bunker basically terrorized local bars by getting into bets with people about whether he could touch his tongue to his eyeball. There's a hilarious one of him on YouTube with Ty Pennington, who was in town to build a house for a veteran who'd saved people at the World Trade site. Bunker hams up the first two tries, twisting his tongue around, leaning his head—it's an Oscar-worthy performance.

Then pulls his "eye" out of its socket and puts it to his mouth, winning the bet.

The star paid off—drinks for all the Marines in the bar.

Bunker stayed in the service after his wounds, continuing to be a Marine when many people would have left. He even trained to be a sniper. Now he saves lives as a firefighter/EMT.

Old Man Hurley? He's recently retired from a career as a cop. I can't imagine him hanging around the house too much, though; I have a feeling he'll start a third career somewhere—he may have been old man Hurley to us, but he doesn't seem to have aged since.

**MCKENZIE WAS ONE OF THE LAST GUYS I RECONNECTED WITH.**

When he looks back, he remembers no break in our relationship, but I think that's generous. I do feel as if I cut him off, as if I couldn't give him everything I wanted or even felt I owed.

And yet, he made it. What an F'in' Marine.

He'd gone through terrible times when he got back. He ended up in a VA hospital again, was stopped twice for DWI, and generally fell into an unspeakably black hole in his first years back. He became homeless, suffered through a divorce—and then with the strength of an incredible Marine, somehow fought himself back to sobriety and sanity.

"I called myself out on my bullshit" is how he describes the process, gliding past a lot of the struggle. "I realized that I didn't have it as bad as a lot of guys."

He looked at his life and he saw these things: He was still alive. He had his Christian faith. He had his kids. He had the support of his Navajo community. It was up to him to make something of all that.

Or as he put it:

"I called myself out on my bullshit."

He stopped abusing alcohol, he went to school, he got remarried. He's currently working toward a Ph.D. in history. Maybe he'll analyze the war for us.

I didn't know all this for a long while. Finally, I reached out to him on Facebook to see how he was. He responded back. That first contact wasn't exactly a deep conversation, or anything I can even remember. But it was a start. We've kept the connection ever since.

I've only found the strength to visit Grant's wife once. It was so painful I've never been able to return.

I feel guilty that I let him die. I told her that I would take care of him.

I said I would.

I could have been at the exact same spot Grant was sitting. I should have been right there. That's where I always was. That's where I was meant to be.

But I wasn't.

He had two children. A wife who needed him. I was single. Unmarried. I should have been the one to die. I'll never get beyond that fact.

If Grant were still around, he'd be proud, he'd be bustin' me, and he would not let me slack. He'd have an opinion on everything. At his core, he was a very good man.

## MEMORIAL DAY

Memorial Day sucks.

It's the day we honor and remember our war dead. Maybe it should suck. But it sucks especially for me, and I'm sure for the families of the Lima men who died.

It's the only day of the year I go to church, praying for my friends, praying for myself. The rest of the day I spend alone, unless I'm with my son, in which case I force myself to be as normal as possible until I'm alone.

I'm often asked to speak at ceremonies honoring the fallen; I turn them down. I'll talk about veterans and our needs, about PTSD, about my experiences, about what we owe those who have fallen—but I don't do it that day. That day is for my own memories, grief, and soul.

Sometimes, little miracles happen. Last year on Memorial Day, another kid swam up to my son in the condo pool and asked what his name was. For the first time ever, Michael gave his full name, Michael Grant Gallego.

It came completely out of the blue. It was as if Grant was giving me a message.

Michael is too young right now to really know about the man

he's named after. At some point in the future, I'll take him to the gravesite, maybe kneel down with him, and explain. I'll tell him how we were best friends, how we made all these plans together.

I'll tell him that he was a man with a pure heart, who thought the best of everyone. Who was never mad the whole time I knew him.

I'll take him to the mountains near Santa Fe, and show him where Grant and I hiked to get ready for Iraq. I'll pick up rocks like Grant did, and tell Michael how he'd put them in my pack and make me hike. I'll tell him how Grant was the only person who didn't give up on me after I failed the fitness test, the person who knew I could make it through the deployment.

I'll take my son to Grant's grave at the Santa Fe National Cemetery and tell him what happened.

If my son were to become a Marine, how would I react? Knowing the anguish my mother went through while I was deployed, could I withstand that myself?

I have no answer for that.

A FEW OTHER DAYS ARE BAD. MAY 8, WHEN DEATH HOUSE WENT DOWN. MAY 11, when Grant died. Mother's Day. August 3. I generally try to get to Arlington National Cemetery on those days. Sometimes with other people, but mostly by myself. Eight of my friends are buried there, and it takes time to talk to each one.

I leave quarters for the guys I sat with. Marlboro Reds for Goodwin.

Bourbon for myself.

## SYDNEY

In June 2018, I went to play in the congressional baseball game. It's an annual affair, pitting Republicans against Democrats for fun and a few laughs. While I was there, I met a young woman named Sydney Barron who'd come with a friend to watch. She wasn't much of a baseball fan—probably something that worked in my favor, since I'm not all that good a player.

We hit it off. Within a few weeks, we were dating seriously. In February 2019, I asked her to marry me.

Like my son, Sydney has been a very positive influence on my life. I don't talk about Iraq that much with her; mostly she has picked up things about my service from random conversations with friends. But she has endured some of my struggles—talking and crying out in my sleep, my still-existing paranoia about where I sit in a restaurant, my down moods. Like a lot of spouses, she has learned to give me space, and to let me talk when I feel the need.

There are times I'm sure it's difficult for her. It may even seem bizarre—like the night we were watching *Game of Thrones* on television, and I had to get up and leave because the scene of warriors foretelling their own deaths was just too real.

The most helpful thing she's ever said to me was this: *I know I don't understand everything you're feeling, but I am here for you.*

I think those are words every veteran with PTSD should hear from someone they love.

Sydney thinks that I've gotten better at dealing with things over the course of our relationship. I hope that's true, and if so, she deserves some credit.

## WHAT DID WE ACCOMPLISH?

Was it worth it?

I like the Iraqi people. I like Iraqi food. But I don't feel nostalgic or even generally charitable toward them. I know most have a hard life, and that their country has a long way to go before it reaches some sort of peaceful stasis. I think we helped them move in that direction. Sometimes I don't know.

Intellectually, I'd known what war was like before going. Now I know what it means emotionally.

On the helicopter riding to the dam, my vision was blurry—literally because of the haze and dust, but figuratively as well. I had a blurry idea of the country. Going out, my vision was sharper. I could see Haditha as a place. Attached to that place were memories of what had happened there. And attached to those memories were the emotions of that experience.

Fear and loss were in sharp relief, defined for me by the loss of friends.

Hatred of the enemy—of people who wanted to kill me—had been defined and made specific. Added to that was firsthand knowledge of mistakes we'd made, and the bigger mistakes our command chain had made. Knowing these as specific things rather than generalities changed my knowledge and deepened my emotions. It changed me.

Not that I could sort all of that out on the helicopter or the plane ride home. That would take years—that is still ongoing, happening even now as I work on this book.

THERE WERE SOME WHO CRITICIZED THE FACT THAT A RESERVE UNIT WAS SENT into combat. I think the fact that we were reservists made us better equipped to do our job as an occupying force. Reserve Marines, and soldiers for that matter, generally have a wider range of experiences dealing with civilians than "regular" servicepeople do. Our unit included a number of guys who were cops and other emergency responders in civilian life; I think that helped them dealing with Iraqis and gave us some good examples to follow.

Looking at the photos of our operations now, the first thing that strikes me is how young we were. Even so, we were generally older than the Marines in regular divisions. You can argue whether it was a good idea to send eighteen- and nineteen-year-olds into an area that had been in strife for a couple thousand years, a place used as a war and transit zone by everyone from the Mongols and beyond. Or how effective any foreign force is going to be patrolling an area used by smugglers for eons, or how they will interact with a culture used to war, oppression, and corruption. But that's an argument about the war, not the people who fought it.

If I had to make an assessment of our tactics and performance—with the caveat that I'm not an expert in the first and obviously prejudiced on the second—I think we did fairly well in urban combat situations, where the enemy was clear, present, and committed to engage. Where we didn't do as well was in the majority of the situations we found ourselves, where the enemy freely mixed in with civilians. There we were playing a cat-and-mouse game, which often got frustrating.

The Corps in general fought well in the war, even in places like Fallujah and New Ubaydi where the enemy was well-prepared. There are always difficult situations in urban warfare; plenty of opportunities for ambushes, human error, and just dumb luck. But our objectives were taken.

Marines are not policemen, though. Nor are we social workers, construction crews, government infrastructure, job programs—all of those things were greatly needed in Iraq, and surely would have helped the people and maybe stopped the insurgency sooner, but we weren't there to provide them.

I think the dumbest thing we did over there was to clear a town or a city, and then leave. What happened next? The insurgents came back. And the whole cycle began again.

Our biggest vulnerabilities were the amtracs. We never should have had to use them in the first place. That was on the politicians and the administration, and the generals. More should have been done to replace those vehicles earlier in the war. Or better, before it. That was the most serious defect in our overall operations, and we paid dearly for it.

After that, Command. There were times when we were used when we shouldn't have been, when more time between operations would have left guys less exhausted and more prepared to deal with the challenges of combat, both physical and mental. And some of the decisions—most notably those that led to the trac strike in August, but others as well—made no sense.

Some of that was due to inexperience in the chain of command above us. Some of the decisions, I'm convinced, were motivated not by a careful evaluation of our capabilities, but by overeagerness to please higher ups.

Obviously, I don't have access to all the information and the circumstances; I can only give my honest opinion. I would have done things differently, but I was not in the position to make the call.

There are two facts about our deployment that are indisputable: we saw a lot of action, and we took a lot of casualties. The numbers speak for themselves. There were eleven battalion-level operations during our time there. Out of those, Lima Company was the main effort on ten. The company had another twenty-five missions, which doesn't count "routine" patrols and the like. It was a pretty torrid pace.

As for the casualties, even one would be too much. We had the dubious honor of being the hardest hit unit in the Marine Corps since the bombing at Beirut. We had the equally dubious honor of being the hardest hit unit in the Iraq occupation.

There was another toll, far harder to measure. The war changed everyone who was in it. A few of those changes may have been for the good. A number were not. People like McKenzie, all of us really, found we could never really go back to the person we had been in the past. As Marines, we wanted to face the future with bold resolve. As human beings, we knew we had great vulnerabilities an enemy could exploit.

## ELEVEN IS MY LUCKY NUMBER

On that trip out, I counted the number of times I should have died. There were eleven.

1. CAG mission where the IED missed because of the sandstorm
2. The IED at Quick Strike, which hit another vehicle
3. Our trac missing the switchblade IED
4. The IED explosion as the helo landed
5. The mortar attack after the snipers were killed
6. The sniper missing me in the field
7. The IED that blew up Grant during Matador
8. The RPG on our first firefight
9. The incoming mortar rounds at the dam when we arrived after a mission
10. The IED during Operation Sword that didn't go off because we were with the kids
11. The shots that landed around me as I scoped New Ubaydi

As time has gone on, most of those have lost their sharp edge of remembered fear. Sometimes I even forget the specifics of certain incidents; occasionally I leave a few out as I list them.

But I always know there were eleven. It's a lucky number.

In the casino, that is.

You go into some politicians' offices, and you'll see photos of them with their old unit. You won't see that in mine.

It would feel fake. And the constant reminder would be too much.

Friends, family, awards I collected—those are on the wall. But the truth is, those things are there for a specific purpose, one that is meant to evoke a certain image in the viewer: the successful congressman.

It's not a fake image, but let's be honest, it is a bit contrived. All politics is contrived, and showing pictures and mementoes to remind people who you really are is hardly the biggest political sin.

Somehow, bringing the war into that picture would taint the war. The war can only be real. It cannot be used. The death of my friends, Lima Company's seven-month tour of hell—that is a reality that must not be blemished by being used for anything. Its meaning is its meaning, and nothing else.

I don't fully understand what I went through, let alone how I survived. It's crazy to think I was in war. It's also crazy to think I'm in Congress. Certainly, the kid on the floor in the southside of Chicago would be amazed that he grew up to do either of those things.

I live now between those two realities, war and politics; the most intense moments of my life have been spent in both, though it is the former that has left the deepest mark. It's war I measure myself against, war and its effects, war and its children.

I have learned, though, that there are other measurements that matter. I do not know all of them. Nor can I say what role time has to play. It seems the most fickle measure imaginable.

*And luck?*

Luck for me is confined to games, to the roulette wheel or card tables. I've had my run of luck in real life and exhausted it. I've lived my eleven lives and will try my best to make my twelfth a good and happy one.

John Bailon told me about a Navajo story relating to the beginning of the world, when two brothers had to fight evil spirits or monsters oppressing the earth. They fought the worst, but there was not enough time to vanquish all of them. Those they could not reach remain with us: greed, anger, hunger, disease—all the evils that torment us today.

It is up to us to continue the fight against them.

There is another Navajo tradition that seems relevant to me, though not being a Native American, I have a limited understanding of it. After returning from battle, warriors take part in a four-day ceremony that restores them to their people. It is an ancient recognition that war changes men, and to return to what we call the normal life we must undergo another passage.

I know intuitively that there's a lot of truth in that, but I'm not sure it's possible to ever get back to normal after war. Even men who have been through that ceremony tell me that they have dreams of war, and continue to struggle to make sense of what they have been through.

And yet . . .

For years, I didn't think the hole in my soul from the loss of Grant and the others would ever be filled. But Michael changed that. Having this little man to raise somehow gives me a purpose beyond grief. It's not closure or a substitute; it's more a transition, a recognition that grief is not the only fact that informs my life.

Loss will always be there, but there are other things that can drive me. There is some incalculable worth and joy in the responsibility of raising a child that doesn't negate evil and loss, but answers to a deep need for hope.

Words don't entirely explain my experiences in Iraq. Maybe these are close:

My Marine Corps service was about service for me. It was one of the purer things I did in my life—not for money, not for ideology, just for my country. It will always be that.

# POSTSCRIPT

## THE LUCKY AND THE DEAD

All told, the battalion lost forty-six Marines and two corpsman in the months we were in Iraq. These are the men who died from my company, Lima:

- Lance Corporal Timothy M. Bell Jr.
- Lance Corporal Eric J. Bernholtz
- Lance Corporal Nicholas William B. Bloem
- Lance Corporal Michael J. Cifuentes
- Lance Corporal Wesley G. Davids
- Corporal Dustin A. Derga
- Lance Corporal Christopher J. Dyer
- Private First Class Christopher R. Dixon
- Lance Corporal Nicholas B. Erdy
- Lance Corporal Grant B. Fraser

- Staff Sergeant Anthony L. Goodwin
- Lance Corporal Jonathan W. Grant
- Lance Corporal Jourdan L. Grez
- Sergeant Bradley Harper
- Sergeant Justin F. Hoffman
- Staff Sergeant Kendall H. Ivy II
- Sergeant David Kenneth J. Kreuter
- Lance Corporal Christopher P. Lyons
- Lance Corporal Aaron H. Reed
- Lance Corporal Edward A. Schroeder II
- Corporal David Stephen "Bear" Stewart
- Lance Corporal Kevin Waruinge
- Lance Corporal William B. Wightman
- Corporal Andre L. Williams
- Sergeant David N. Wimberg
- Petty Officer 3rd Class Travis Youngblood (Navy corpsman)

That's a horrendous total, the worst for a Marine unit and we believe the highest for any American military unit during the war. The battalion had roughly half of all Marine casualties during that period; roughly a quarter of all Marine KIAs those months were my brothers in Lima.

Marines worked in some of the worst parts of Iraq during some of the worst times of the occupation. Largely because of this, they took a disproportionate number of casualties—representing seventeen percent of the American force, they had twenty-five percent of the overall casualties. As of August 1, 2020, 852 Marines were killed by hostile forces. The lower your rank, the younger you were, the greater the odds were that you would not make it through the war.

Those are the numbers of the dead. Total casualties including the wounded were far more. And of course that doesn't count those of us wounded mentally and emotionally, whether formally diagnosed with PTSD or not.

All of our lives were changed. Those who were lucky enough to live have pushed on. Some succumbed to their injuries and their burdens; others fight on each day.

SINCE RETURNING FROM IRAQ, LIMA HAS LOST A NUMBER OF OTHER MEN; MOST recently, Vincent Knapp, who took over as commander during some of the company's most difficult days. He passed away while we were working on this book.

Captain Knapp restored energy and hope to the unit during some of its darkest days. His leadership sustained the men, ensuring that Lima could continue to fulfill its missions with the efficiency and excellence expected of Marines. During his career, Major Knapp earned the Joint Service Commendation Medal, the Navy and Marine Corps Commendation Medal (2) with Combat V Distinguishing Device, the Navy Marine Corps Achievement Medal, the Good Conduct Medal, and the Combat Action Ribbon. Like all of Lima's Marines, he made the world a better place while he was alive, and is sorely missed with his passing.

# CODA

## DEMOCRACY SURVIVES—THE INSURRECTION,

## JANUARY 6, 2021

Are you OK?

I t was shortly before two p.m., January 6, 2021, when I got that text from my wife, Sydney, back in Arizona. It was already an extraordinary day, already a day unprecedented in our history, a day the country knew would test the resilience of America's collective soul.

Are you OK?

One thing you have to know about Sydney: she's not a person to panic or raise alarms out of thin air. She's no conspiracy theorist. And she's not a wife who interrupts her husband at work, especially when she knows he's on the floor of the U.S. House of Representatives, about to deliver one of the momentous and historic speeches of his life.

Congress had met to accept the results of the Electoral College, which had certified the presidential election and awarded the presidency to Democrat Joe Biden. We were just starting the debate over Arizona's election, expected to be the opening round of a daylong attempt by a faction of the Republican Party to overthrow the results. Sydney knew I would be making the closing argument in our defense and was watching C-SPAN to see me do it. What she saw, and what I was experiencing at that moment, was certainly extraordinary, but not alarming in a physical way.

That was inside the chamber. Outside was a different matter.

Knowing that pro-Trump groups were planning protests in the city today, I'd taken the precaution of following a circuitous route to the Capitol, avoiding the crowds and possible craziness. But never did I envision the madness that was about to unfold in the Capitol itself.

I could hear the noises of the crowd outside as I texted my wife to tell her I was fine. A short time later, security entered the chamber and escorted Speaker Pelosi out, locking the doors behind them.

And yet, the reality of what was going on didn't hit me until some minutes later, when a security guard came in, breathing hard, hands shaking, clearly doing his best to pretend to be calm . . . and failing.

Stay inside, he told the congresspeople on the floor. People have broken into the Capitol. We're under lockdown.

Right around then, I heard pounding on the doors of the gallery upstairs, where several representatives and news reporters had gathered to watch the debate. A third security guard came in. This one had a dire message:

Rioters have broken into the building. Chemical agents are being used to thwart them. Put on your gas masks.

Masks were stored under the seats in the chamber. We'd never had a drill on using them. Very likely a number of those on the floor of the House and in the galley overlooking us didn't know they were there, or at least had forgotten about them.

I grabbed one and put it on, reminded of the drills I'd had early in the Corps with tear gas. Congress's masks were large and clear, far more comfortable than the goggle-style most people are familiar with. But one of the more subtle points of using the mask is to keep your breathing as even as possible.

Seeing that many of my colleagues were confused, I jumped up on one of the desks and loudly began giving instructions.

"Tear gas will not kill you," I reminded them. "But it's important to remain calm. If you hyperventilate, you may pass out."

I turned to my friend, Congressman Eric Swalwell, a California Democrat from the Castro Valley area, and made sure he was all right. The night before, his wife had said something in passing that came back to me—"take care of him."

I'd said of course I would.

Those words came back to me as the pounding on the doors to the gallery upstairs grew louder and more violent: it was the same promise I'd given Grant's wife before we left for Iraq.

BACK IN ARIZONA, SYDNEY WATCHED THE TURMOIL AROUND THE CAPITOL WITH disbelief and anxiety. She had CNN on the TV and CSPAN on her computer, trying to make sense of the confusion. She pulled up Twitter and looked at her feed. People on the scene were sending photos and streaming images of the assault on the government's house.

The insurrectionists had gone past the barriers and were flooding into the building. It was clear their intent was far beyond noisy protest. There were reports of the Capitol police being pummeled, of pipe bombs being discovered at other government sites nearby.

Her heart was breaking for our country.

THE CROWD RUSHED THROUGH THE BUILDING IN A CHAOTIC MASS, AT PLACES MILL-ing aimlessly, in others piling forward with venom and massed malice. The security personnel barricaded the entrances to the legislative chamber with whatever furniture they could find. Their weapons were drawn. Outside we could hear banging, shouting, flash-bangs or something similar going off—it was a war zone.

Before I'd been assigned to 3/25, I'd trained for riot control. One of the key things I learned was that in a riot, the crowd itself is a weapon, and often the most dangerous one. Crowds have their own logic, their own sort of madness—a "hive mind" we called it. Violence was inevitable past a certain point.

The Trump supporters pushed against the doors of the chamber, aiming to get in. Anyone they managed to grab, especially a Democrat who opposed Trump, was likely to be killed. Understanding that, security cleared a path for us to leave and reach a more defensible safe room.

Up in the gallery, Congressman Jason Crow, a former Army Ranger, was helping the reporters and congresspeople there with their masks and urging them to remain calm. I climbed up on a chair and shouted to them, making sure they knew the plan to leave.

As our older colleagues began filing out, I made sure Eric was still next to me. At that point, I was almost certain we were going to have to fight our way out.

We waited for the others to clear through the narrow passage—there was a lot of fear and apprehension, not to mention confusion. The line moved slowly. Meanwhile, the pounding at the doors grew louder. I heard glass breaking. The chamber doors couldn't hold out much longer.

The only weapon I had was a pen. Worst case, I could use it to take a better weapon from a rioter. Finally, Eric and I were the last people on the floor. As we moved to the doorway, I caught a glimpse of the mob slamming against a door nearby, trying to get at us.

I stopped and took a photo. Crazy, I know—but I wanted people to know this was real.

As security rushed us to a safe area, I lost track of Eric. I turned a corridor looking for him and saw one of the security supervisors instructing two young officers to draw their weapons.

"Anyone comes down this hall, you shoot them."

I looked at the young men's faces. They looked like kids—they were certainly no older than I was in Iraq, and most likely younger. Were they willing to shoot?

I thought of asking if they wanted to trade places. I'd already killed people; I knew I was capable. And surely I'd do better at living with the aftermath.

But that wasn't my job now. I left, caught up with the others, and finally found Eric in the safe room.

BACK IN ARIZONA, SYDNEY TALKED TO ERIC'S WIFE, WHO HAD HEARD FROM HER husband. Eric's wife told her he was next to me. "He's a good person to be standing next to in this."

But nothing Eric or I could tell them could ultimately relieve the anxiety they felt, not only watching what was going on, but realizing there was no way they could help. Friends and relatives checked in; Sydney drew some comfort from their encouragement. My former wife, Kate, helped tremendously, looking after our son, and offering advice and support that Sydney greatly appreciated. I imagine Kate, too, had great anxiety, and undoubtedly memories of the long days and nights she'd spent without word from me when I deployed.

THE SAFE ROOM WAS CROWDED. I WAS NEAR ONE OF THE ENTRANCES WHEN THE security people opened the door for Virginia congresswoman Abigail Spanberger, who'd escaped from the gallery. She had several people with her; journalists, it turned out.

The security guards would not let them in.

Hearing the commotion, I went over and heard the congresswoman explain that she feared for their safety. But the guards were adamant, acting under orders: they would admit her, but not them.

Come with me, I told the journalists. We'll go somewhere safe.

I lead them out of the room, walking in combat-mode—deliberate, wary, quickly. I scanned ahead, worked out solutions to potential surprises, just *went*, ready for whatever happened. We moved quickly through a labyrinth of corridors, halls, and stairways to my office. There, I told them to make themselves comfortable—not an easy task under any circumstance—and gave them a few security tips. We established a protocol for coming and going, and I went back out to scour the halls for others stranded in the tumult.

THE CAPITOL POLICE, NATIONAL GUARD, AND OTHERS GRADUALLY REGAINED control of the building. Several of us began insisting that we go back on the floor to finish our business. It was our duty to see the electoral process through.

If we didn't, who knew what the next day would bring? Even if it was only more delay, the insurrectionists still would have won. We didn't want them to have even a symbolic victory.

Finally, leadership called us back. The debate resumed. When it was my turn to speak, I delivered my words from the heart. I talked about my oath as a Marine, where I swore to protect the country from enemies foreign and domestic.

Never had I thought I would have to protect America from within. Yet here we were.

After the vote, which of course upheld the validity of the election, I went to my Republican colleagues and urged them to stop the charade and insult to our country—drop the nonsensical arguments over the votes in other states. They already knew the contentions were phony and they were sure to lose the votes.

It was time to come together and end the madness. Time to preserve our Union.

Instead, they continued through to Pennsylvania, embarrassing themselves and making a mockery of the oaths they had sworn upon taking office.

AS THE NIGHT WENT ON, THE RESULTS IN EACH STATE CERTIFIED BY THE COLLEGE were approved. Finally, we got to 270 votes, ensuring Joe Biden's election. At that point, Vice President Pence adjourned the proceeding.

Back at my apartment, I was too wound up to sleep. I found a bottle of Scotch, and put on Otis Redding's "(Sittin' On) The Dock of the Bay." You never know where war will find you, or where your oath as a Marine will be tested.

For Sydney, the sense of danger really didn't abate until I returned home from Washington. As more information has come out about the crowd, about Donald Trump's actions, about the people involved, her concern for me and the country has only grown deeper. I think that's true for a lot of people.

In the days following the insurrection, members of Congress and their families have continued to be threatened. We've all had to increase security precautions to a level most of us never thought necessary.

And yet, I remain optimistic. I think this was the last gasp of a dying attitude and impulse of hate and division. The future is strong—if we persevere.

I'm not naïve. In no way do I feel that our country is in a good place. Facts are still being manipulated, and much of the Republican Party continues to push looney theories and back ridiculous positions. But in the end, the American spirit is to persevere. We will have a stronger, better union as we see this through.

Am I being too optimistic?

I don't think so. I'm an American, and a Marine. We fight like hell, and we don't give up.

# COLLABORATOR'S NOTE

## THERE IS NO SUCH THING AS A "PART-TIME" MARINE

I've had the privilege of knowing some great Marines over the years—my father-in-law and my godson for starters—but I'd never known one who humped a copy of Shakespeare's complete works in his ruck with mortar shells until I met Ruben. I'm also reasonably sure I never met one, or a corporal at least, who graduated from Harvard. And certainly not one who wanted to listen to the Buena Vista Social Club and Sarah McLachlan on the way to battle.

Wonderful artists, certainly, but their music isn't what most fighters would use to rev themselves up for war.

That's the thing, though—he didn't want to rev himself up for a fight. He wanted to be calm, clear-headed, and professional.

That is Ruben Gallego. Or, as he was known in the Marines, Corporal Ruben Marinelarena.

I met Ruben for the first time in the late winter of 2020. We spent that morning visiting the graves of some of his friends, men we've written about here. He wanted me to know who they were before I even knew who he was.

That's Ruben, too.

No politician is without ego or an agenda, but whatever the qualities that make him a successful politician are somehow split away from his identity as a Marine. As a Marine—and once you earn that insignia, you are a Marine for life—he is deeply loyal to the men he fought with. Skeptical of many of the officers and often derogatory of the civilians above them, he remains an idealist when it comes to the Corps and especially the "grunts" who bore and still bear the brunt of the fighting.

For good reason. They were among the best men this country has ever produced.

I doubt Ruben ever weeps in Congress. He wept in the cemetery, and cried several times recounting his experiences in the war.

There is a tendency among some of the uninformed—and even those who should know better—to look down on reservists from all branches. They're called "part-time soldiers" or "weekend warriors," implying that they are not only less trained than "regular" servicemembers but are less capable and dedicated as well.

Lima Company's service is the obvious answer to that slander. The unit saw more action than many "regular" units of all services during the war. Nor were their casualties due to any lack of experience. By the time the fatalities began to mount, the company had been in several engagements; combat experience is always the most important factor in a unit's performance. One can argue with how the unit was used, but the argument would apply whether it was "regular" or Reserve.

Any number of statistics demonstrate the importance of Reserve units in the war, not just to the Marines, but to all American forces. By the end of March 2005 when 3/25 deployed, there were some 23,630 Marines and sailors in Iraq. Just under 13,000 of them were reservists. Pentagon officials said that, of the 152,000 U.S. troops in Iraq that year, about half were in the Reserve or National Guard. It's not surprising, then, that a high percentage of casualties were from those two types of units. This was a matter of poor timing, coming just before the surge at a point where, candidly, the U.S. was unprepared. Al Qaeda in Mesopotamia was at its high point, escalating an offensive that would not be adequately countered until after the "Surge" brought more American fighters into the country, the U.S. changed tactics, and the Iraqis themselves decided to unite and counter the al Qaeda foreigners.

The people who study troop readiness and performance have developed what is called an "ideal dwell time." It's a ratio of deployment in a combat zone to time training and resting at home. In the simplest terms, it's generally believed units are most efficient when deployed seven out of every twenty-one months. The Marines deployed at a rate about twenty-five percent higher than that; the Army was even worse. In any case, even those deployment rates could not have been achieved without the use of Reserve units.

While many reservists like Ruben remain in the Reserve corps their entire military careers, a large number come to the Reserves after duty in "regular" units. This is especially true for NCOs, something the unit structure of Lima demonstrates—in many cases, fireteams were led by Marines who would probably have rated higher slots if they were serving elsewhere. Unfortunately, the opposite is often true for officers across the different services, who more commonly simply leave service completely when they go off active duty. Lima's experience immediately before the war, when it went through a succession of commanders in the year or so prior to activation, illustrate this as well.

Ruben is unique as a Marine—Harvard and all. But in other ways, he's far more typical of Marines than most people realize.

They are all well-trained, dedicated, patriotic, and, yes, among the world's best fighters, which means they kill when called on to do so. But they are also more complicated than the recruiting posters and television advertisements suggest. Articulate or not, they feel deeply. One of the great tragedies of our time is that many who have been to war feel guilt at having let their comrades down because they couldn't save them; that misplaced guilt and PTSD have led a number to end their lives prematurely, depriving the world of a lot of what they might have accomplished.

Until recently, the problem was often compounded for reservists, who, like Ruben and McKenzie, face the burden of proving that they were in combat and can be held up by slow, inadequate, or inaccurate paperwork. The rules have been changed to make it easier for them to get help. Unfortunately, the stigma remains.

The Marines who served in Lima never lacked for courage. Aside from what they did in actual combat, the greatest testimony of their bravery may have come every day when they put their gear on and boarded vehicles they knew were potential deathtraps.

"Not one of them hesitated," Gunny Hurley told me at one point. There was a bit of awe in his voice, and deep respect. "They did their job. They did what they had to do."

Hurley himself is a testament to the best of the Marines: a matter-of-fact, let's-get-it-done leader. There's a certain well-deserved aura to gunnery sergeants in the Corps; talking to Hurley and the others about him, you can see why. "Old Man Hurley" was always in the mix of things, whether in the streets of Haqlaniyah or at the front of Hell House. He got no medals—though he deserved them. He did his job, and the men who served under him respected him for it. He stayed on after he blew out his leg; the injury could have easily earned him a trip home. He got in trouble with higher ups because he stuck up for his men. He was that one guy on the battlefield whose judgment you could trust when the shit hit the fan.

He was a Marine. Nothing part-time about it. And nothing part-time about the men he took to battle.

As McKenzie told me, "These were the best men I ever knew."

They were Marines.

# SOURCES

The main sources for this memoir are the personal memories of Ruben Gallego, refreshed at times by consulting other members of 3/25 and his family.

Andrew Taylor graciously shared a contemporaneous journal of the deployment, which was relied on for detail and clarification at various point. He kindly gave us permission to use the material quoted here.

Scott Bunker generously shared an essay recounting some of his experiences at Death House and afterward.

Both Taylor and Bunker supplemented their material with lengthy interviews. Other Marines who assisted with extended, formal interviews included John Bailon, Cheston Bailon, Chuck Hurley, and Jonithan McKenzie. Additional in-depth interviews included sessions with Kate Gallego, Ruben's first wife, and Sydney Gallego, who selflessly shared memories and observations.

Other written sources include:

Ardolino, Bill. *Fallujah Awakens: Marines, Sheiks, and the Battle Against Al Qaeda*. Naval Institute Press, 2013.

Brooks, Ian P. *The United States Marine Corps Reconnaissance Reserve: Adaptation and Integration for the Future*. Master of Military Studies Research Paper, USMC Command and Staff College, Marine Corps University.

Camp, Dick. *Operation Phantom Fury: The Assault and Capture of Fallujah, Iraq*. Voyageur Press, 2009.

Estes, Kenneth W. *U.S. Marine Corps Operations in Iraq, 2003–2006*. History Division, United States Marine Corps, Quantico, Virginia, 2009 (available via the web at https://fas.org/irp/doddir/usmc/iraq03-06.pdf).

———. *U.S. Marines in Iraq, 2004–2005: Into the Fray, U.S. Marines in the Global War on Terrorism*. History Division, United States Marine Corps, Quantico, Virginia, 2011.

McWilliams, Timothy S., and Nicholas J. Schlosser. *U.S. Marines in Battle: Fallujah, November–December 2004*. United States Department of Defense, 2014.

Thimbault, Glenn F., M.D. *Sword in the Lion's Den*. Publish America, 2008.

News stories and articles in the *New York Times, Washington Post, Wall Street Journal,* and numerous local newspapers.

Video and film:

*Combat Diary: The Marines of Lima Company,* directed by Michael Epstein, Viewfinder Productions, 2006. The documentary includes footage in Iraq and accounts from a number of Lima Company Marines.

Video footage taken by Lima Company Marines during the tour has been posted on YouTube, generally without commentary or description. The images were extremely helpful in describing scenes and prompting memories.

AS OFTEN IN BATTLE, MULTIPLE VIEWPOINTS, GENERAL CONFUSION, MEMORY lapses, and occasional errors cloud the exact reality of what precisely happened. While we've striven for the most accurate and precise accounts, we have had to make judgment calls at several points in the narrative, choosing between conflicting accounts. While the differences in all cases were minor, nonetheless we acknowledge that there may be other versions of some of the action.

In examining conflicting sources, we tended to give more weight to contemporaneous and near contemporaneous accounts (Andrew Taylor's diary, for example), followed by eyewitness accounts not recorded at the time, reports written after the fact, news reports, and information from secondary and tertiary sources originating from eyewitnesses.

Here's a much simplified example: Most of the eyewitnesses, including Ruben, believe the incident where the trac struck the IED during Quickstrike occurred on August 3. However, at least one eyewitness believes it was August 5, and there have been written accounts saying it was August 4. We chose August 3 because of the preponderance of eyewitness accounts as well as news reporting from the time.

The quotes used here are from memory, and while we are sure they carry the gist of what was said, it is impossible at this point to present the exact words used.

So much happened on Lima Company's deployment that by necessity we have had to limit ourselves to those we've told here. There are many tales still out there, waiting to be told.

We have generally used the common spellings of place names Marines used during the time of Ruben's deployment, except when that would cause confusion.

# THANKS

In addition to the sources named previously and other members of Lima Company, 3/25, and the Marine Corps community, the authors wish to thank the following people:

Members of Lima Company who urged Ruben to write the book and contributed anecdotes to the authors for inclusion in the work.

Debra Scacciaferro, who conducted background research and assisted with comments on the manuscript in progress.

Bob DeFelice, for first suggesting the title.

Our editor, Peter Hubbard, who supported the project from day one, and the rest of the team at Custom House/HarperCollins: Molly Gendell, Maureen Cole, Kayleigh George.

David Larabell and the staff at CAA, who helped make this a reality.

Ruben's mom and sisters: Elisa Gallego, Liza Lynch, Alejandra Gallego, and Laura Marinelarena.

And most especially Sydney and Michael Gallego, for their patience, love, and support.